IMAGES
of America

JEFFERSONTOWN

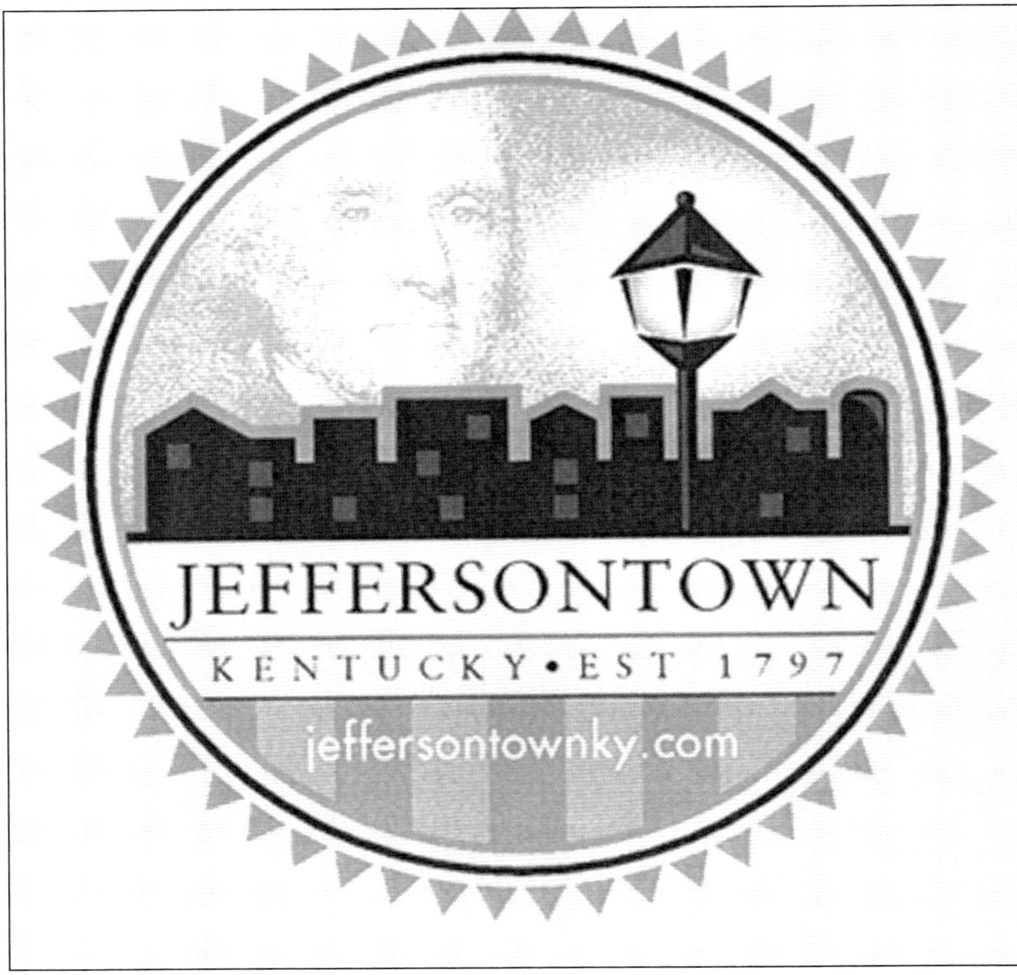

Jeffersontown is a city proud of its history, which dates back over 200 years. Originally a crossroads for travelers on their way to the port city of Louisville, Jeffersontown quickly developed into a town complete with all the industry necessary to settlers at the time. Jeffersontown was incorporated as a city on May 3, 1797, and named for Thomas Jefferson, who was then vice-president, even though the accepted practice at the time was to name new cities after the current president of the United States. The official logo of Jeffersontown represents the city quite well, bearing an image of Thomas Jefferson, as well as a cityscape and Jeffersontown's very popular gaslight motif. (Photo courtesy of the City of Jeffersontown.)

IMAGES
of America

JEFFERSONTOWN

Beth Wilder

ARCADIA
PUBLISHING

ISBN 978-0-7385-1774-2

Published by Arcadia Publishing
Charleston, South Carolina

Printed in the United States of America

Library of Congress Catalog Card Number: 2004116494

For all general information contact Arcadia Publishing at:
Telephone 843-853-2070
Fax 843-853-0044
E-mail sales@arcadiapublishing.com
For customer service and orders:
Toll-Free 1-888-313-2665

Visit us on the Internet at www.arcadiapublishing.com

Contents

Introduction

Kentucky was one of the first places early pioneers explored in a move to expand our country's borders westward. The beautiful land and crystal-clear water to the east of Louisville were too tantalizing to pass up, so by the late 1700s, many Revolutionary War veterans began to settle in the area that would become known as Jeffersontown. Since the area was a crossroads for travelers on their way to Louisville, townsmen saw the potential for a city, so in 1794, Abraham Bruner purchased 122 acres and divided the land into plots to be sold for business purposes. The lots sold quickly, establishments sprang up immediately, and Jeffersontown soon became something of a "county seat" in its own right—rather than make the arduous journey to Louisville to buy goods, people from the surrounding areas opted to conduct business in Jeffersontown.

Times change, and over the next 200 years, Jeffersontown adapted. Although it remained primarily a farming community, by the 1950s, subdivisions and shopping malls emerged all over town. City leaders began exploring the possibility of bringing even more business to the area, and in 1967, Bluegrass Research and Industrial Park officially opened, marking the start of Jeffersontown's reign as a leader in industry.

Jeffersontown has been a progressive city since its founding, yet it has managed to retain all the charm of a rural town. This is due, in large part, to the people who have resided here throughout the years. People may picture buildings when they hear the word "city," but in truth, a city is actually made of the people who inhabit it. Jeffersontown is blessed to be comprised of thoughtful, intelligent citizens who are passionate about their home.

The book you hold in your hands is an excellent example of how proud the residents of Jeffersontown are of their hometown. A call was put out for photographs of the city's history, and the residents of Jeffersontown swung into action, bringing in their family photos and relating bits of history that might otherwise have gone unrecorded. The City of Jeffersontown is extremely grateful to them for all their assistance.

This book is by no means a definitive account of Jeffersontown's history. It is a compilation of photographs put together to give the reader a broad overview of Jeffersontown's past and its people. A special note of thanks deservedly goes out to two of Jeffersontown's most prominent historians, Lt. Col. Robert C. Jobson and Mrs. Joellen Tyler Johnston, whose prior research of the city's history remains an invaluable asset to the entire community.

—Mayor Clay S. Foreman

One

Business and Industry

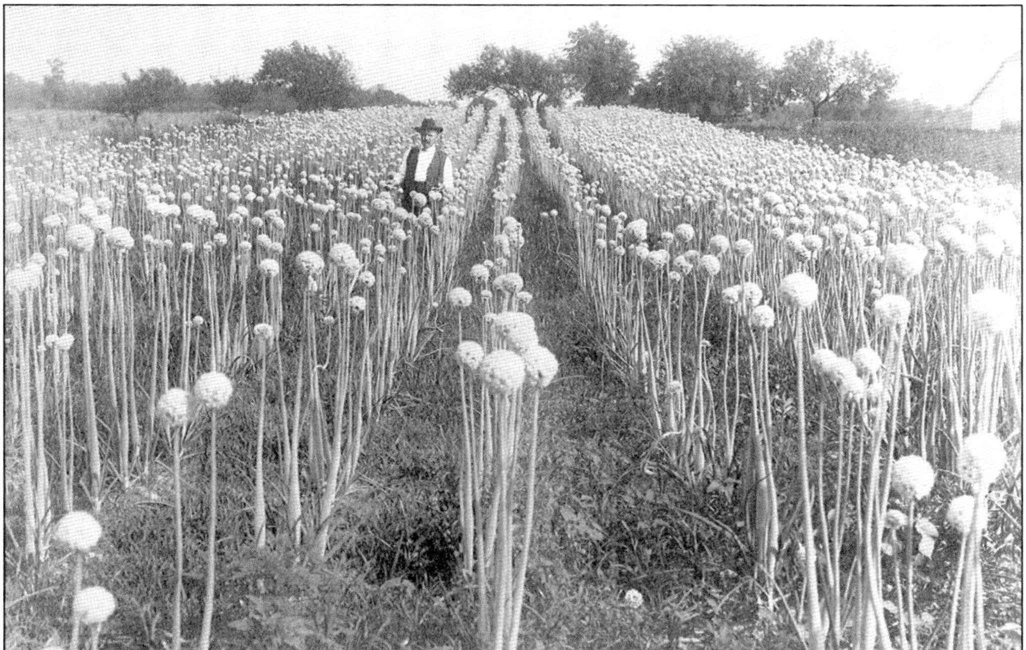

Jeffersontown has gained worldwide recognition for its massive industrial park, which opened in 1967, but at the turn of the 20th century, Jeffersontown's primary industry was onion and strawberry production. This photo shows onions gone to seed at the Oechslin farm, which was located where J-town Center (now Jeffersontown Commons) stands. (Photo courtesy of Tillie Meffert, Mary Boring, and Fred Oechslin.)

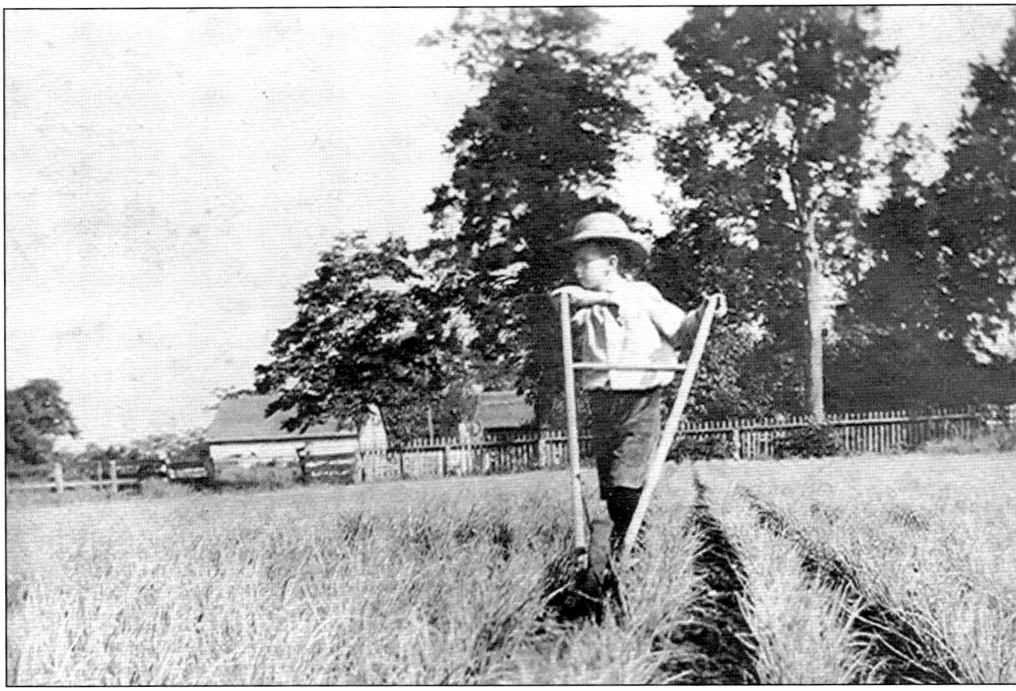

Plowing fields was a common sight in the early days of Jeffersontown. Here, Claude Hobson Hunsinger, born in 1898, is seen cultivating his family's onion field. (Photo courtesy of Marjorie Hunsinger Weeks Babson.)

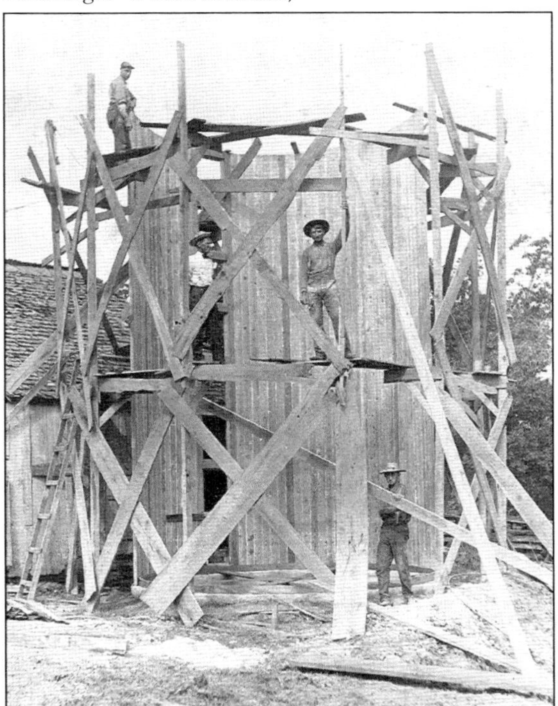

Farmers were the primary landowners in Jeffersontown throughout the 19th and most of the 20th century. Herbert Leonard Goose (wearing a white shirt) is shown supervising the construction of a second silo next to one of the three barns on his property in the 1890s. (Photo courtesy of Sallie Cheatham Smith.)

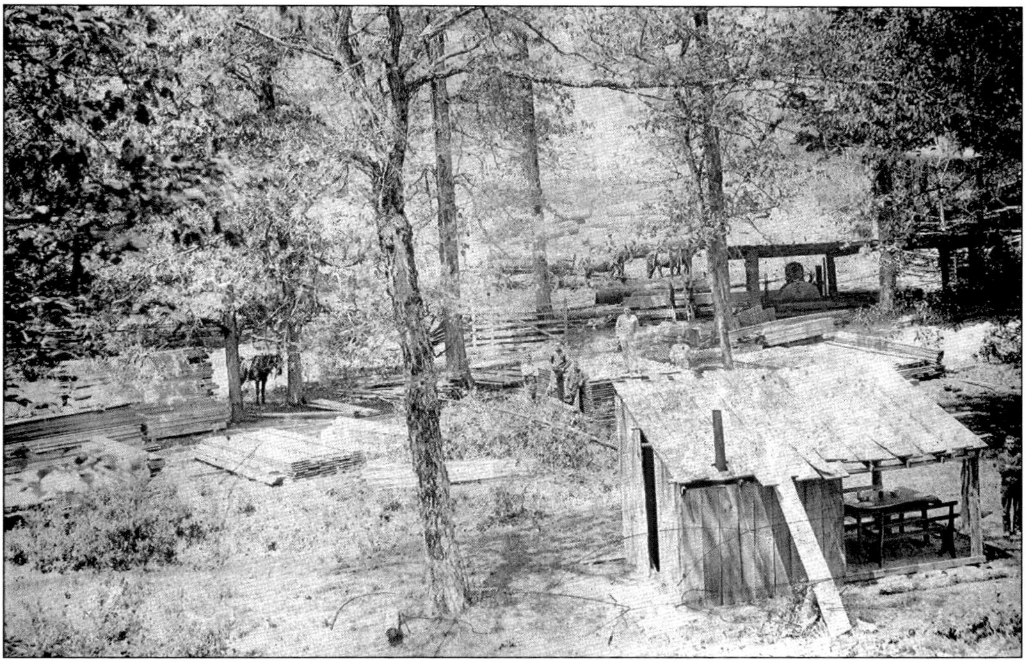

The Goose family owned two mills in Jeffersontown. One was located at the Goose family farm, while the other, located on what is now Billtown Road, was owned by William Goose Jr. in partnership with Henry Woolet. (Photo courtesy of Sallie Cheatham Smith.)

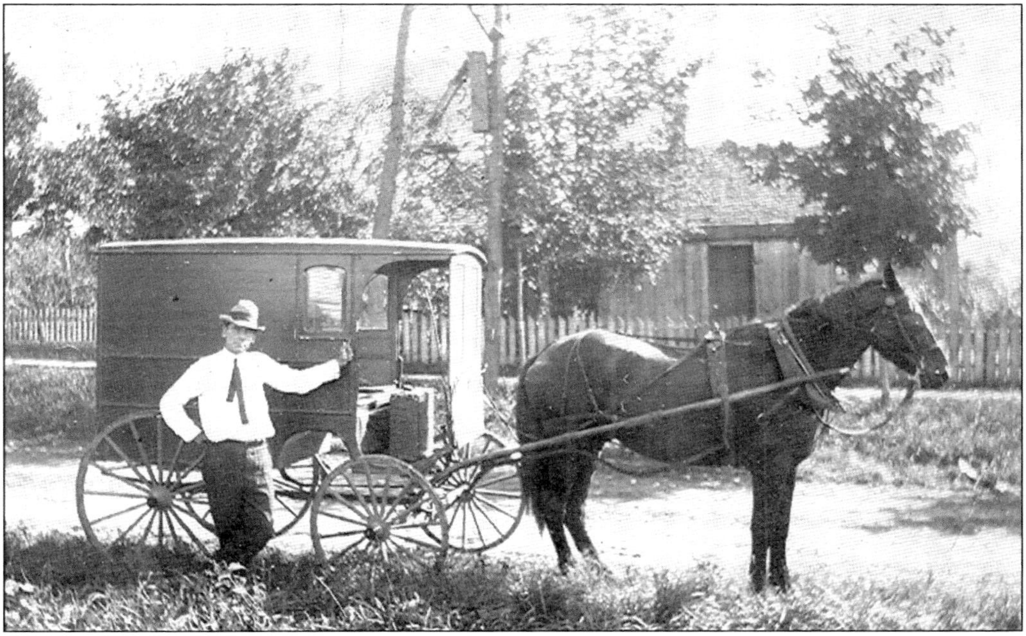

Hucksters' wagons were a popular sight in the old days. Peddlers sold their wares—typically meat, poultry, eggs, and produce—door to door as they traveled about in their horse-drawn wagons. Here, Eberhart Mittler is seen standing next to his wagon in the early 1900s. (Photo courtesy of Jack Mittler.)

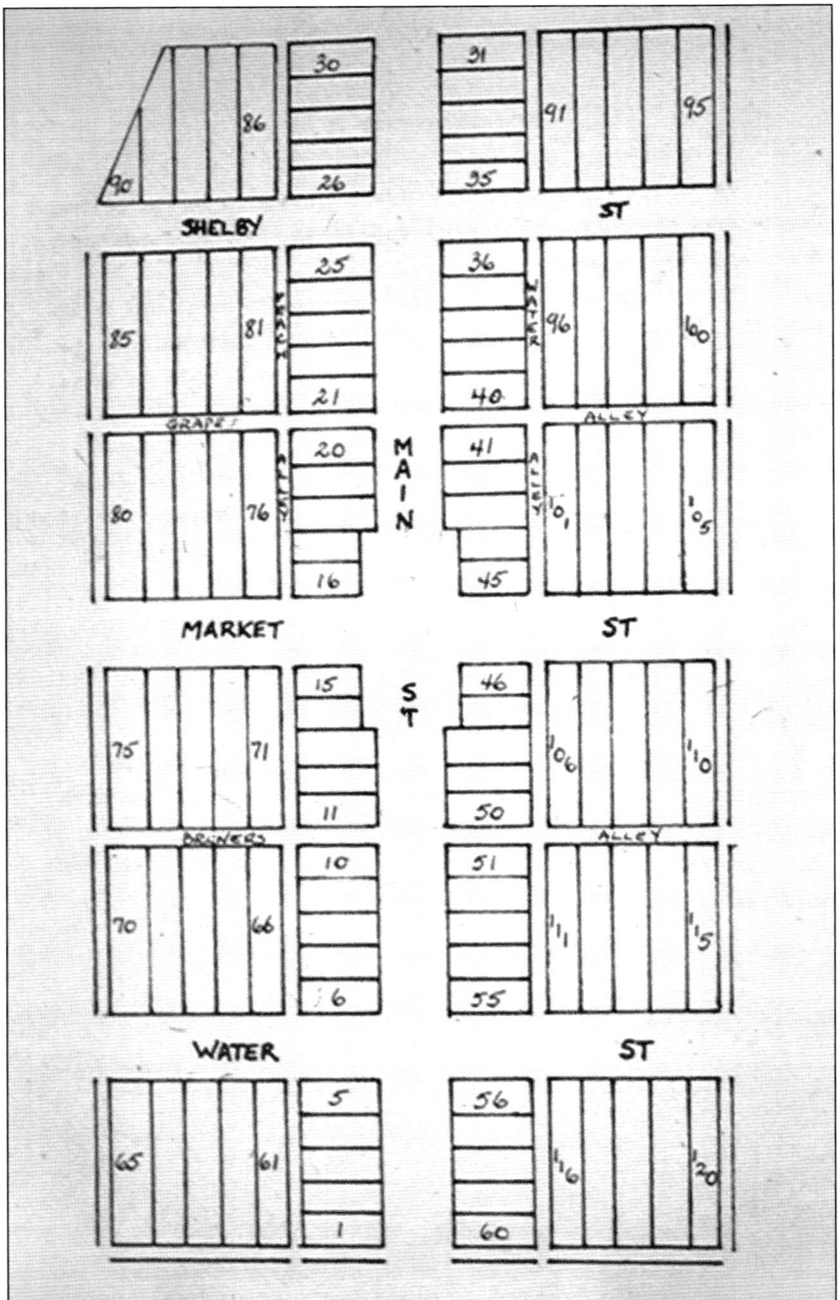

FIGURE 4. The Town Lots

This plot map is commonly referred to as the Brunerstown Layout. In 1794, Abraham Bruner purchased 122 acres with the intent of selling lots to businessmen in order to create a city. Main Street and Market Street are now known as Watterson Trail and Taylorsville Road. The spot where they cross is known as Gaslight Square, which is considered the heart of Jeffersontown. (Photo courtesy of Lt. Col. Robert C. Jobson.)

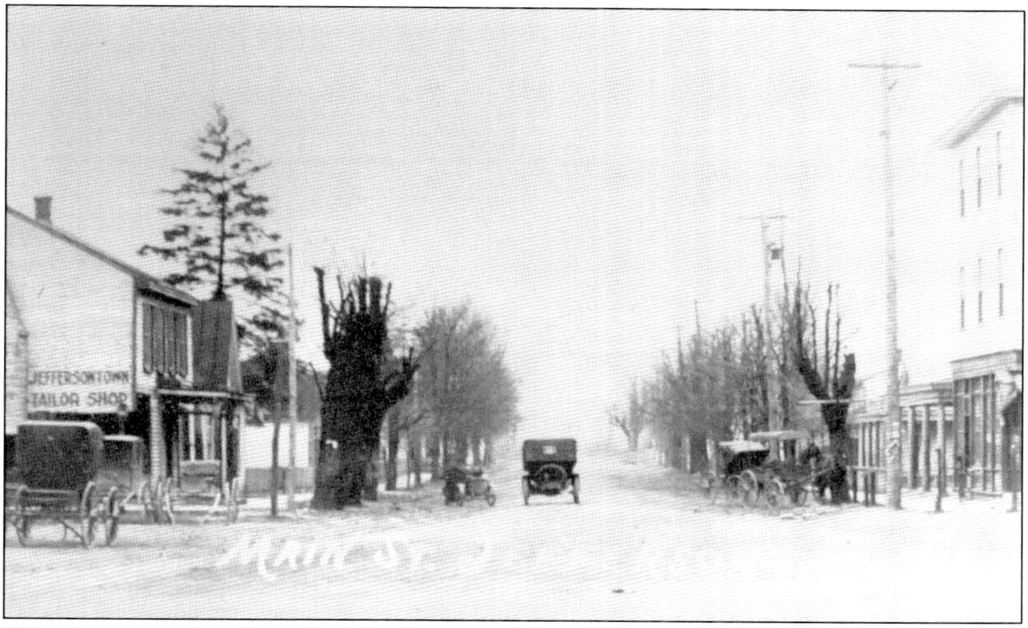

This photo was taken from Gaslight Square and shows the view looking north on Main Street, or Watterson Trail, which was still a dirt road at the time. The Jeffersontown Tailor Shop on the left stood in the space now occupied by Jeffersontown Hardware. The Bruce Building is seen at the far right. (Photo courtesy of the Jeffersontown Historical Museum.)

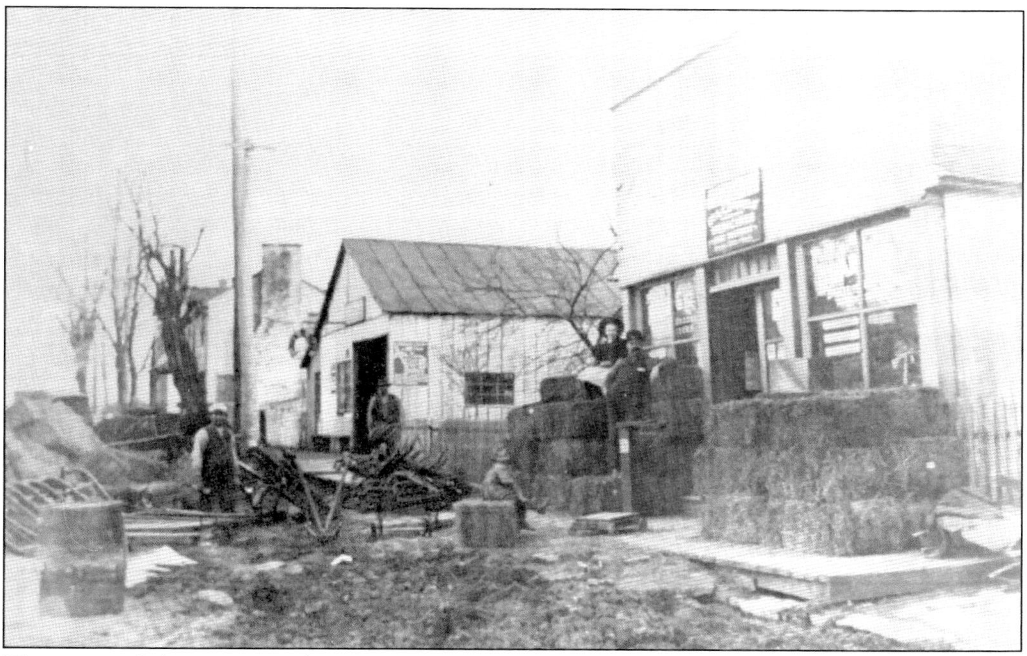

This view of shops on Market Street, or Taylorsville Road, was taken just west of the town square while work was being done on either the dirt roads or the wooden sidewalks. Note the extensive use of advertising on the buildings, including a sign for medicines at the far right. (Photo courtesy of the Jeffersontown Historical Museum.)

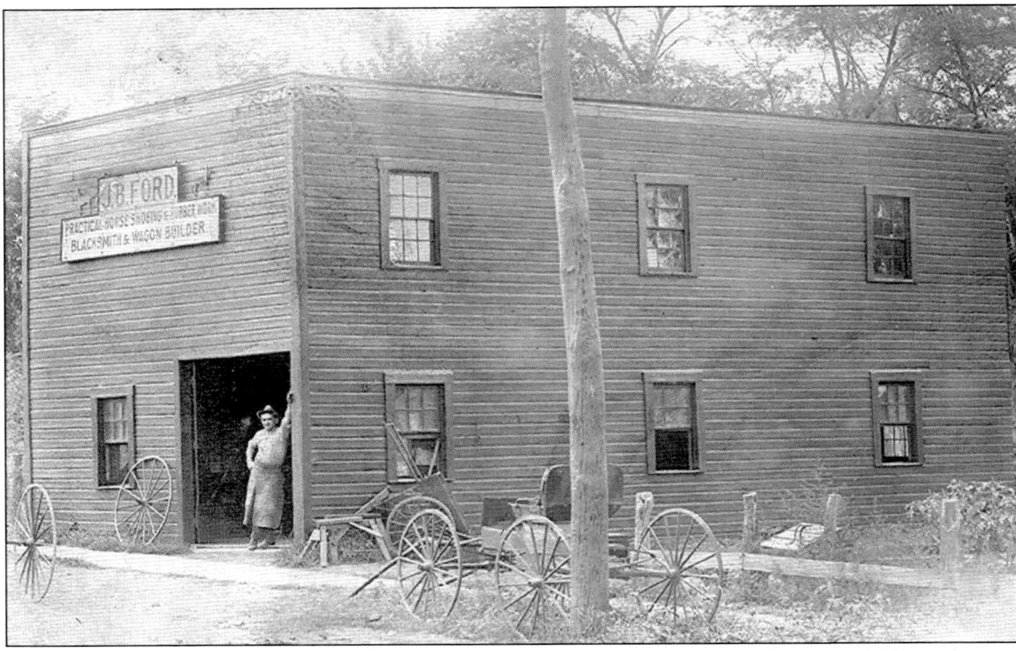

Lewis Salem Ford stands in front of his father's business, titled J.B. Ford Practical Horseshoeing & Rubberwork, Blacksmith & Wagon Builder, c. 1899. The building was located next to the Jeffersonian newspaper office. (Photo courtesy of Betty Ford McClain and Patricia Ford Atchley.)

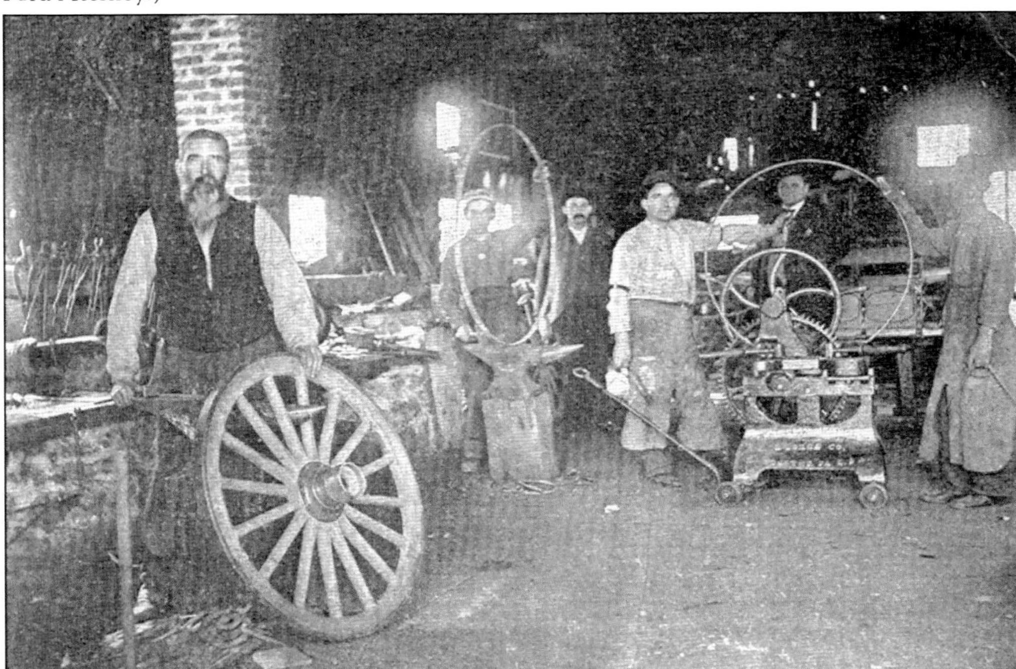

Here is John B. Ford (on left) inside his blacksmith shop. His son, Lewis Salem Ford, is third from left. (Photo courtesy of Betty Ford McClain and Patricia Ford Atchley.)

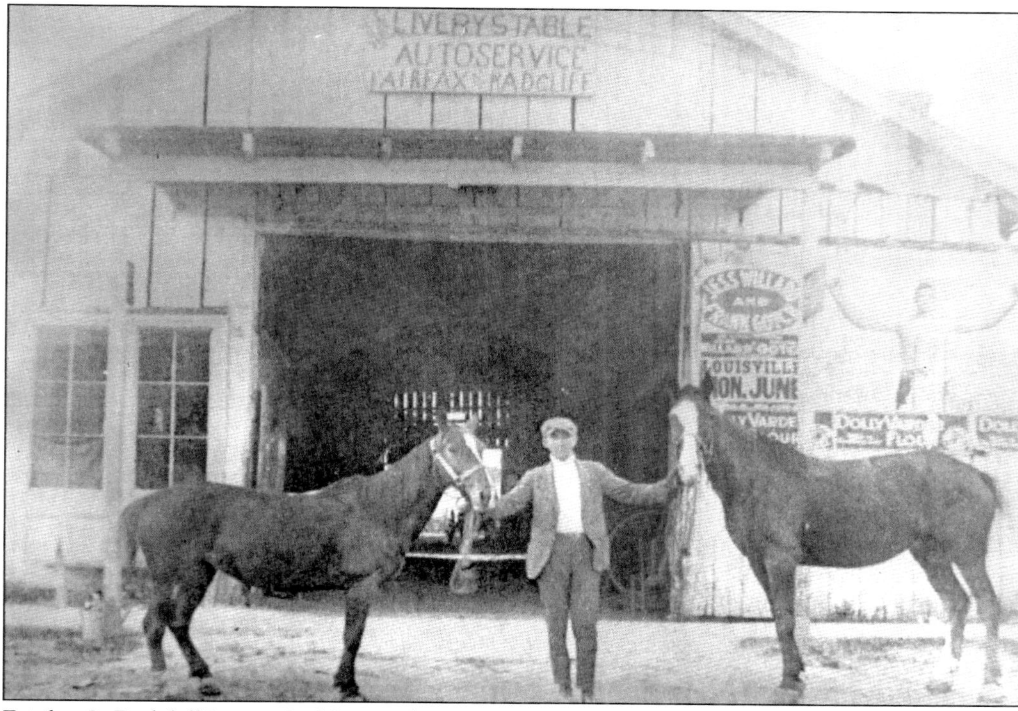

Fairfax & Radcliff Livery Stable stood next to the old Jefferson House hotel on the northwest corner of the town square. The sign above the door shows that the livery stable had already adapted to automobile service by 1914, when this photo was taken. (Photo courtesy of the Jeffersontown Historical Museum.)

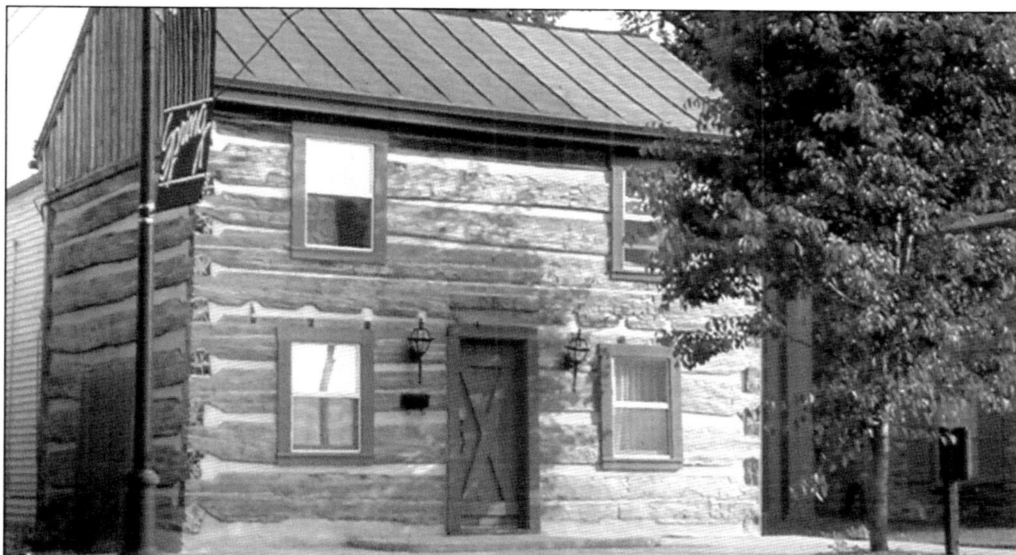

The Leatherman log cabin is probably the most easily recognizable building in Jeffersontown. Located on the north end of Watterson Trail, this two-story log house was built c. 1826 by blacksmith John B. Leatherman. He sold the house in 1841 to his nephew, John Leatherman, a wagon maker. (Photo courtesy of Jane Smith.)

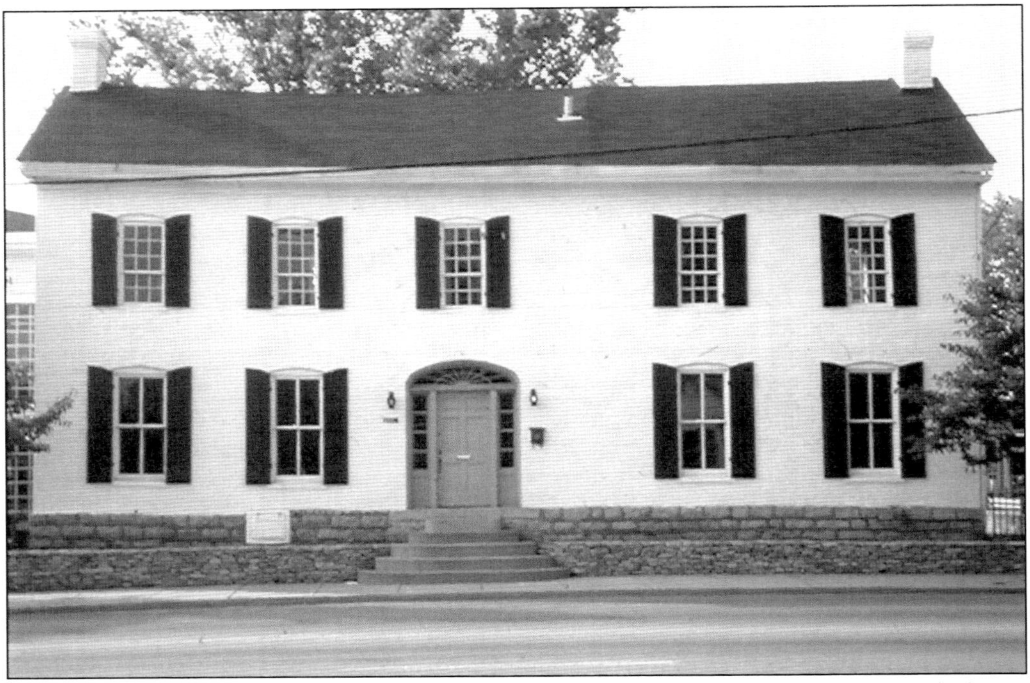

The Seaton House, which stands on the south end of Watterson Trail, was built around a home originally constructed by brothers William and Valentine Conrad, potters whose wares were shipped primarily to New Orleans for sale. In 1844, the property was bought by Dr. John S. Seaton, who enlarged the house. Several people have owned the house since then, but the name "Seaton" has stuck with it. (Photo courtesy of Jane Smith.)

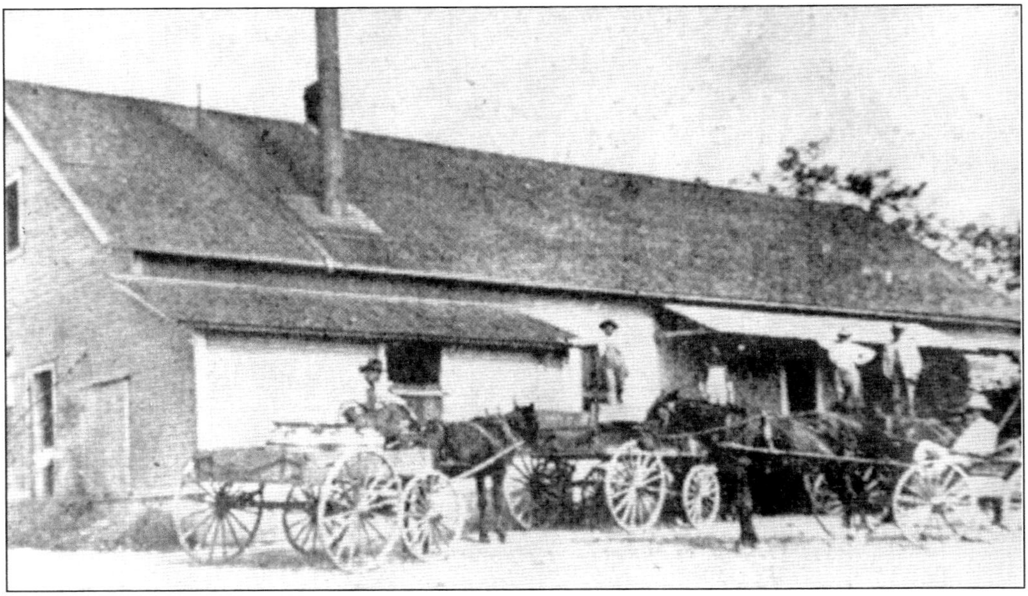

The Jeffersontown Creamery was located south of the Seaton House on the corner of Billtown Road. Before it was destroyed by fire in the 1920s, the creamery was known for the high quality of the butter it produced. (Photo courtesy of the Jeffersontown Historical Museum.)

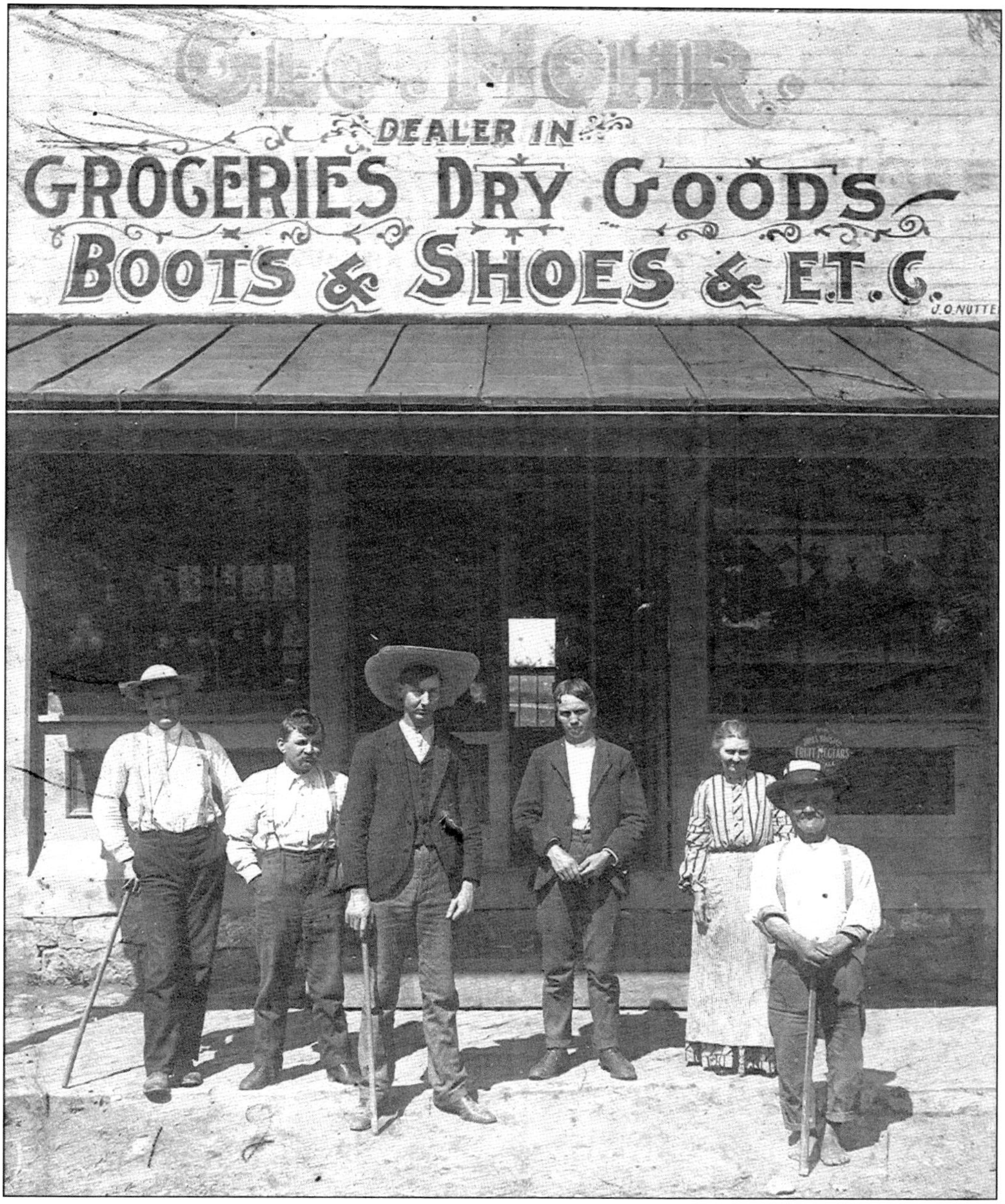

Ownership of businesses tended to change hands rather frequently in the early days of Jeffersontown, so although the top of the sign in this photo says "Geo. Mohr," Fred Bauer actually owned this general store at the turn of the 20th century, when this picture was taken. Standing left to right in front of the store are the following: unidentified; Fred, the brother of Sallie Bauer Bennett; Bruce Hoke; H. Knauer; unidentified; and Elias "Duck" Thompson. (Photo courtesy of Jack Mittler.)

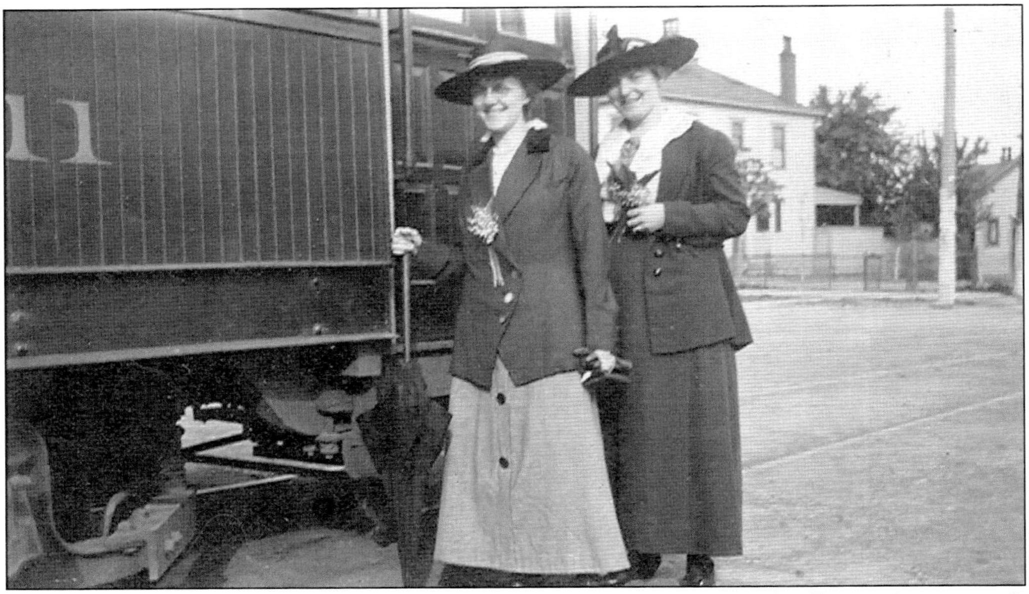

The Louisville & Interurban Railroad connected the outlying areas of Jefferson County with Louisville. Jeffersontown's interurban was the first line put into operation on May 2, 1903. Travelers boarded at the southeast corner of the square, where a lovely Victorian-style clock now stands. The interurban was abandoned in 1932 and replaced by a bus line operated by Blue Motor Coach Company. (Photo courtesy of Tom Lovett.)

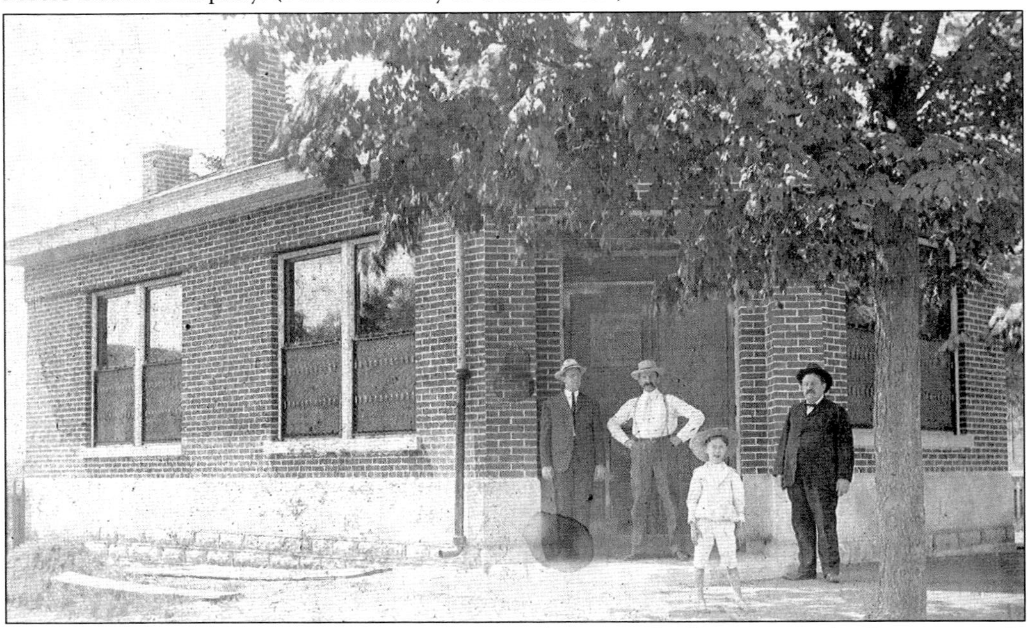

The Jefferson County Bank was organized in 1904 by some of Jeffersontown's leading citizens. It moved into a new building on the northwest corner of Taylorsville Road and Watterson Trail in 1927, but closed September 24, 1931, due to hard economic times. Pictured left to right in this 1907 photo are bank president H.N. Reubelt, E.R. Sprowl, William Bryan, and bank cashier D. Price Vanarsdale. (Photo courtesy of Marcia Bryan Horton.)

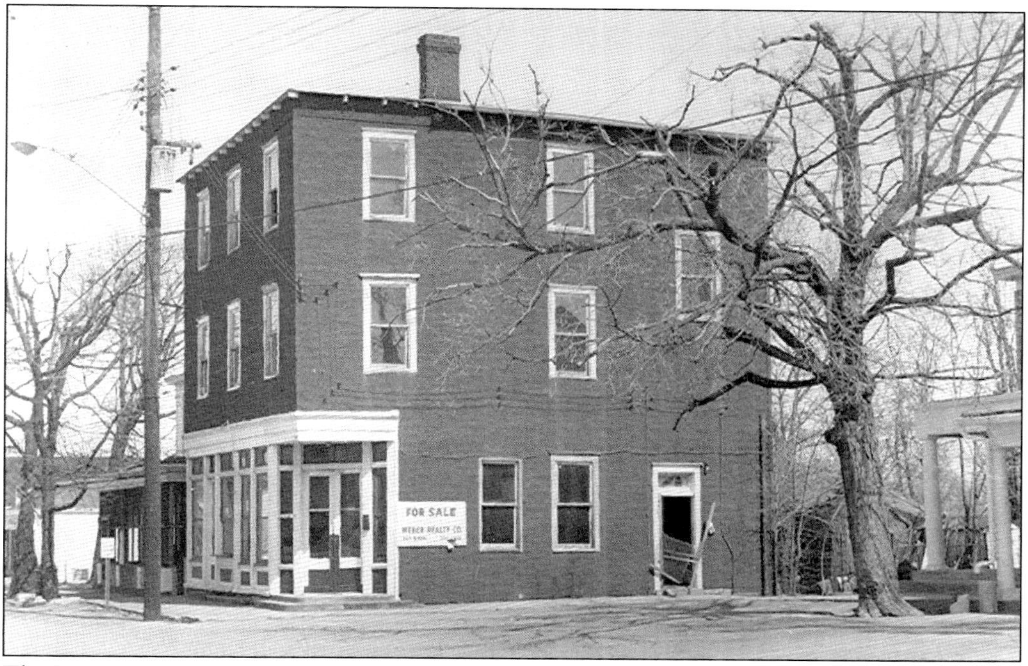

The Bruce Building was constructed on the north end of Watterson Trail in 1907 by J.C. Bruce. Over the years, it housed many businesses, including the *Jeffersonian* newspaper, the town's first public library, the office of E.R. Sprowl, Dr. Oatey's drug store, and Kozy Korner tavern. (Photo courtesy of Lt. Col. Robert C. Jobson.)

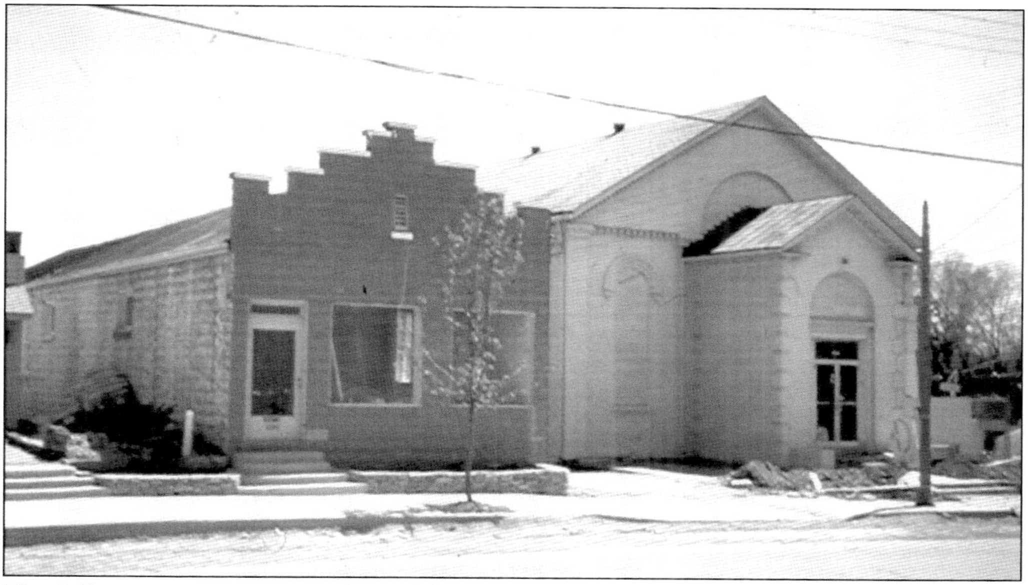

The *Jeffersonian* newspaper made its debut June 13, 1907, and was moved to the building on the left in 1913. The paper remained a staple in Jeffersontown until 1959, when it was merged with the *Voice* of St. Matthews. The building on the right was constructed in 1837 to house the Christian Church, but when the congregation outgrew the building, it was sold to the Moose Lodge. (Photo courtesy of Jane Smith.)

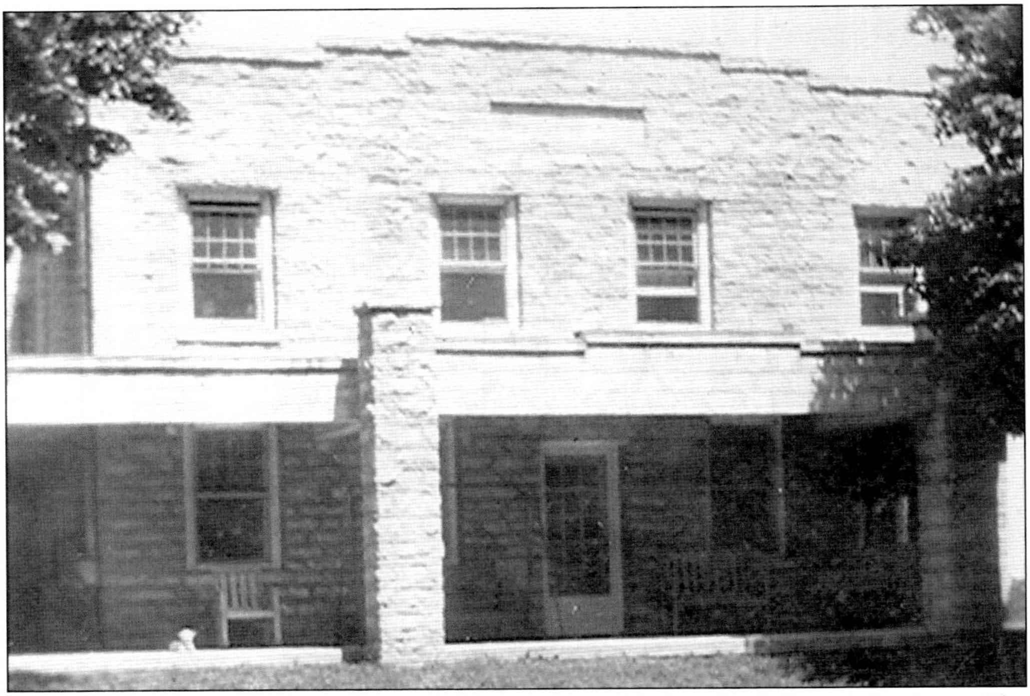

Christ Lutheran Home was originally built in 1836 to house the Jefferson Academy. The Mittler family purchased the building in 1905 and made it their home until 1925, when they sold the property back to the Lutheran Churches of Louisville and Jefferson County, who rebuilt the house and opened it in 1927 as a home for the elderly. (Photo courtesy of Elizabeth Bishop.)

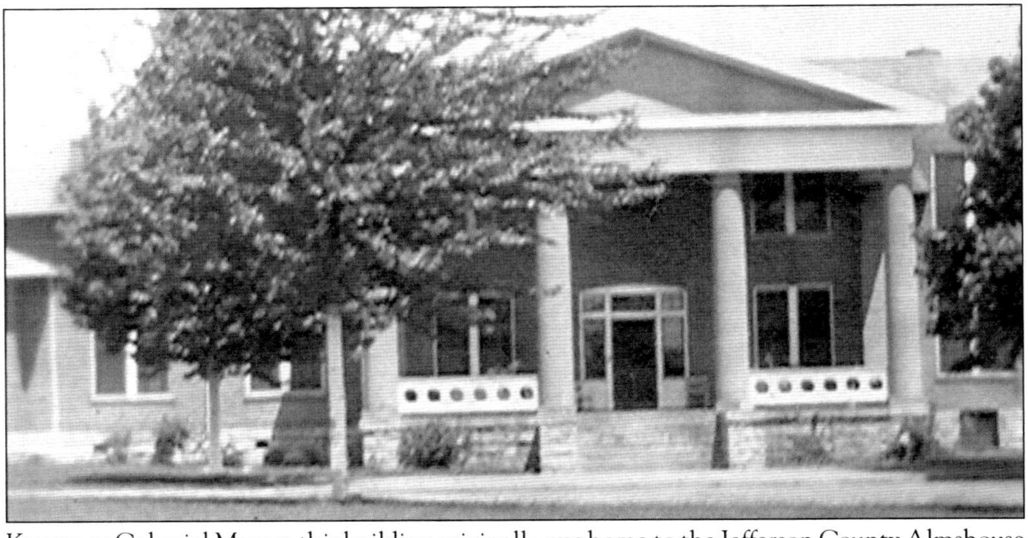

Known as Colonial Manor, this building originally was home to the Jefferson County Almshouse from 1914 until the 1920s, when it became the Jefferson County Home for the Aged. In 1970, the Jeffersontown Branch of the Louisville Free Public Library moved into the building, where it remained until 1995. The building was renovated and reopened in 1998 as the Daniel H. Ruckriegel Senior Citizens Center. (Photo courtesy of Elizabeth Bishop.)

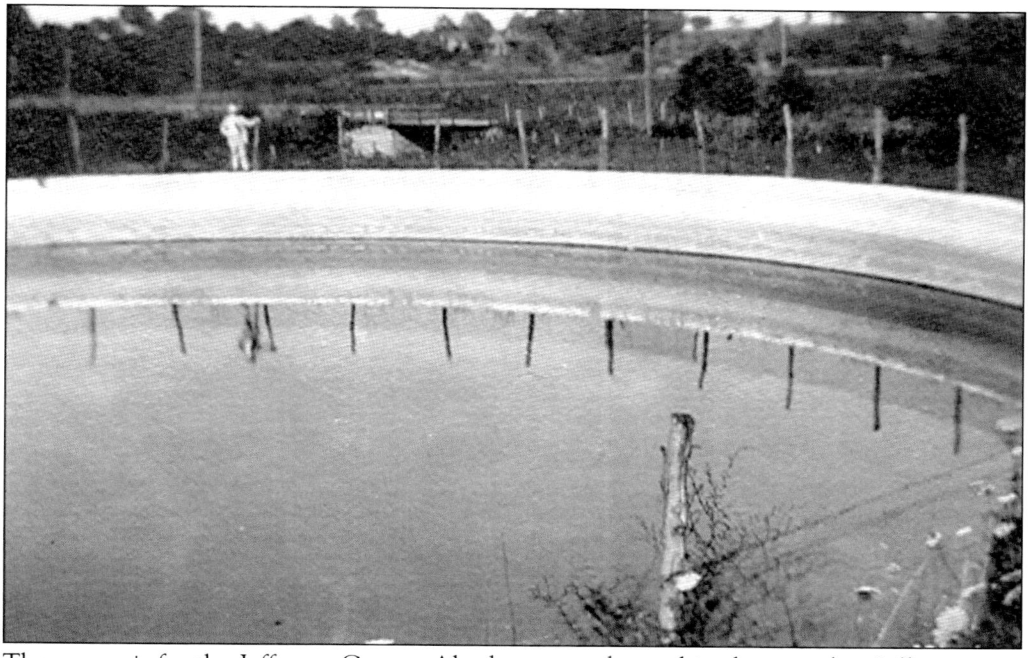

The reservoir for the Jefferson County Almshouse was located in the area that Jeffersontown Public Works now occupies. The reservoir supplied the residents of the almshouse with water for personal use as well as fire protection. (Photo courtesy of Julia Smith.)

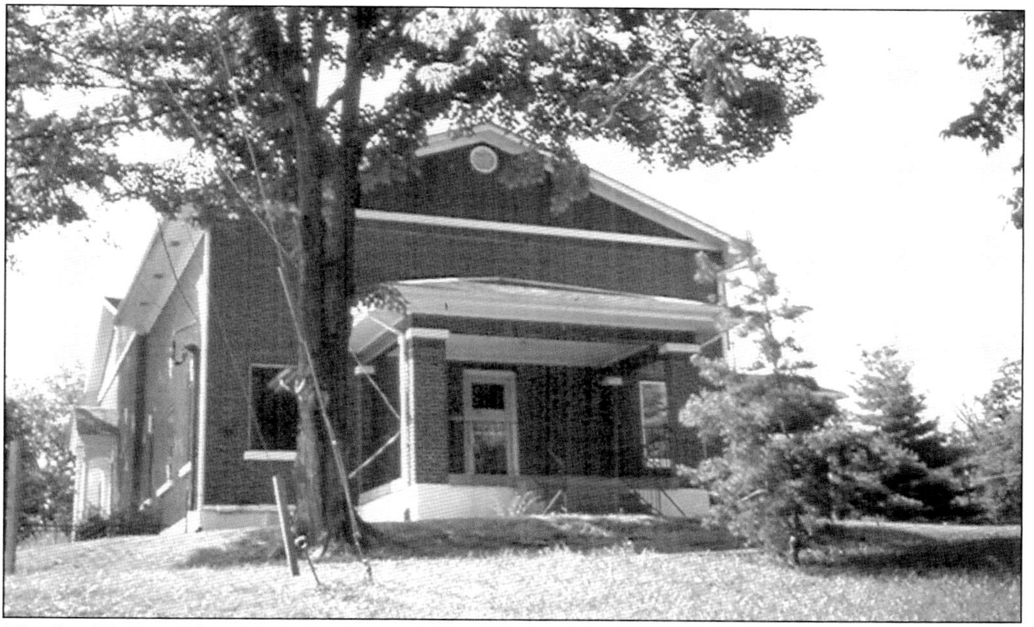

This building was home to the African-American residents of the almshouse. In later years, the building was renovated by the County Welfare Department, and in 1946 it was dedicated as the Sunshine Lodge, which provided immediate temporary care for children in need. More recently, the building housed the Jeffersontown Police Department until it moved to a new location on Taylorsville Road. (Photo courtesy of Jane Smith.)

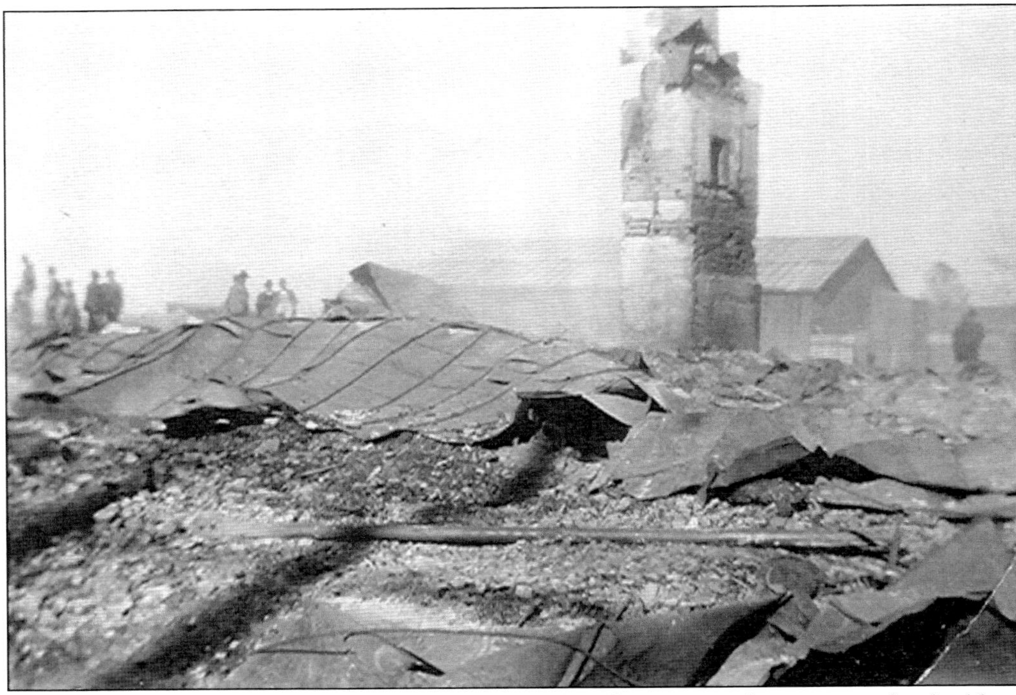

In November 1921, a devastating fire swept through Jeffersontown, leaving very few buildings standing. This photo shows residents walking amid the ruins on the square. (Photo courtesy of Julia Smith.)

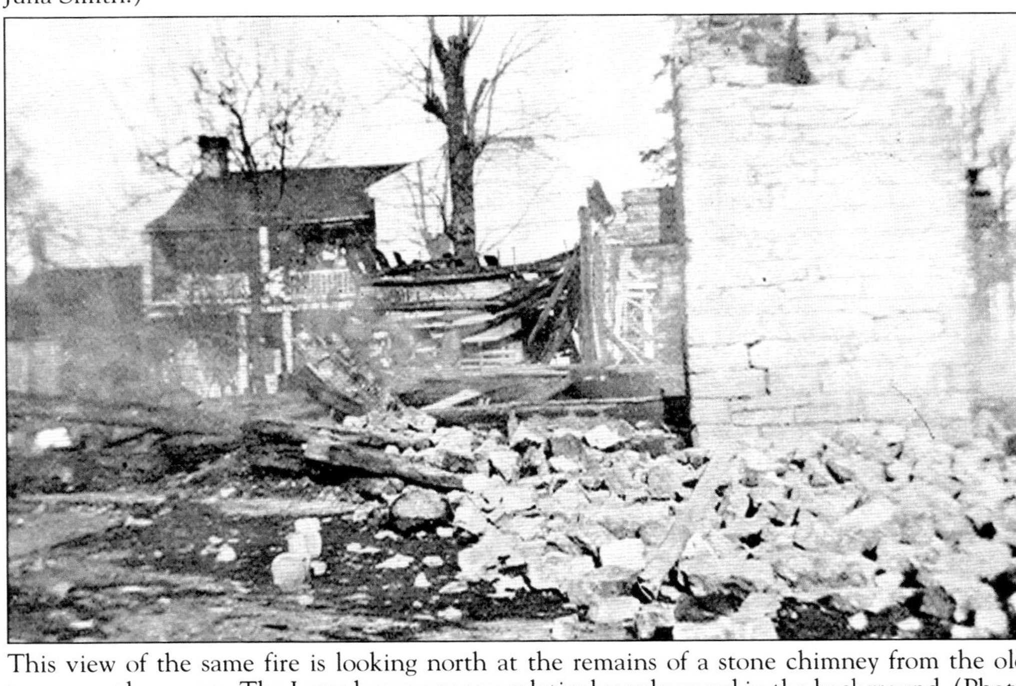

This view of the same fire is looking north at the remains of a stone chimney from the old tavern on the square. The Lutes house appears relatively undamaged in the background. (Photo courtesy of Julia Smith.)

The Municipal Building occupied the southeast corner of the town square and housed the fire department and town meeting hall. Machine guns and field pieces from World War I were put atop the roof of this building, which was completed in 1926. (Photo courtesy of Chief Fred L. Roemele.)

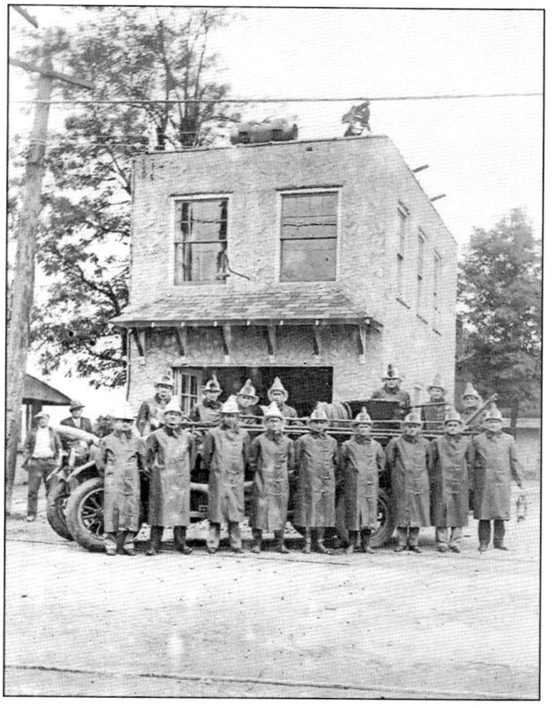

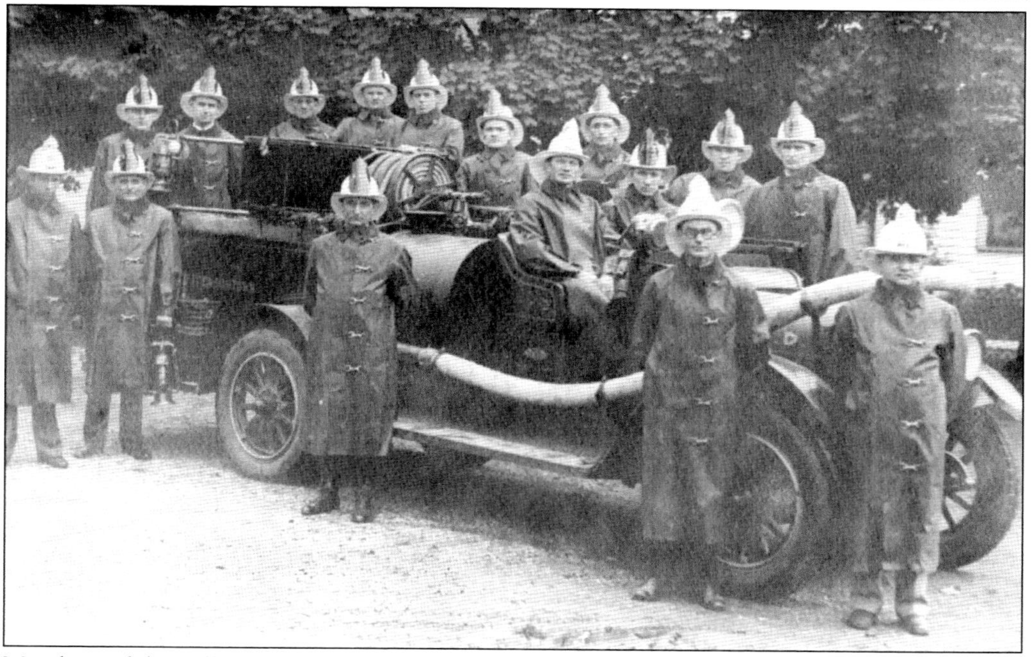

Members of the Jeffersontown Volunteer Fire Department, pictured here c. 1926, are, from left to right, as follows: (front row) George Bowles, Fred Myers, ? Seitz, Emery Smith, and ? Bruce; (back row) Lawrence Miller, Melvin Hawes, Levy Brooks, Roy Montgomery, ? Eddleman, ? Ellaby, Sam Brooks, Marshall Floore, Larry Tyler, Noel Quisenberry, and Marion Floore. (Photo courtesy of Chief Fred L. Roemele.)

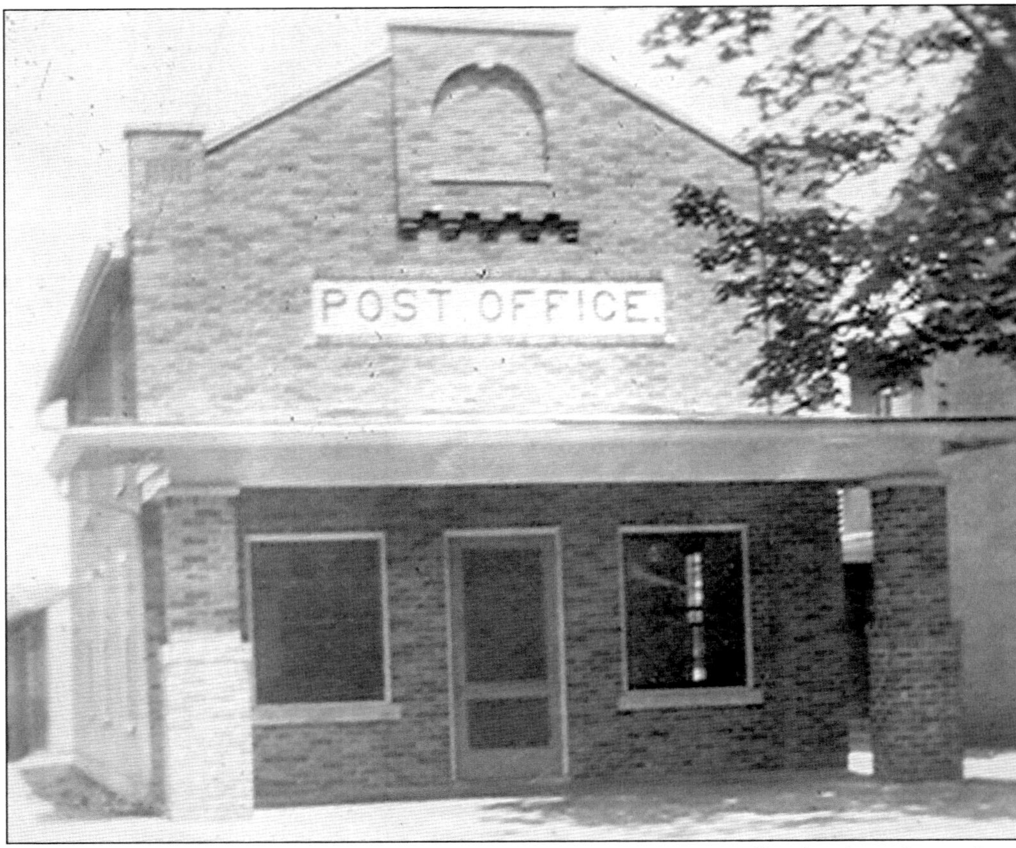

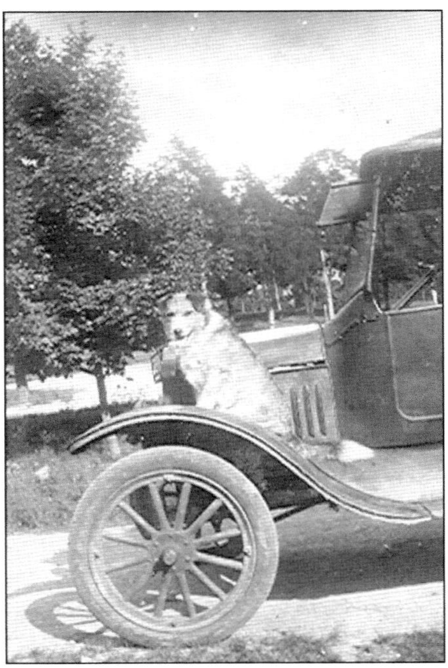

The Jeffersontown Post Office has been located in several different buildings throughout its existence. This photo was taken at its location in the 1920s. (Photo courtesy of Elizabeth Bishop.)

Brownie Bryan was known as the assistant mail carrier, Jeffersontown R.F.D. #13, from 1924 to 1930. He took it upon himself to help Lud Bryan deliver the mail once Lud switched from riding horseback to his new Model T Ford. Brownie liked to ride on the running board by the engine, where he could keep warm. (Photo courtesy of Marcia Bryan Horton.)

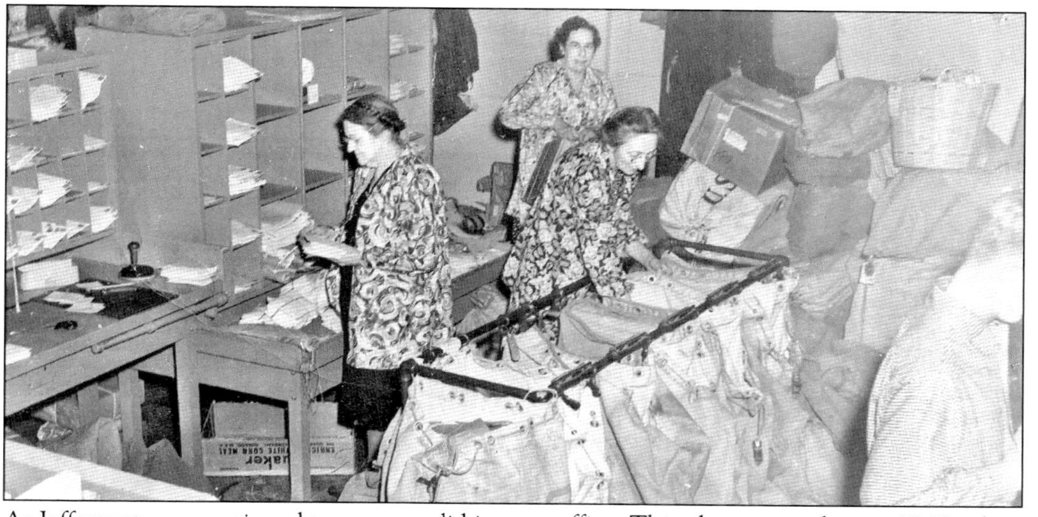

As Jeffersontown continued to grow, so did its post office. This photo was taken in 1949, when the post office was located in the Masonic Building on Watterson Trail. The postal clerks pictured here, from left to right, are Fanny Tucker, Mary Baumlisberger, and Ethel Sprowl Bryan. (Photo courtesy of Marcia Bryan Horton.)

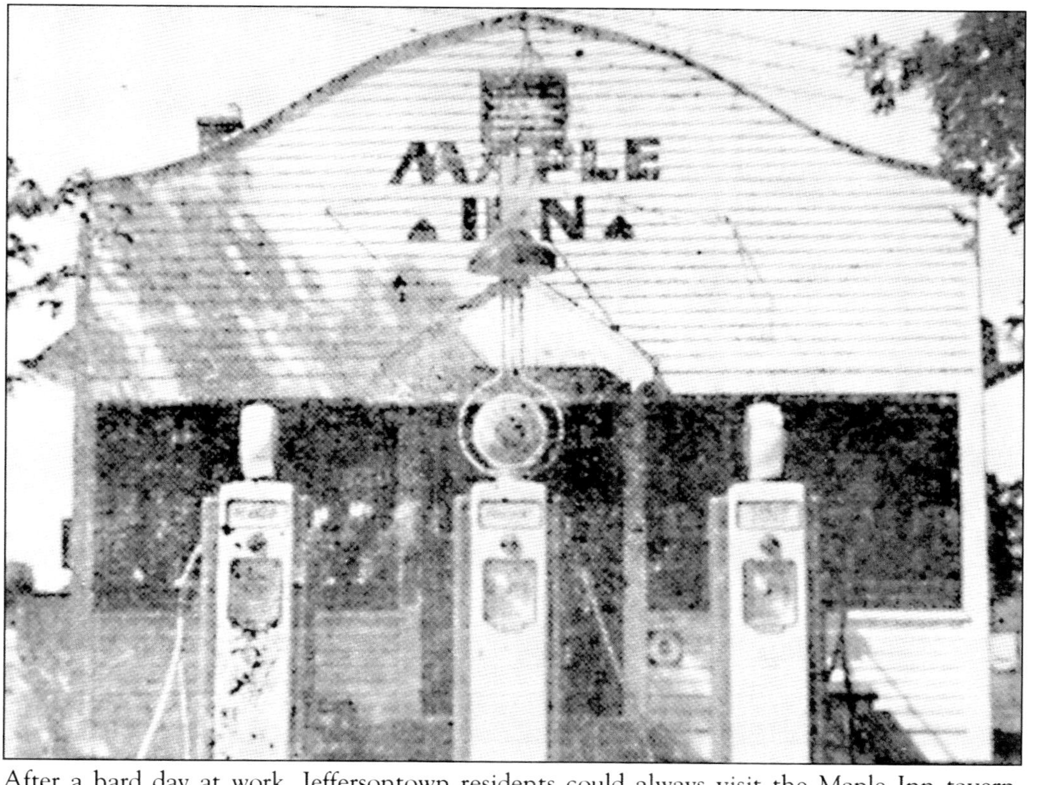

After a hard day at work, Jeffersontown residents could always visit the Maple Inn tavern. While the building had several incarnations along Taylorsville Road, this photo was taken in the 1930s, when the building was located a little closer to the square in Jeffersontown. (Photo courtesy of the Jeffersontown Historical Museum.)

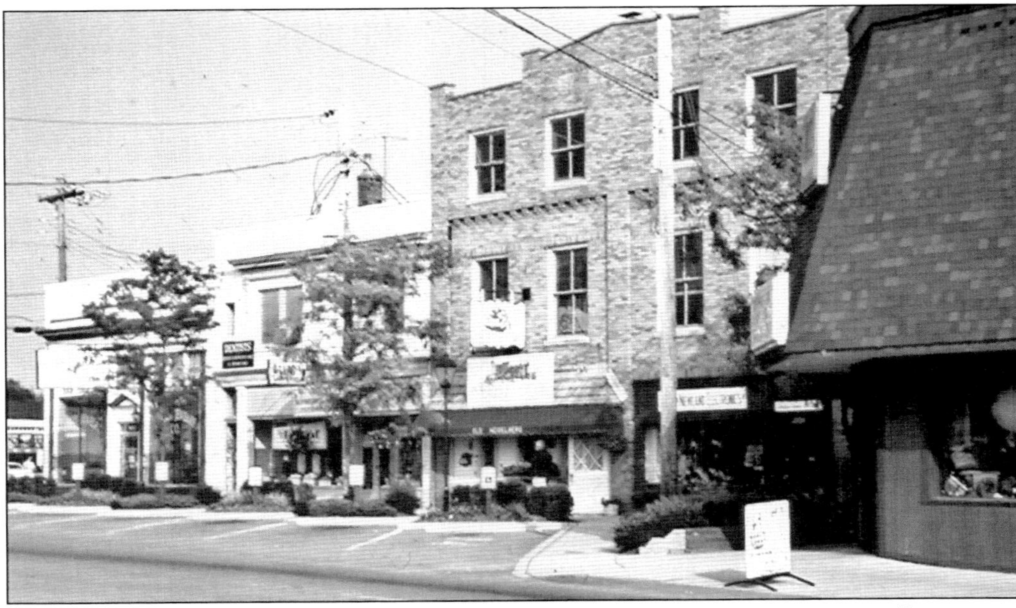

This photo shows a view of what is probably the most recognizable corner in Jeffersontown. Located on the northwest corner of the intersection of Taylorsville Road and Watterson Trail, this strip of buildings has been home to many businesses over the years, including banks, pharmacies, restaurants, grocery stores, and hardware stores, to name just a few. (Photo courtesy of Jane Smith.)

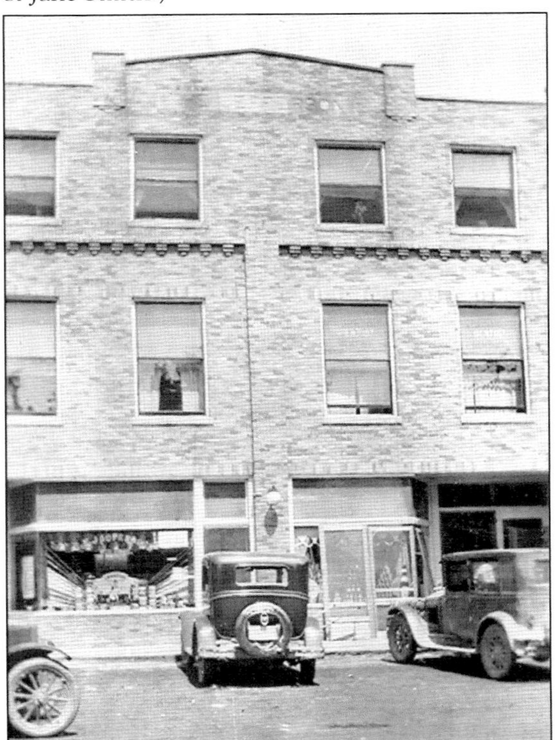

The Jefferson Building was located in the middle of this popular strip. It contained a movie theater and public auditorium on its upper floors, while the first floor was originally occupied by Jasper's Grocery before it moved next to what is now Jeffersontown Hardware, but was originally the Myers and Blankenbaker Funeral Home. (Photo courtesy of Elizabeth Bishop.)

Oatey Drug Store occupied the space between the corner bank and the Jefferson Building. Dr. Oatey's business originally opened in the old Well's store on the northeast corner of Watterson Trail, but it moved to the Bruce Building in 1917, then across the street to the new block of buildings in 1927. (Photo courtesy of Elizabeth Bishop.)

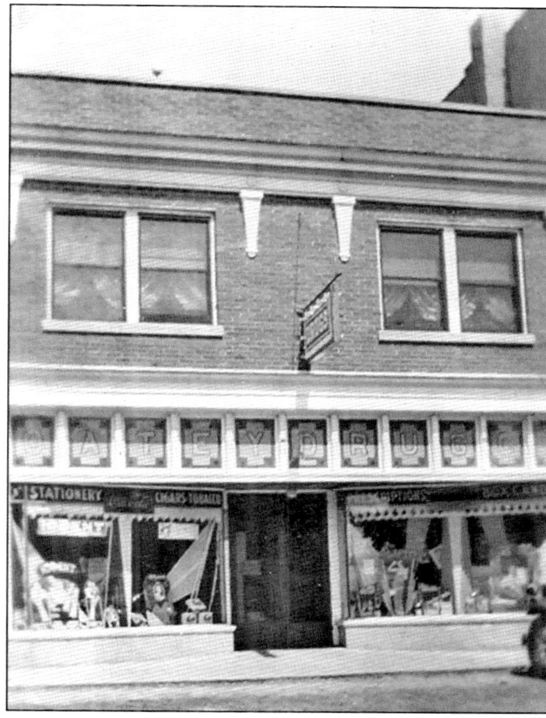

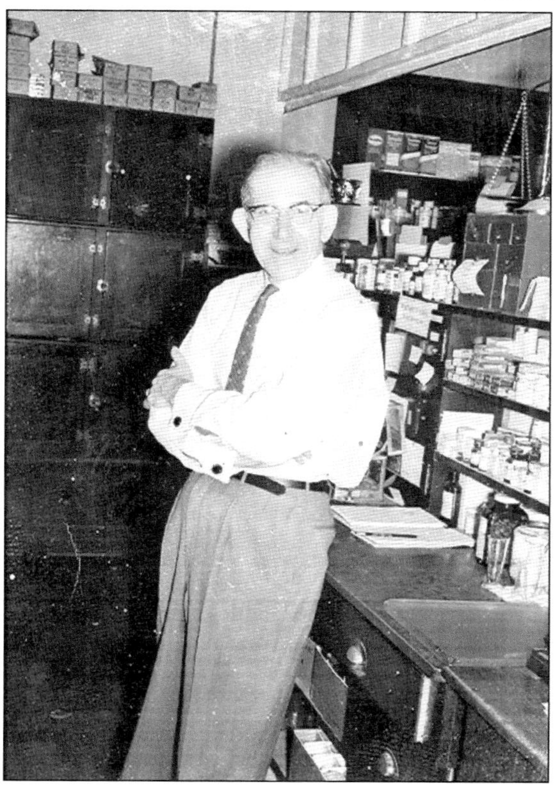

Since Dr. Oatey owned another store on Bardstown Road, he handed over the one in Jeffersontown to William T. Newkirk in the 1930s. Because of its excellent soda fountain, Newkirk's became a popular attraction for visitors from Louisville who were out for a "Sunday drive." (Photo courtesy of Roycelea Newkirk Scott.)

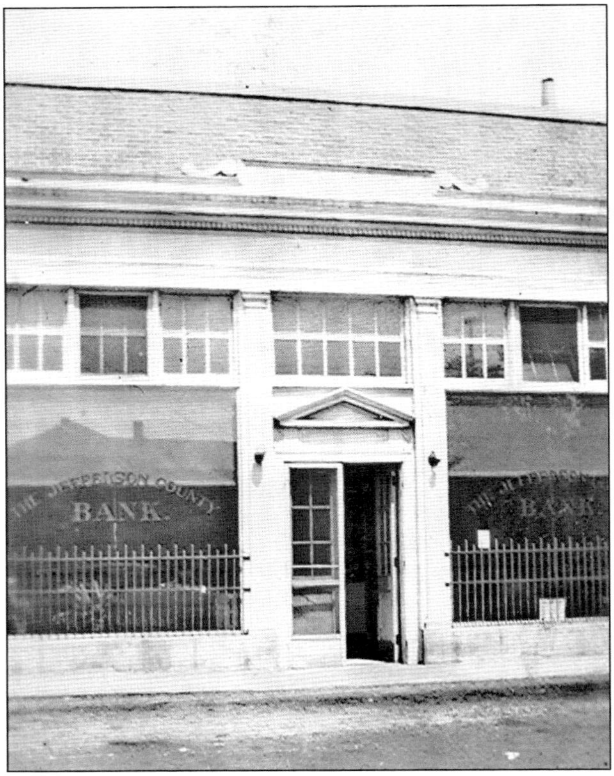

The Jefferson County Bank relocated to the new corner lot on the square in 1927. Hard economic times forced the closure of the bank on September 24, 1931, but by 1941, the new Bank of Jeffersontown opened in the same location. (Photo courtesy of Elizabeth Bishop.)

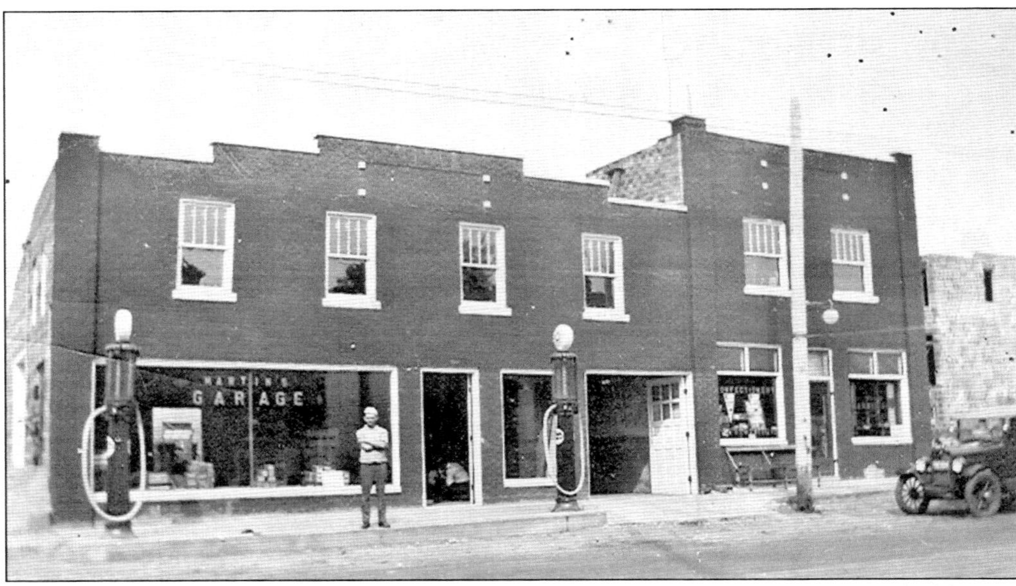

Just behind the bank, the Martin family owned several businesses in a two-story building on Taylorsville Road. William H. Martin's garage occupied the left side of the structure, while the right side housed a barbershop, confectionery, and poolroom operated by his sons. (Photo courtesy of Zita Kay Elder.)

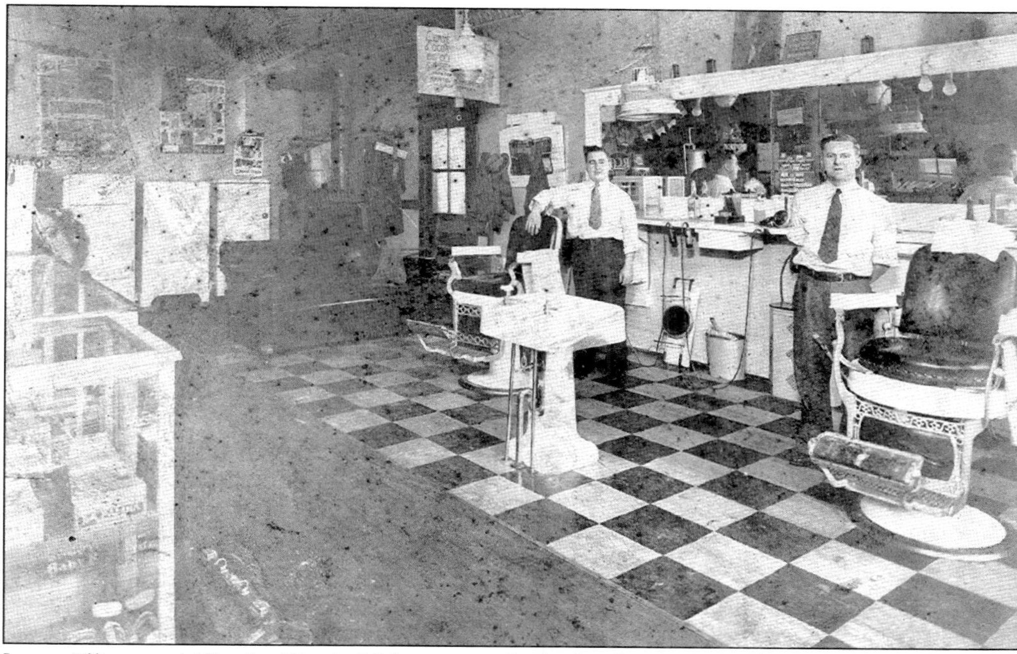

James Elliott and Charles "Bucky" Martin ran the barbershop next to their father's garage. This 1937 photo shows the brothers, Charles and Elliott, next to their barber chairs. Candy cases that held the confections can be seen on the left. (Photo courtesy of Nancy Noel Hood.)

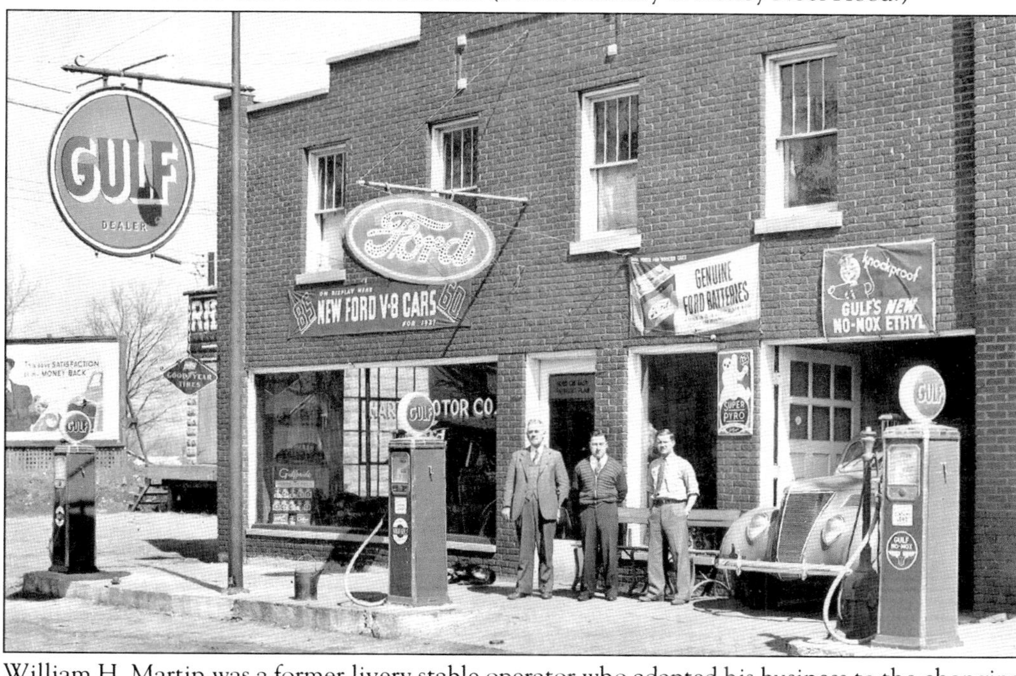

William H. Martin was a former livery stable operator who adapted his business to the changing times. The building, which housed Martin Motor Co., was built in 1925. Pictured from left to right are W.H. Martin, Charles "Bucky" Martin, and Dick Martin. (Photo courtesy of Zita Kay Elder.)

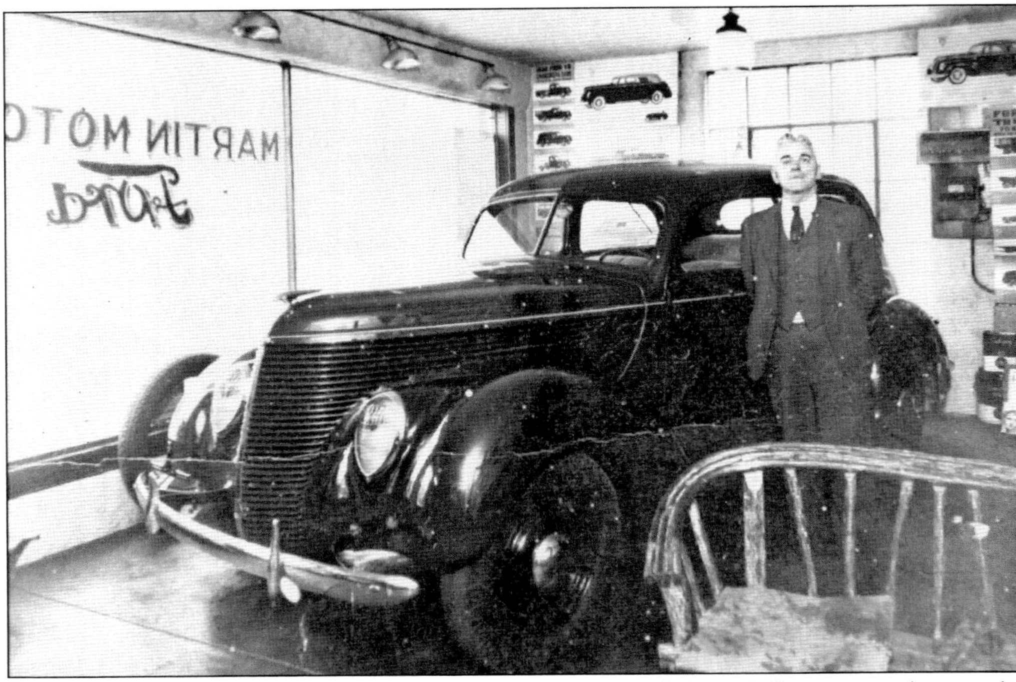

Not only was William H. Martin the first man to sell automobiles in Jeffersontown, he was also the city's first (and only) Ford dealer. Here, Mr. Martin is seen standing next to one of the cars in his showroom. (Photo courtesy of the Jeffersontown Historical Museum.)

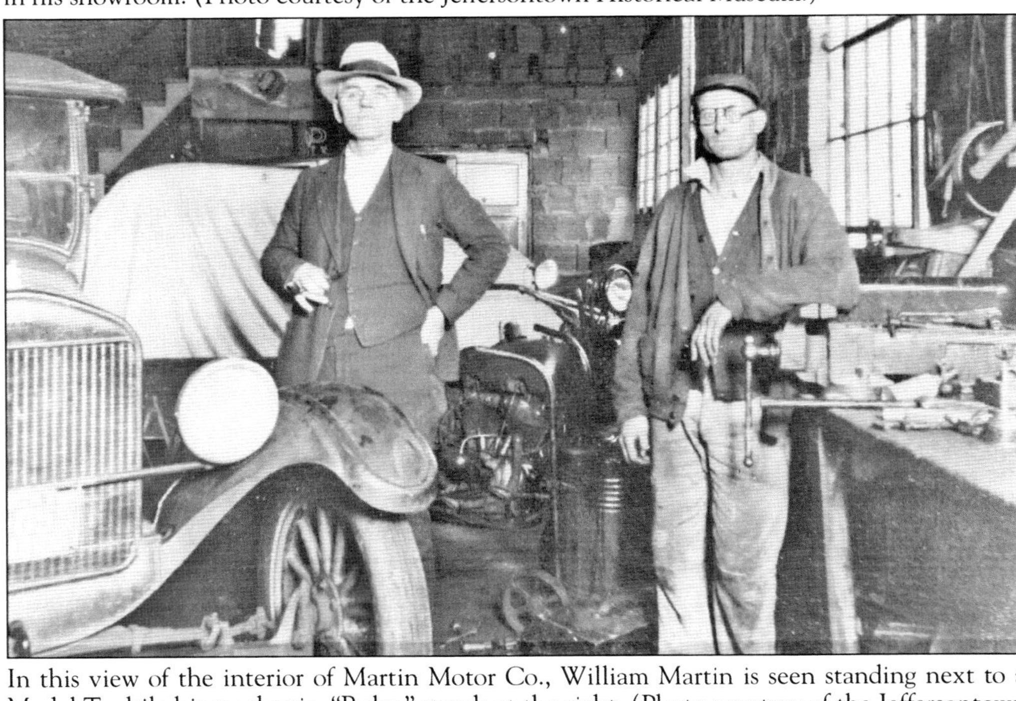

In this view of the interior of Martin Motor Co., William Martin is seen standing next to a Model T while his mechanic, "Roby," stands at the right. (Photo courtesy of the Jeffersontown Historical Museum.)

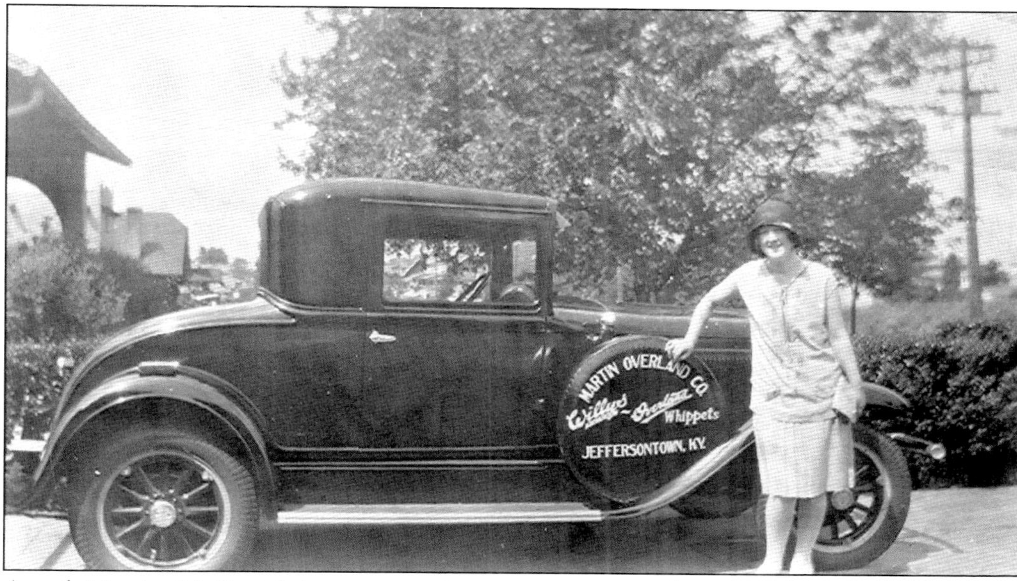

Averil Martin McDaniel is seen standing next to a car bearing advertising for Willys-Knight and Overland cars, which were also sold by Martin Motor Co. (Photo courtesy of Zita Kay Elder.)

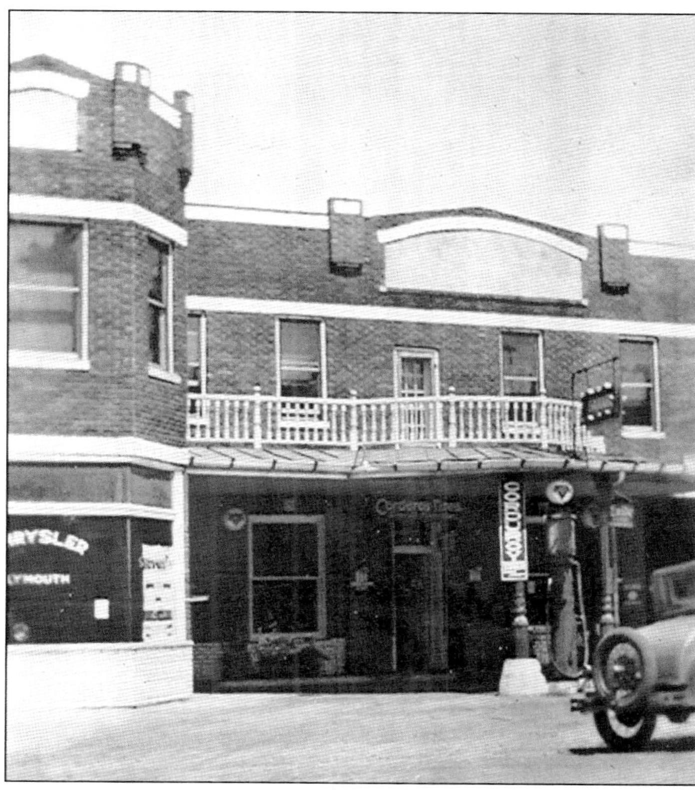

The Jeffersontown Garage was opened in 1915 by Louie C. Coe. Fire destroyed the original frame structure in 1925, so a new brick edifice was built according to stricter standards about 1927. Hudson-Essex automobiles were sold at this location. (Photo courtesy of Elizabeth Bishop.)

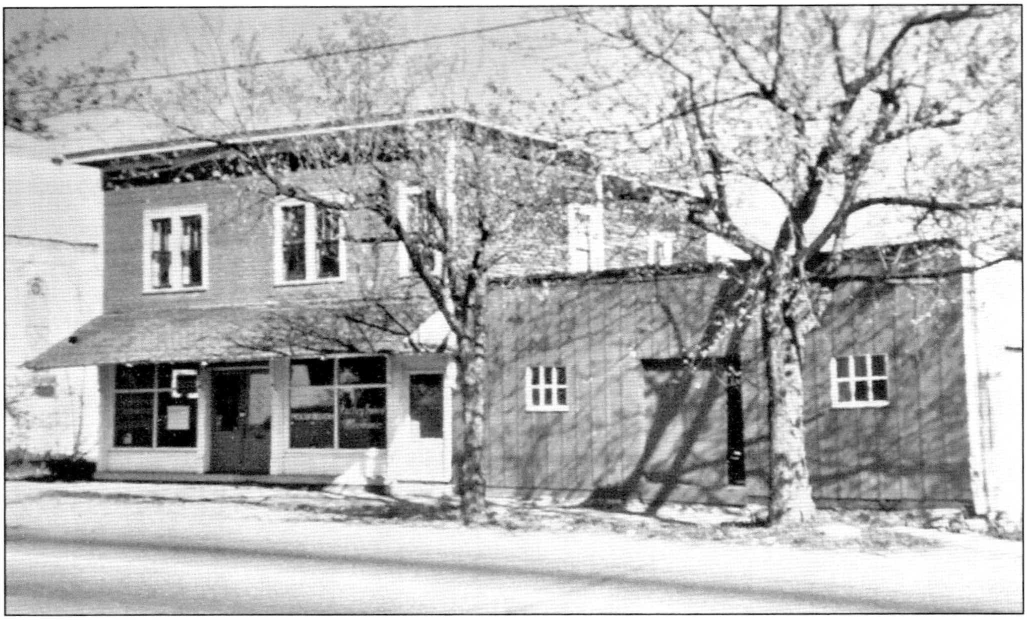

E.G. Hewitt built his hardware store on Watterson Trail in 1915. A pond behind the shop was the square's only source of water for fighting fires at the time. (Photo courtesy of Priscilla Hewitt Becker.)

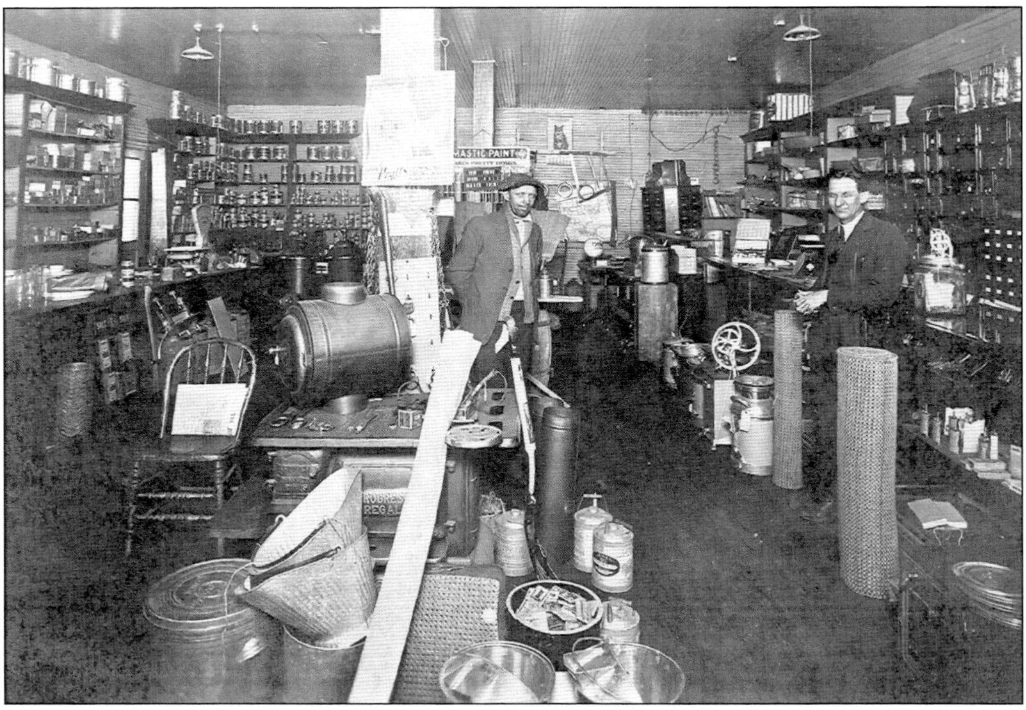

This interior photo of E.G. Hewitt's Hardware Company shows the vast extent of Mr. Hewitt's wares. An unidentified man is in the center of the room, while Mr. Hewitt is seen standing to the right. (Photo courtesy of Priscilla Hewitt Becker.)

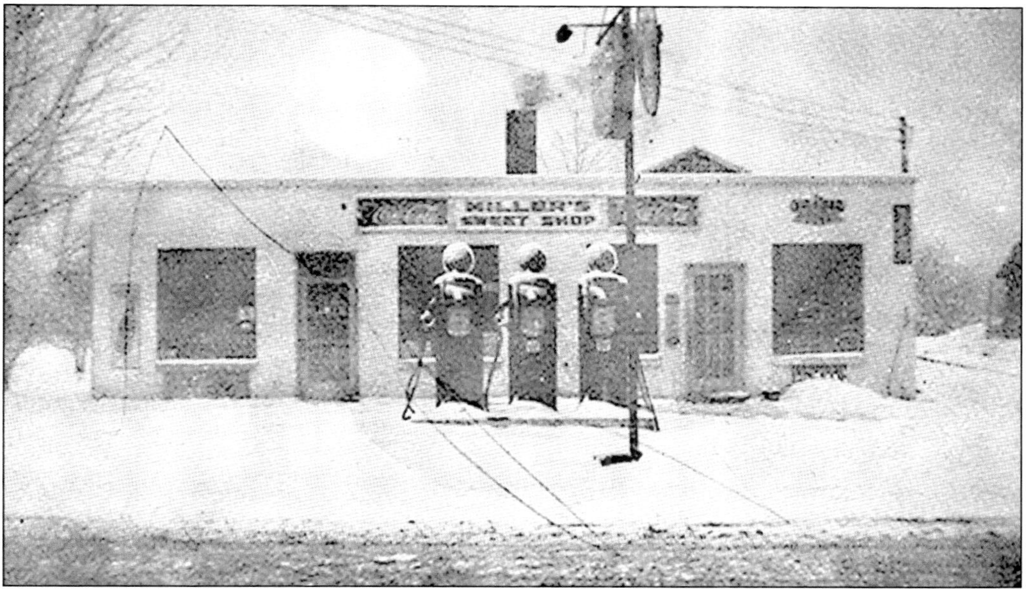

Miller's Sweet Shop, located on Taylorsville Road near the southwest corner of the square, was owned by Carl William Miller and his wife, Lillian. (Photo courtesy of Carole Chambers Davis.)

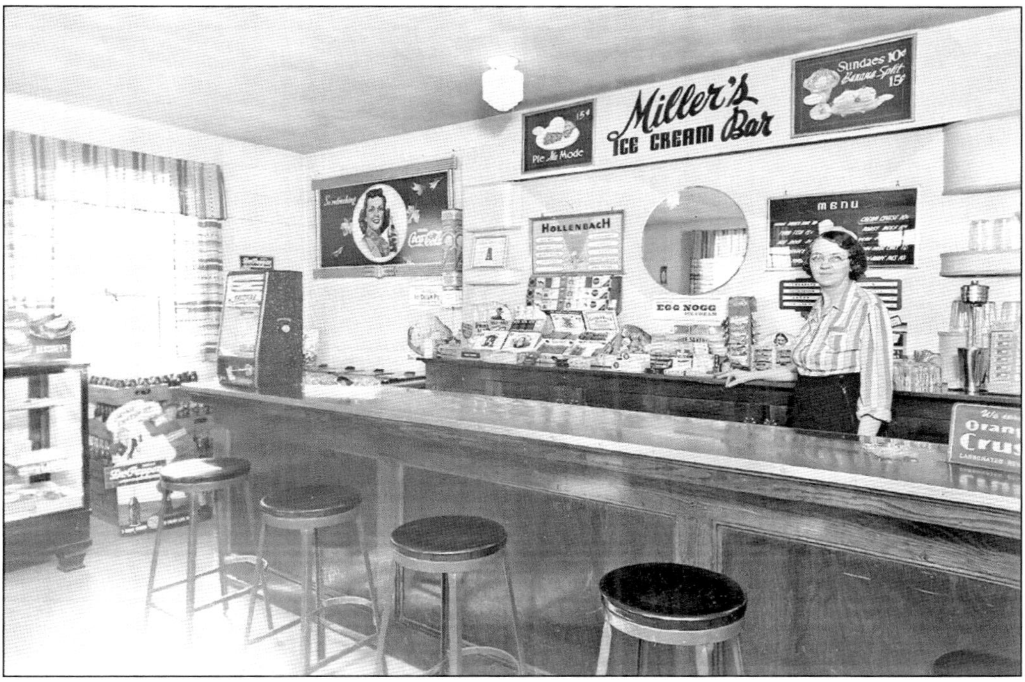

Lillian Holloway Miller is seen standing behind the counter of Miller's Sweet Shop in this 1935 photo. (Photo courtesy of Carole Chambers Davis.)

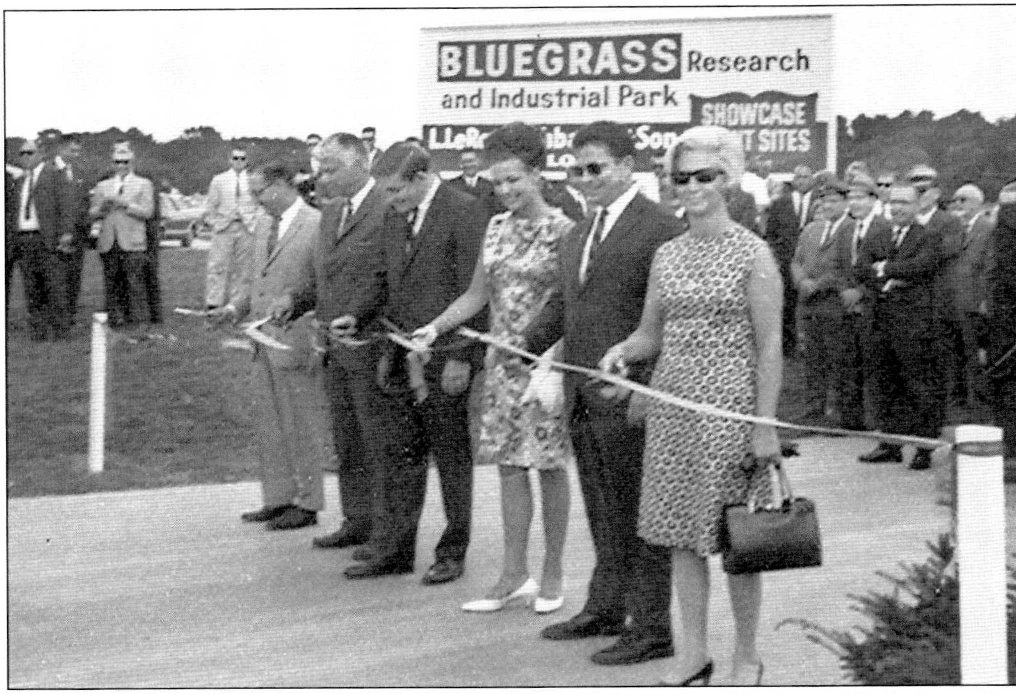

This 1967 photo shows the ribbon cutting at Bluegrass Research and Industrial Park. In the late 1950s, real-estate broker Fred Weber embarked on a mission to bring industry to Jeffersontown, so he approached farmers about selling their land when he could find a developer to purchase the properties. LeRoy Highbaugh bought 627 acres in 1964, and Jeffersontown annexed the land, thus establishing the industry that would make Jeffersontown known worldwide. (Photo courtesy of Carole Chambers Davis.)

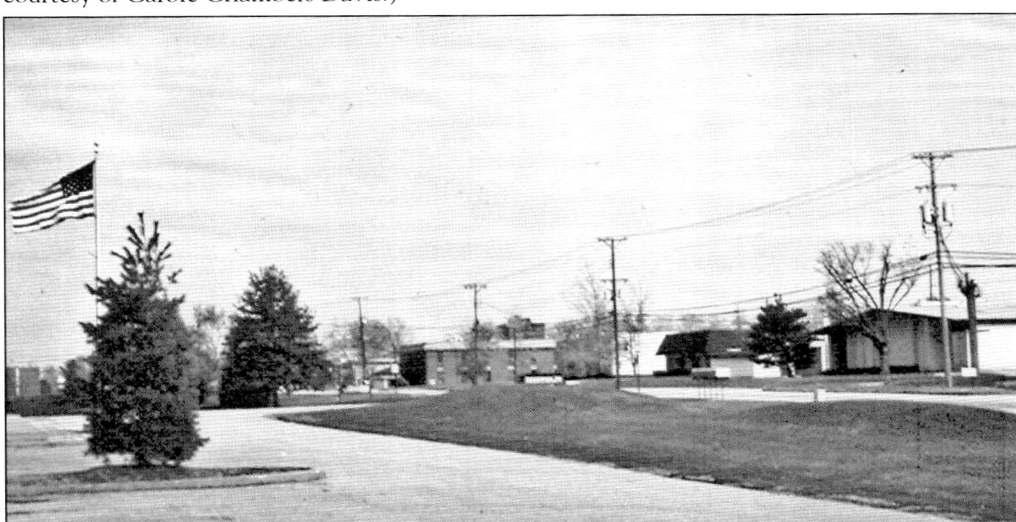

This c. 1990 photo shows a view of the Bluegrass Industrial Park. The park opened in June 1967 with 19 businesses. As of 2004, it boasts approximately 850 businesses, representing over 30,000 employees. (Photo courtesy of Jane Smith.)

Two

SCHOOLS AND COLLEGES

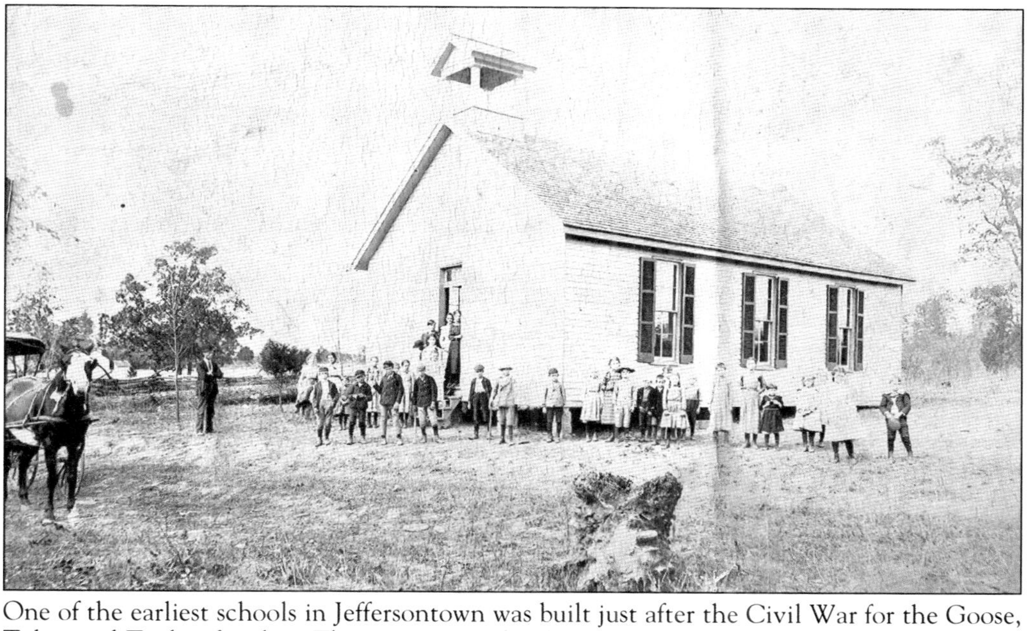

One of the earliest schools in Jeffersontown was built just after the Civil War for the Goose, Tyler, and Tucker families. The one-room school sat on a hill behind the home of William Goose Jr. The children later attended the Jefferson Academy. (Photo courtesy of Sallie Cheatham Smith.)

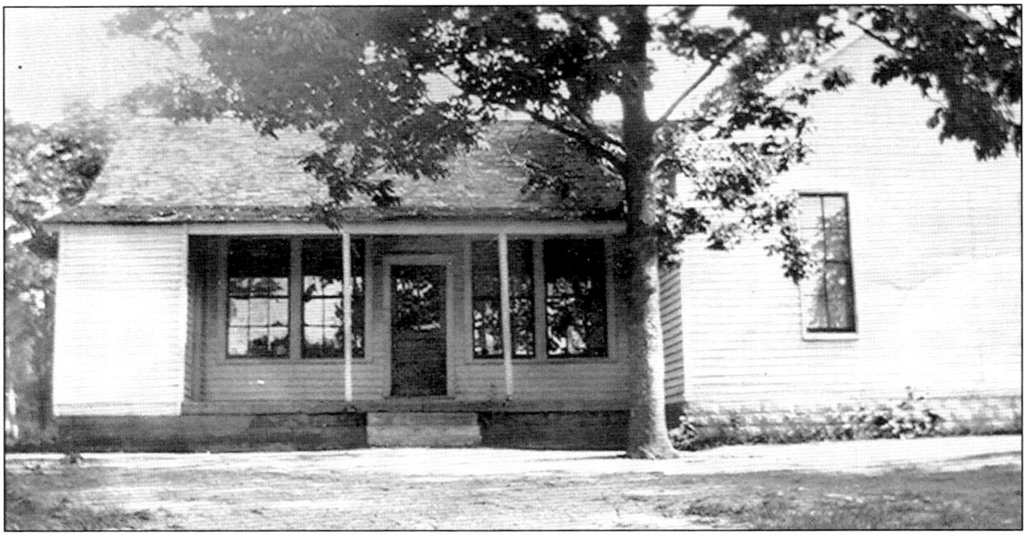

Tucker Station School was located on Rehl Road. This two-room school housed upper grades in the original part of the building, facing the camera, while the lower grades were housed in the addition. (Photo courtesy of Sallie Cheatham Smith.)

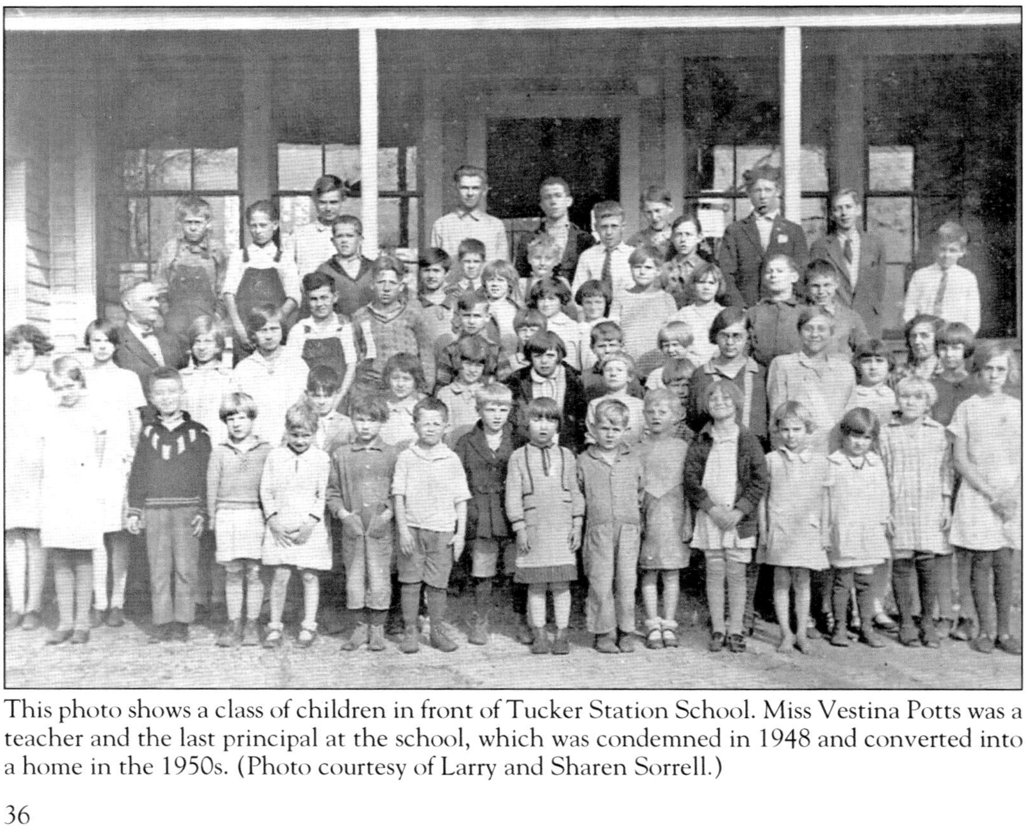

This photo shows a class of children in front of Tucker Station School. Miss Vestina Potts was a teacher and the last principal at the school, which was condemned in 1948 and converted into a home in the 1950s. (Photo courtesy of Larry and Sharen Sorrell.)

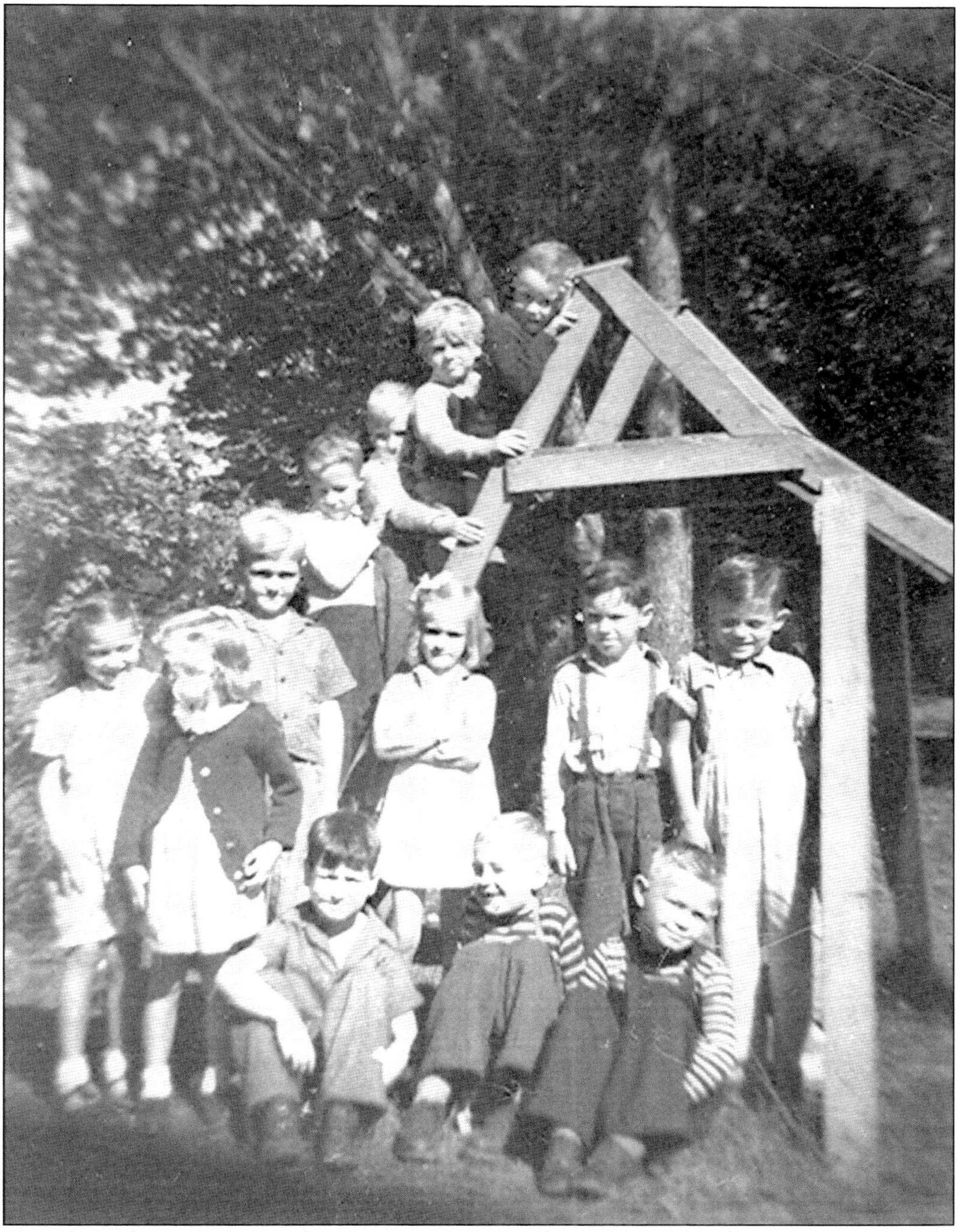

This photo shows the last students to attend Tucker Station School. (Photo courtesy of Sallie Cheatham Smith.)

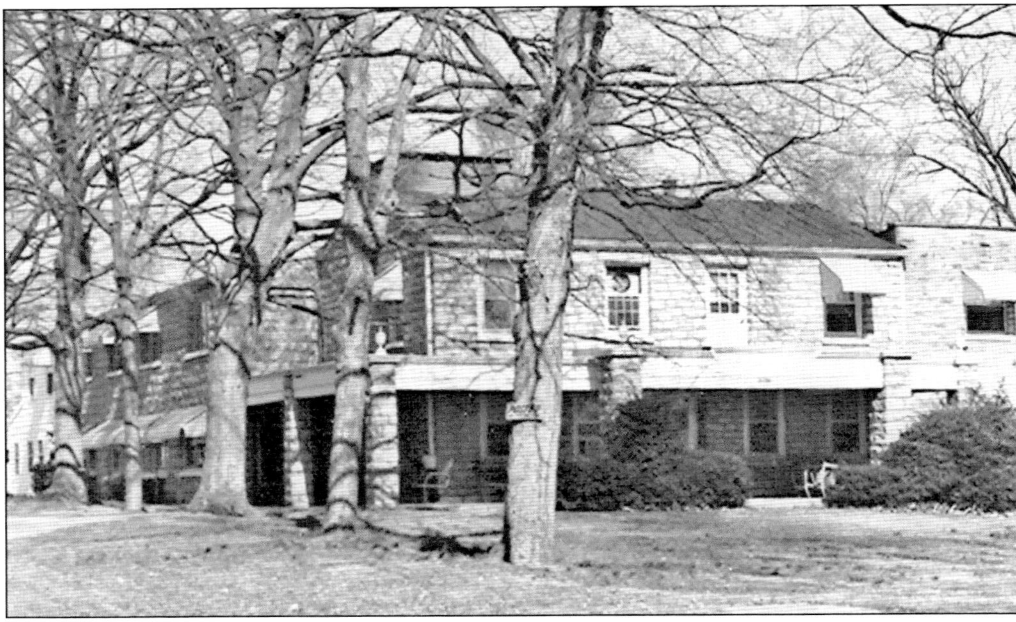

The Lutheran Church Council built the Jefferson Academy in 1836. This nondenominational school was run by Rev. George Yaeger for 24 years, before it was turned over to the Jeffersontown Joint Stock School Company. In 1905, it was purchased by the Mittler family for a home, which became known as "College Heights." (Photo courtesy of Lt. Col. Robert C. Jobson.)

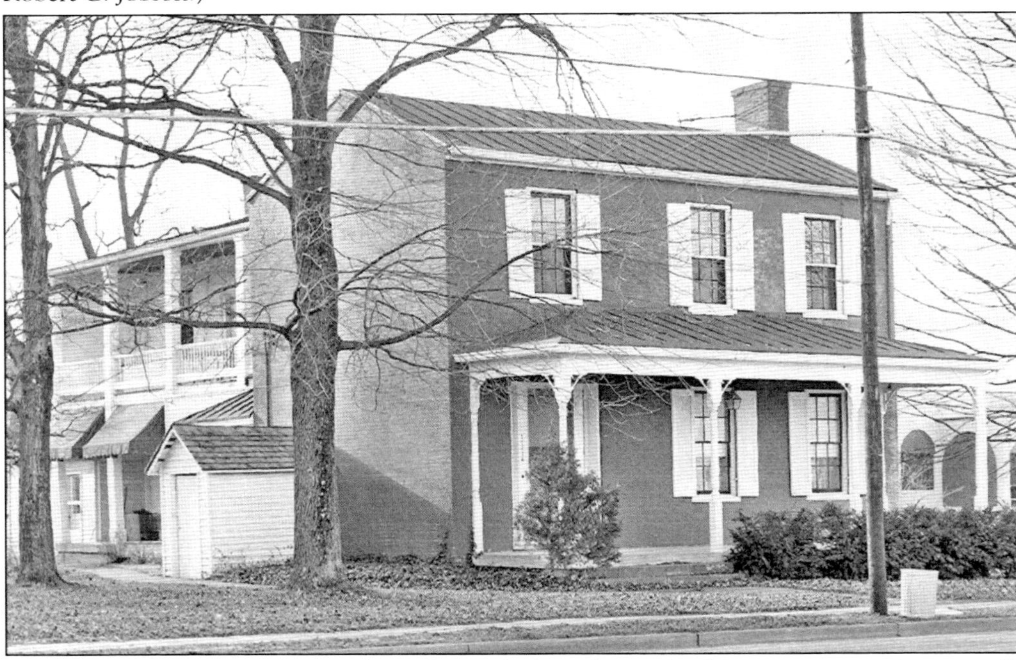

The Floore House, located on Taylorsville Road where the Medical Center now stands, originally served as a dormitory for Jefferson College, which was an early boarding school in Jeffersontown. (Photo courtesy of Louisville Metro Historic Landmarks Commission.)

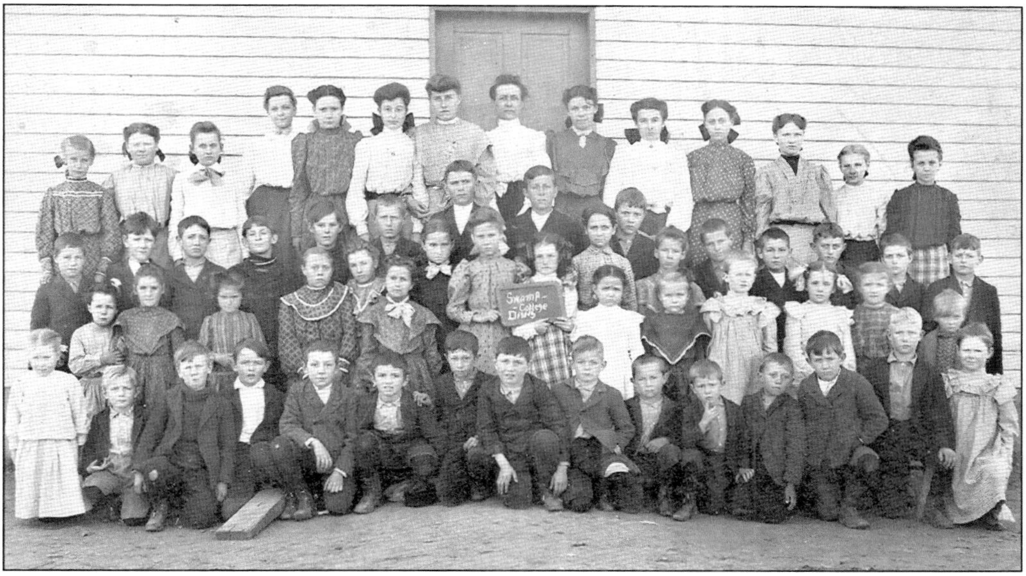

Swamp College was a two-room school located on Lovers Lane near Billtown Road, on land that was not farmable because the soil was too wet (hence the name "Swamp College"). This photo of one of its classes was taken in the early 1900s. (Photo courtesy of Carole Chambers Davis.)

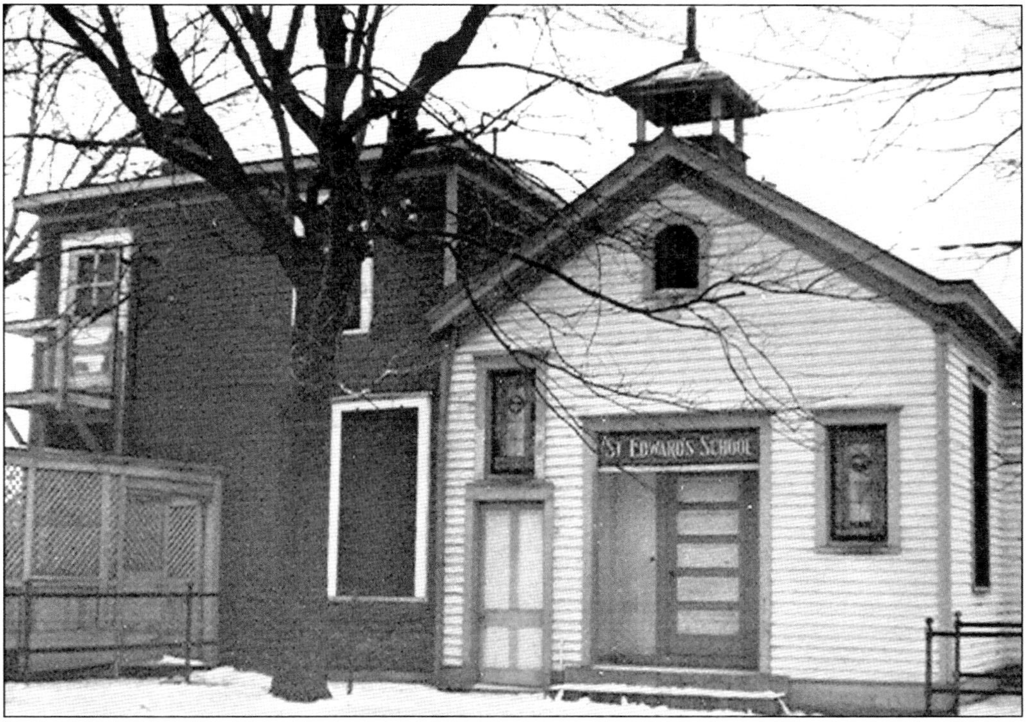

St. Edward's School was built in 1907. This two-room school, located on the southwest corner of the square, housed first through eighth grades. The building to the left is the convent where the nuns who taught at the school resided. (Photo courtesy of Dottie First.)

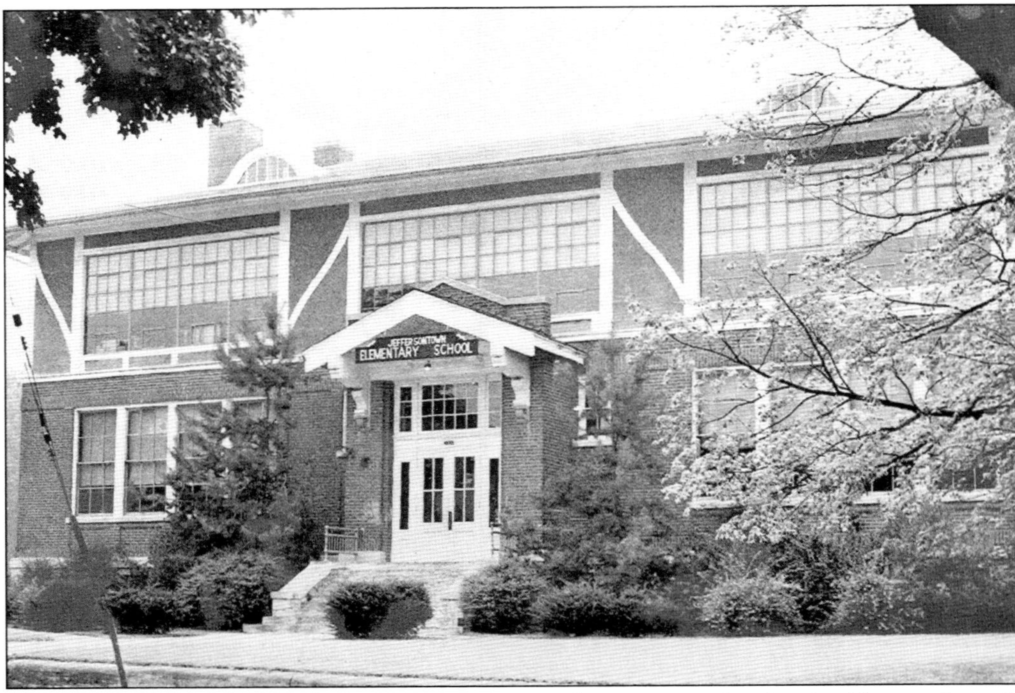

Jeffersontown School opened in 1914 as a one-story, four-room grade school, with two classes in each room. In 1927, a second story was added so the building could house high-school students as well. The school's population grew so quickly that a separate high school had to be built, so in 1950, the building reverted back to an elementary school. (Photo courtesy of the Jeffersontown Historical Museum.)

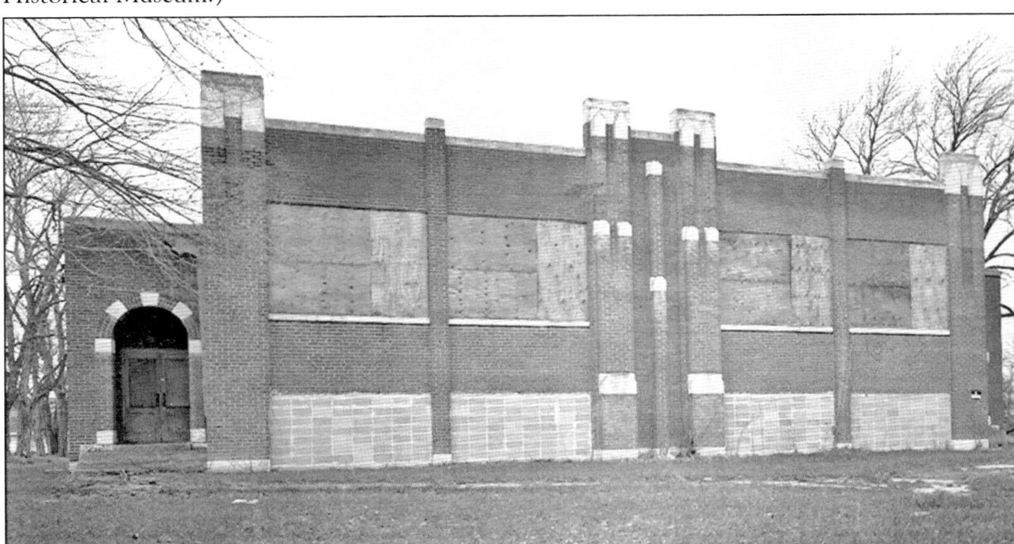

Alexander-Ingram School was constructed on Shelby Street in 1929 for Jeffersontown's African-American students, and was the 13th school for black students in Jefferson County. This art-deco building was renovated in 1985 and added to the National Register of Historic Places. (Photo courtesy of Louisville Metro Historic Landmarks Commission.)

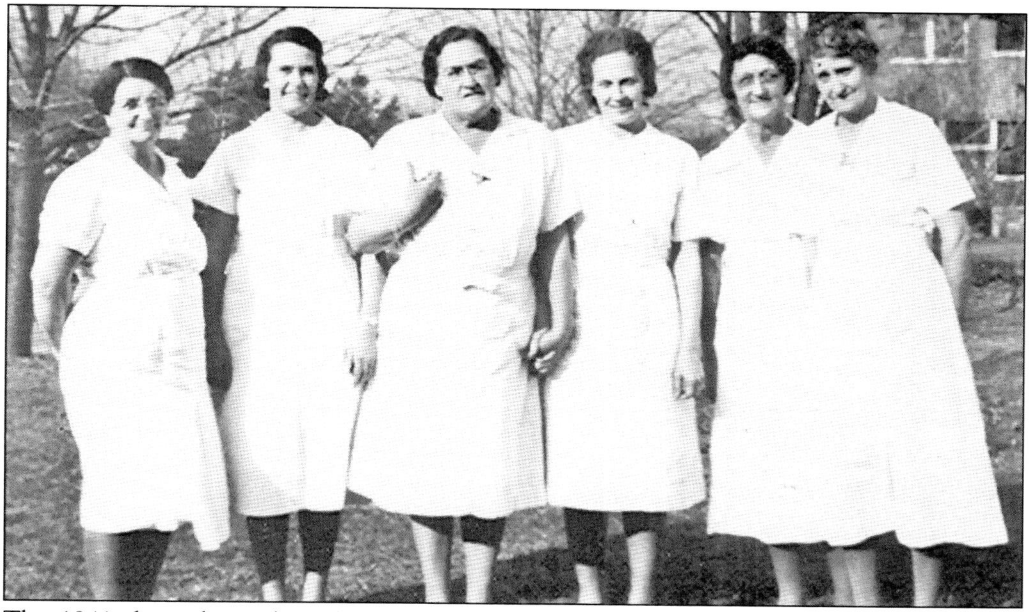

This 1941 photo shows the cafeteria ladies who worked at the Jeffersontown School. Pictured from left to right are Pearl Speer, Mary Romine, Pauline Snider, Ida Roemele, Eva Stucky Smith, and Mrs. Charles Riley. (Photo courtesy of Julia Smith.)

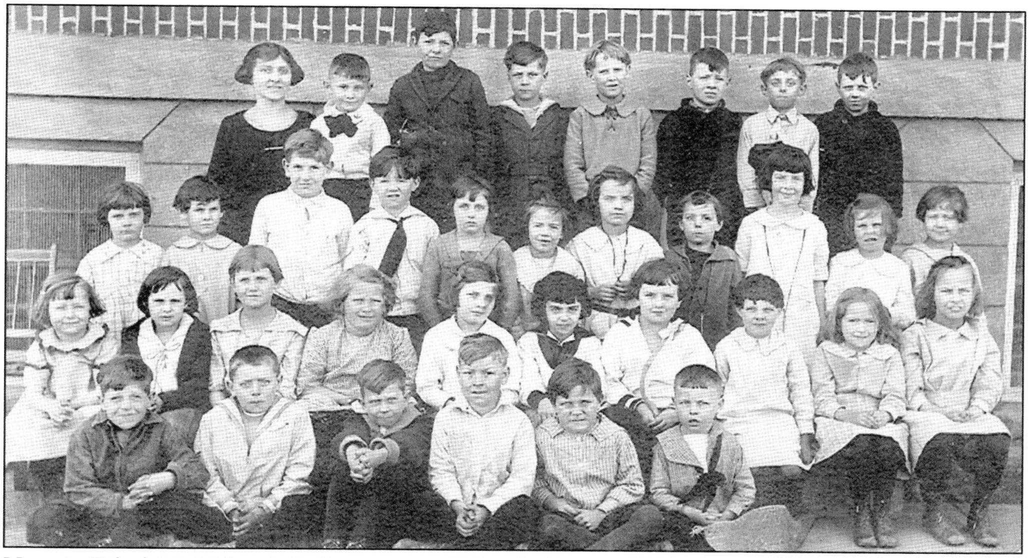

Here is Ethel McMahan's Jeffersontown School class, *c.* 1922. Pictured from left to right are (first row) Willis Spangler, James Floore, Burton Yenowine, Charles Petman, Edgar Coe Jr., and Chester Rohde; (second row) Marcia Bryan, Irma Bryan, Esther Huffine, Evelyn Wigginton, Alice Adams, Eva Stucky, Lucille Shacklette, Alberta Ernspiker, Helen Bridwell, and Mary Elizabeth Bridwell; (third row) Elenora Brooks, Rose Wearren, Kenneth Davis, William Hummel, Anna Agee, Florence Coe, Martha Stomberger, Carolyn Allen, Mildred Casey, Mildred Seitz, and Dorothy Frederick; (fourth row) Ethel McMahan (Jones), Robert Adams, Francis Brohm, Wayne Bolin, Field Leichhardt, George McGee, Fred Fleck, and Stanley Diehl. (Photo courtesy of Marcia Bryan Horton.)

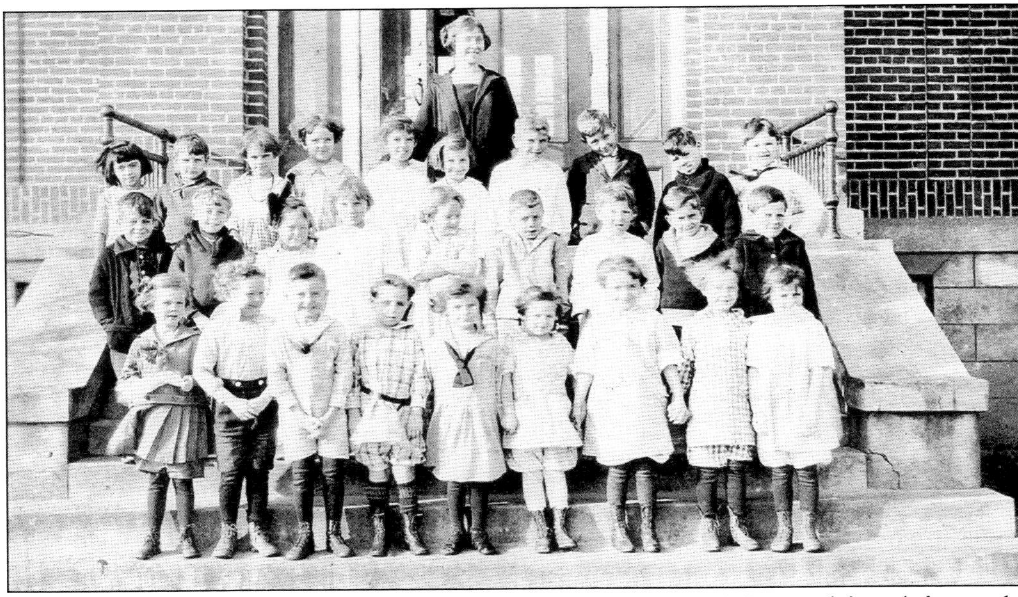

Here are Jeffersontown School first and second grades, 1922–1923. Pictured from left to right are (front row) Mildred Seitz, Earl Hood, Robert Adams, Carolyn Allen, Elenora Brooks, Alberta Ernspiker, Martha Stomberger, Dorothy Frederick, and Anna Agee; (middle row) Willis Spangler, Fred Fleck, Marcia Bryan, Esther Huffine, Eloise Hood, James Floore, Charles Petman, Burton Yenowine, and Edgar Coe Jr.; (back row) Eva Stucky, Stanley Diehl, Charlotte Collier, Lucille Shacklette, Jennie Lee Burkhart, Alice Adams, Kenneth Davis, Francis Brohm, George McGee, and William Hummel. (Photo courtesy of Marcia Bryan Horton.)

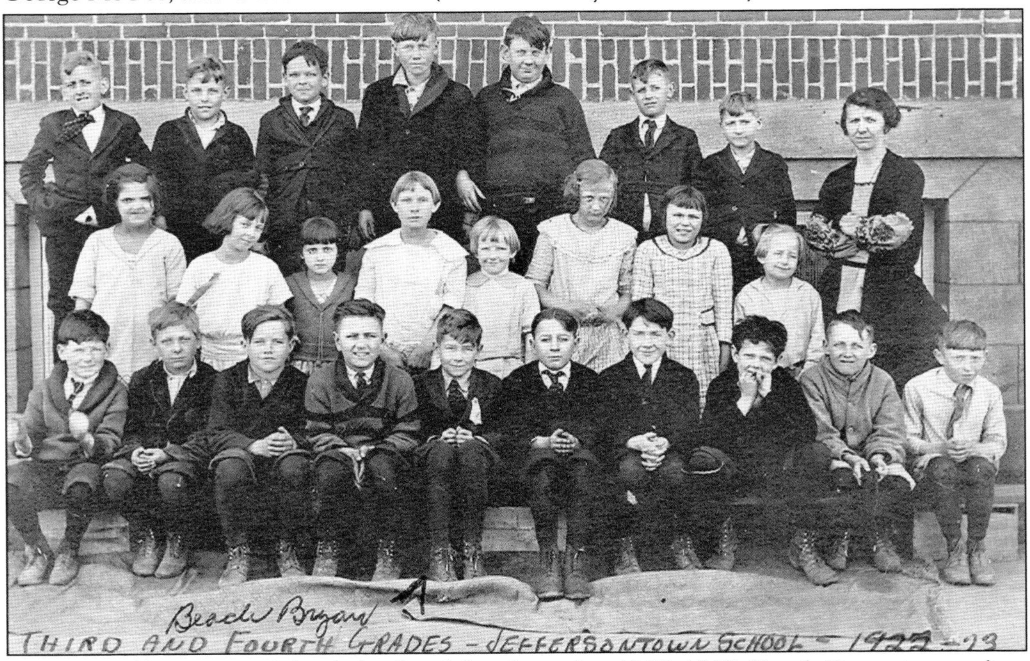

Here are Jeffersontown School third and fourth grades, 1922–1923. Beach Bryan is seated on the front row, fifth from left. (Photo courtesy of Marcia Bryan Horton.)

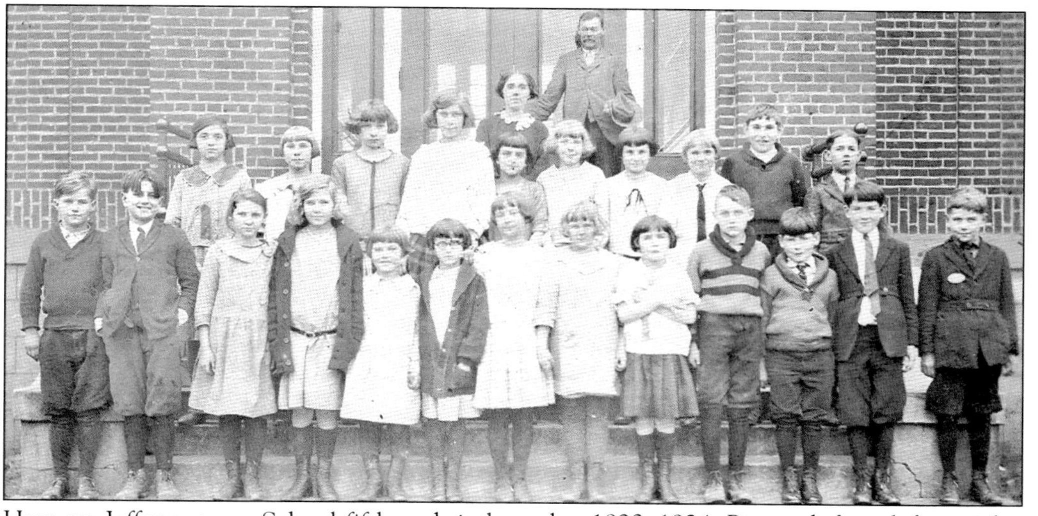

Here are Jeffersontown School fifth and sixth grades, 1923–1924. Pictured, from left to right, are as follows: (front row) Clarence Roemele, Ira Humphrey, ? Wright, Mary Lee Brooks, Alma Brooks, Mary Jane Agee, Juanita Wigginton, ? Wigginton, Dorothy Sprowl, Alfred Humm, Robert Adams, Harold Casey, and Beach Bryan; (middle row) Theresa Herman, ? Huffine, Alberta Henderman, Nellie Beerman, Frances Speer, Rebecca Fairfax, Virginia Wearren, ? Huffine, Everett Thomas, Charles Martin, and Hugh Radcliffe; (back row) Mrs. Vestina Potts (teacher) and J.E. Winand (janitor). (Photo courtesy of Marcia Bryan Horton.)

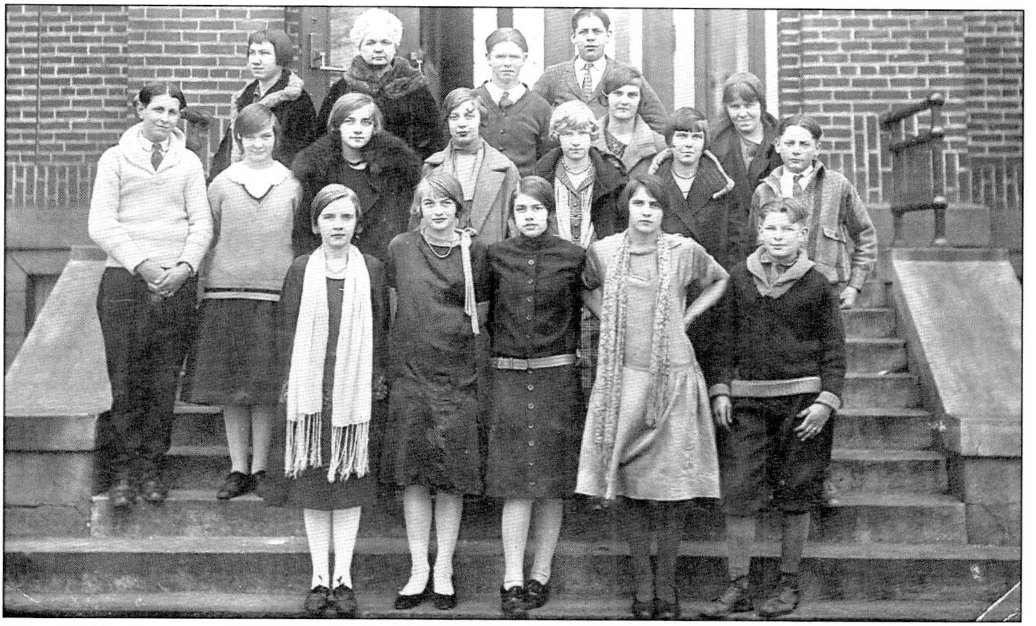

This 1925 photo is of the first high-school class to attend Jeffersontown School. Pictured, from left to right, are the following: (front row) Pauline Hefley, Evelyn Hester, Mariceta Robinson, Ruth Agee, and Hal Leichhardt; (middle row) Kenneth Jasper, Mary Lee Brooks, Katherine Tucker, Cora Reid, Mary Jo Ludwick, Myrtle Miller, and Walter Adams; (back row) Alma Alcorn, Myra Sanders, Charles Comstock, James Eddleman, Eva Lena Knapp, and Sue Willie Comstock. (Photo courtesy of the Jeffersontown Historical Museum.)

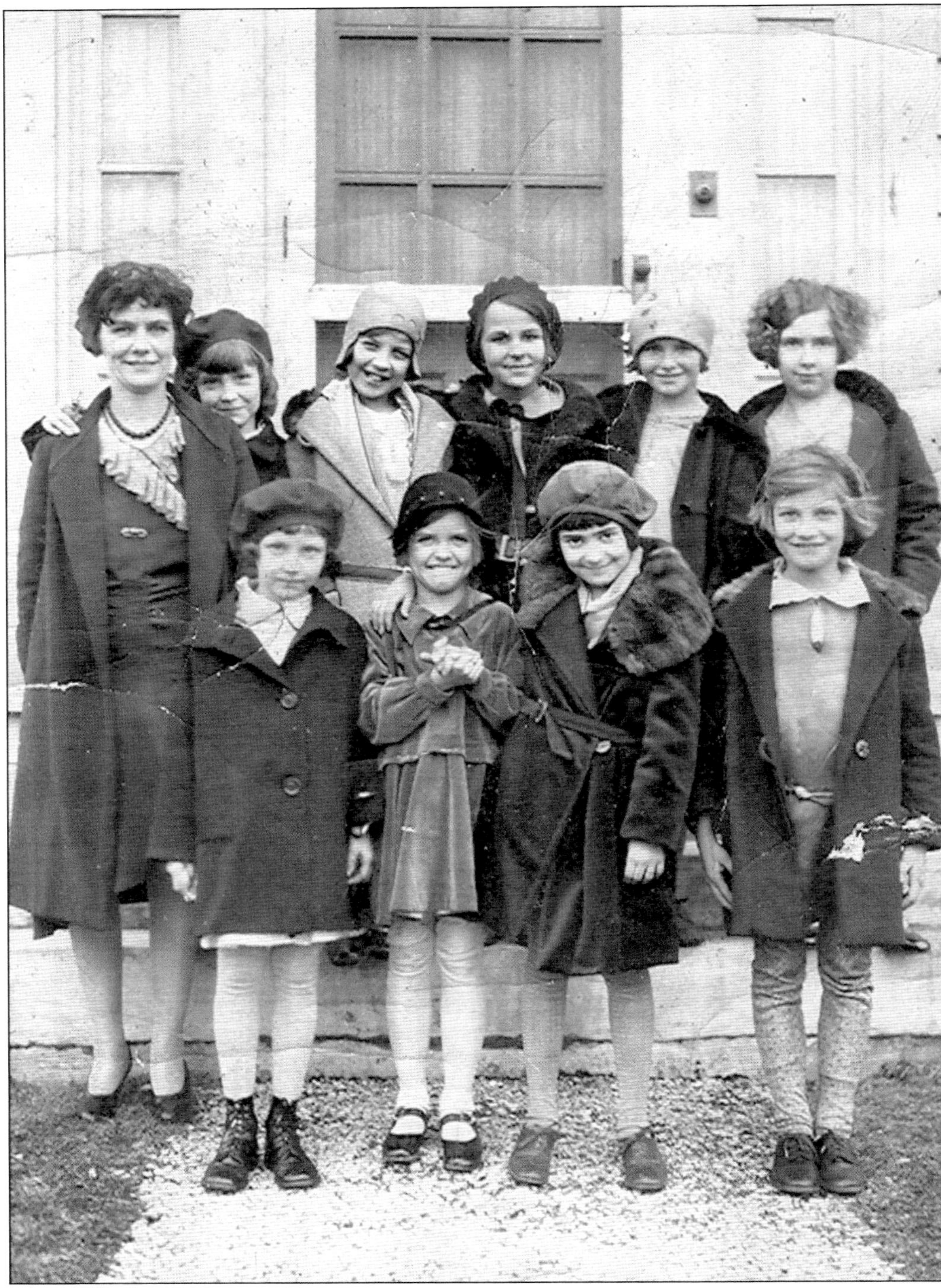

Shown here is the Jeffersontown School third-grade class in February 1931. Pictured, from left to right, are as follows: (front row) Julia Smith, Alzenia Shacklette, Marjorie Finley, and Marie Roederer; (back row) Aldena Barrel (teacher), Mary Ellen Smith, Virginia Miller Chambers, Helen Schneiter, Esther Maeser, and Evelyn Graff. (Photo courtesy of Julia Smith.)

This 1930s photo shows Julia, at left, and Mary Ellen Smith, at right, dressed up for Jeffersontown School's May Day celebration. The dresses were made of layers of paper sewn onto white slips. Note the Maypole directly behind Julia. (Photo courtesy of Julia Smith.)

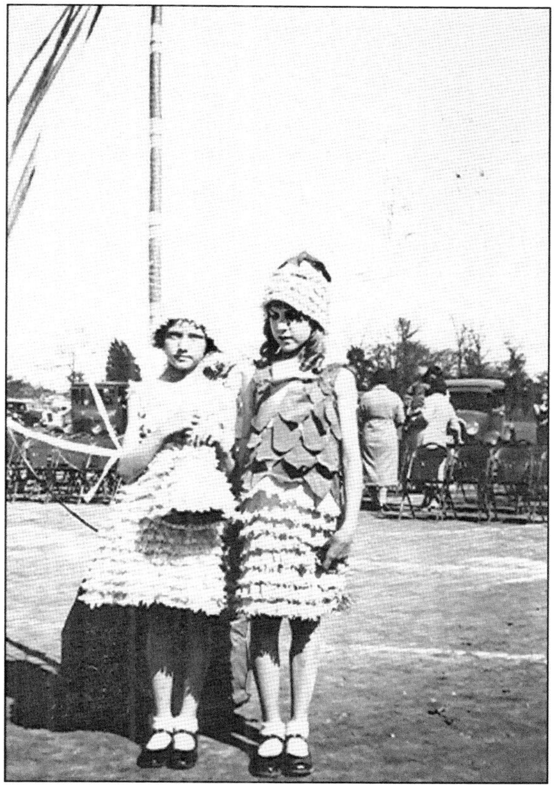

Although the boys' suits were not made of paper, they dressed up for May Day as well. Pictured from left to right are Julia Smith, William Moore, William Stucky, Mary Ellen Smith, and William Smith. (Photo courtesy of Julia Smith.)

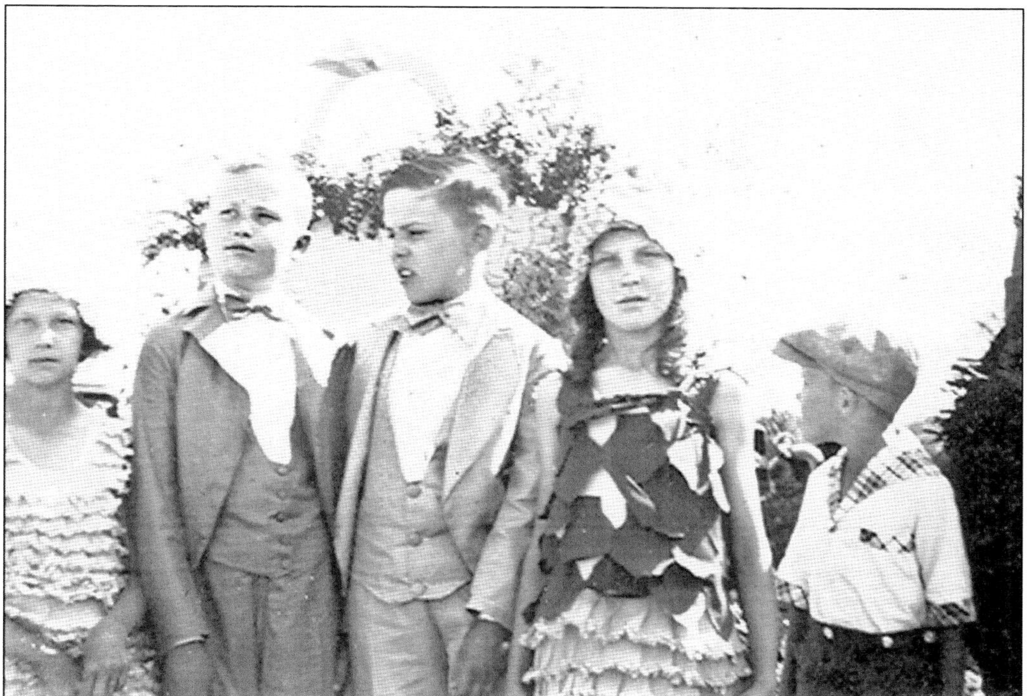

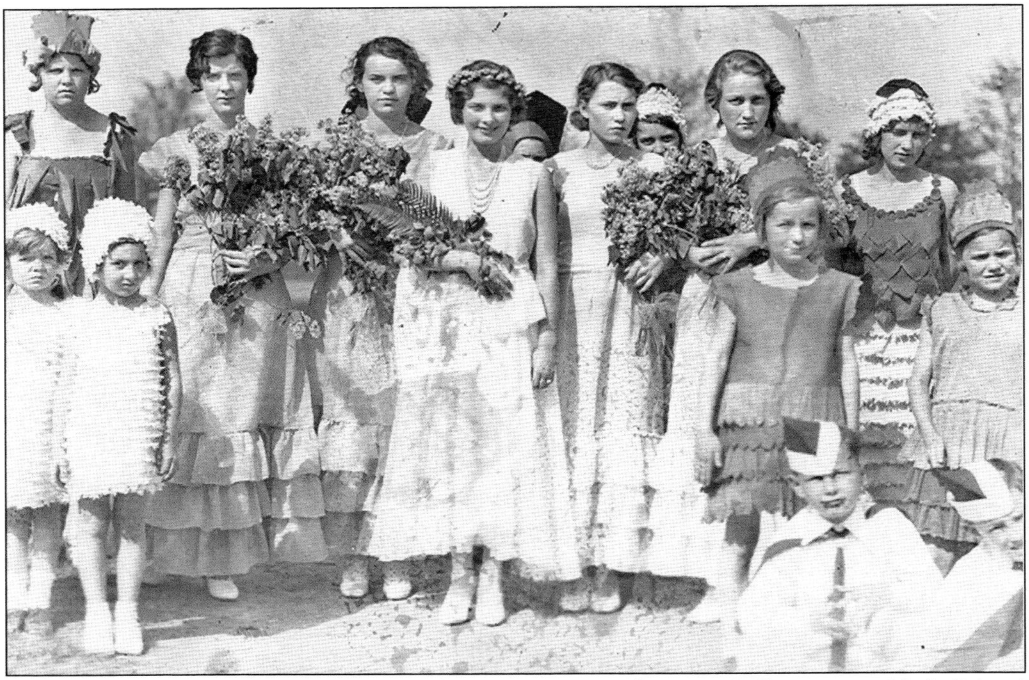

Jeffersontown School had plenty of celebrations. Here is the 1932 Jeffersontown High School May Queen and her court. The smaller children are unknown, but starting at the back row, from left to right, are Mildred Casey, Martha Stomberger, Marie Stout, Alice Adams (May Queen), and Marcia Bryan. (Photo courtesy of Marcia Bryan Horton.)

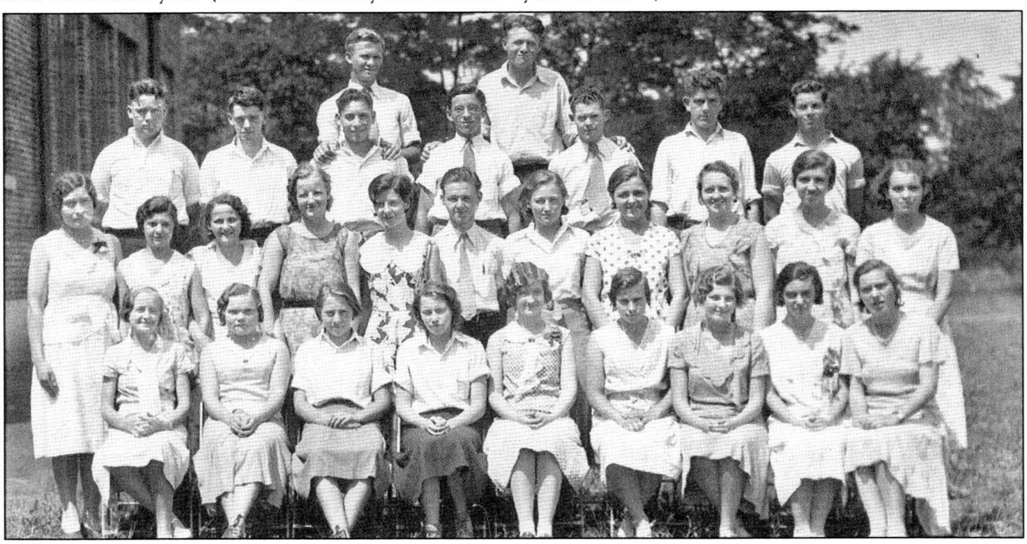

Shown here is the Jeffersontown High School Class of 1932. Pictured, from left to right, are the following: (first row) E. Frederick, I. McMahan, S. Stout, M. Stout, D. Lashbrook, H. Mittler, A. Adams, E. Stucky, and R. Maeser; (second row) K. Walden, M. Stout, M.J. Agee, H. Roemele, M. Casey, B. Hummel, M. Bryan, N. Gentry, L. Shacklette, J.L. Burkhart, and M. Stomberger; (third row) W. Moore, T. Boyd, K. Potts, F. Newton, T. Frazier, K. Davis, and D. Arnold; (fourth row) M. Ludwick and G. Forwood. (Photo courtesy of Marcia Bryan Horton.)

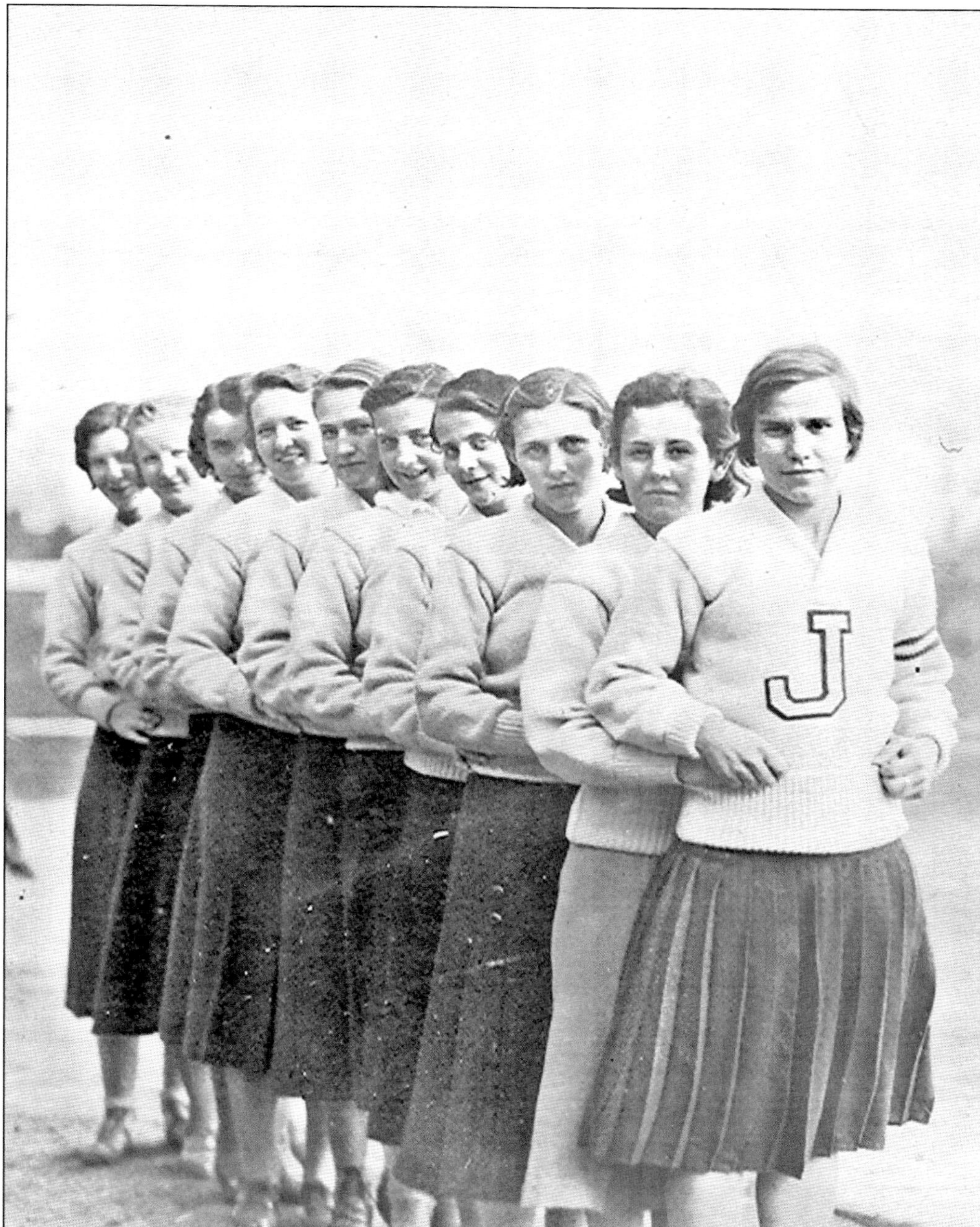

The 1932 Jeffersontown High School girls' basketball team is pictured here. From front to back are Helen Mittler (captain), Rose Wearren, Mildred Casey, Mary Jane Agee, Patty Spangler, Marcia Bryan, Lucille Shacklette, Martha Stomberger, Helen Roemele, and Ann Agee. (Photo courtesy of Marcia Bryan Horton.)

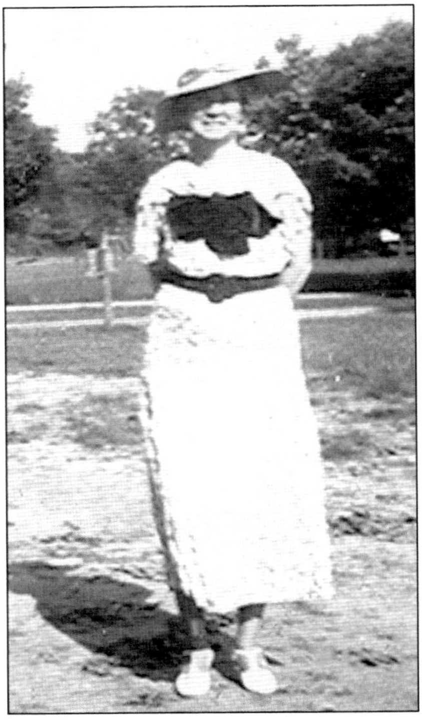

Here is Jeffersontown School eighth-grade teacher, Mrs. E.M. Orr. (Photo courtesy of Julia Smith.)

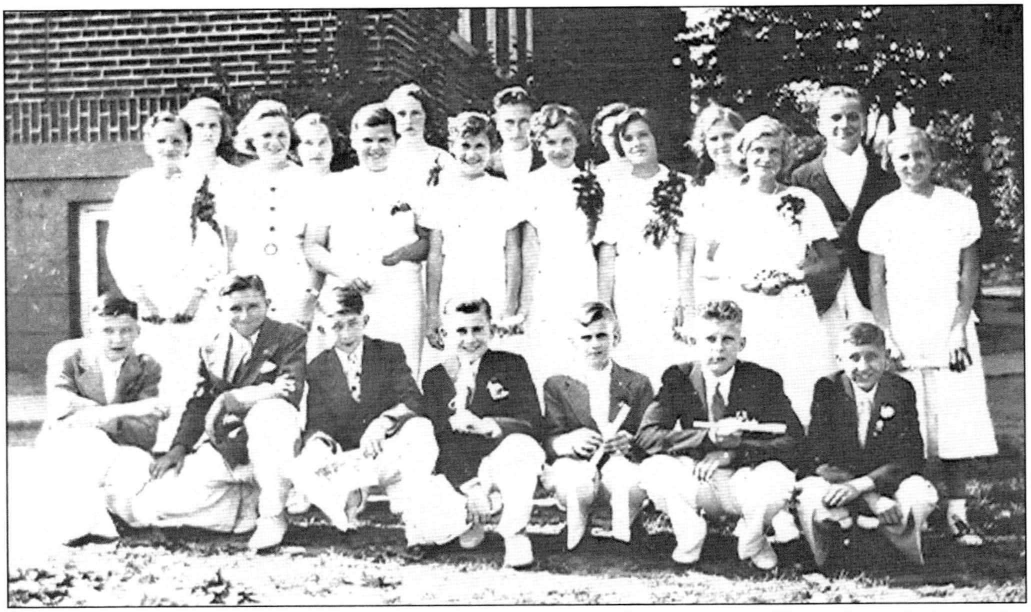

The 1936 Jeffersontown School eighth-grade graduating class is pictured here. From left to right are as follows: (front row) Joe Harley, Leslie Spears, ? Frederick, Billy Arnold, Billy Bryant, William ?, and unidentified; (middle row) Camilla Bryant, Esther Maeser, Eula ?, Mattie Frederick, Josephine Wyatt, ? Reed, Marie Roederer, and Doris Jones; (back row) Gertrude Wooden, Evelyn Graff, Bessie Moffat, Kenneth Gentry, Margaret Wisehart, Mary Ellen Smith, and John Stomberger. (Photo courtesy of Julia Smith.)

Jeffersontown High School custodian Nicholas "Nick" Hobbs Gentry is pictured here, *c.* 1936. (Photo courtesy of Nancy Noel Hood.)

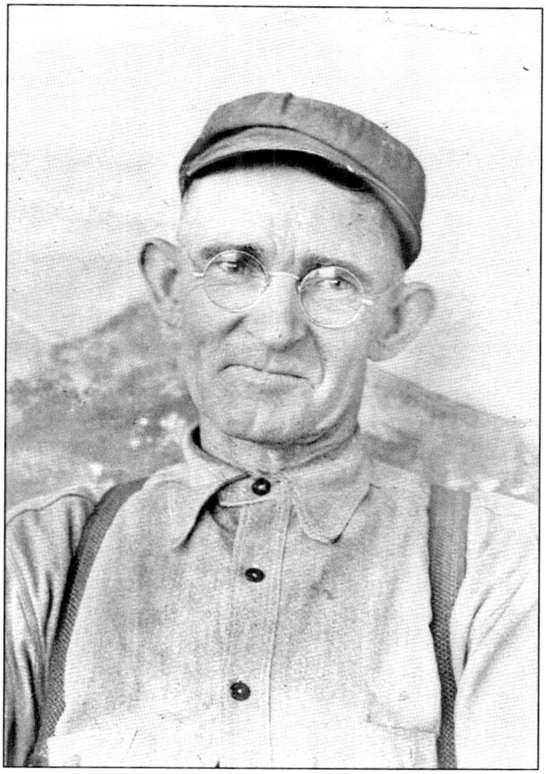

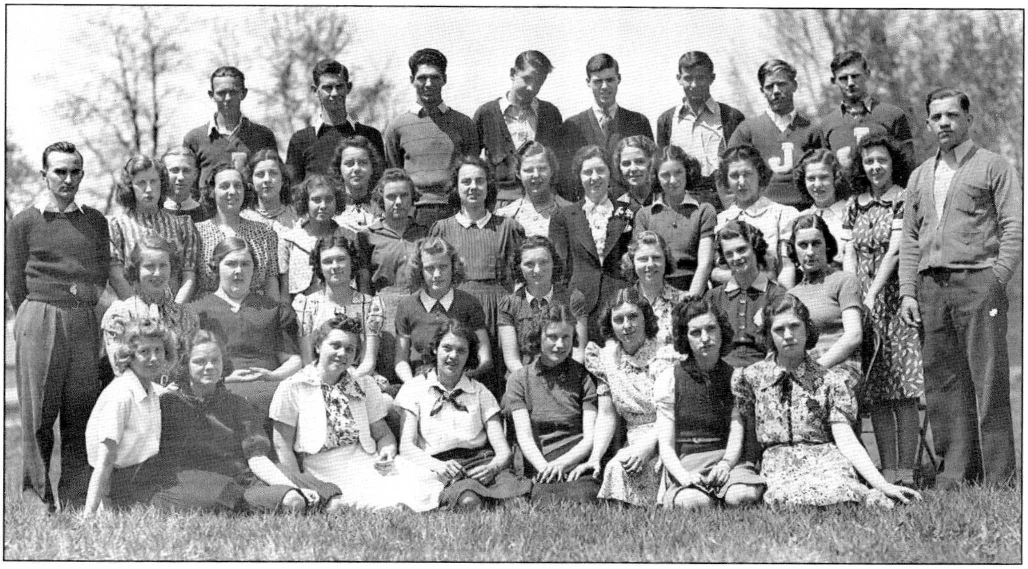

Here is the Jeffersontown High School Class of 1939. (Photo courtesy of Carole Chambers Davis.)

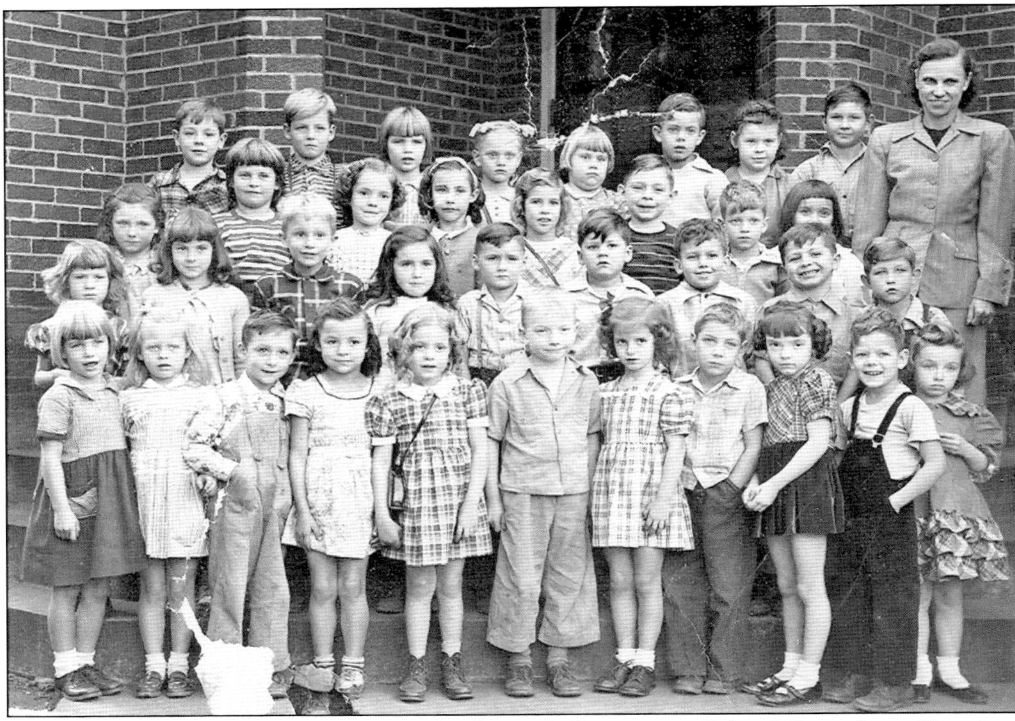

This c. 1940s photo shows the first-grade class at Jeffersontown School. Betty Jean Cheatham Modesty is on the front row, fifth from left. Myrtle Shake (upper right) is the teacher. (Photo courtesy of Sallie Cheatham Smith.)

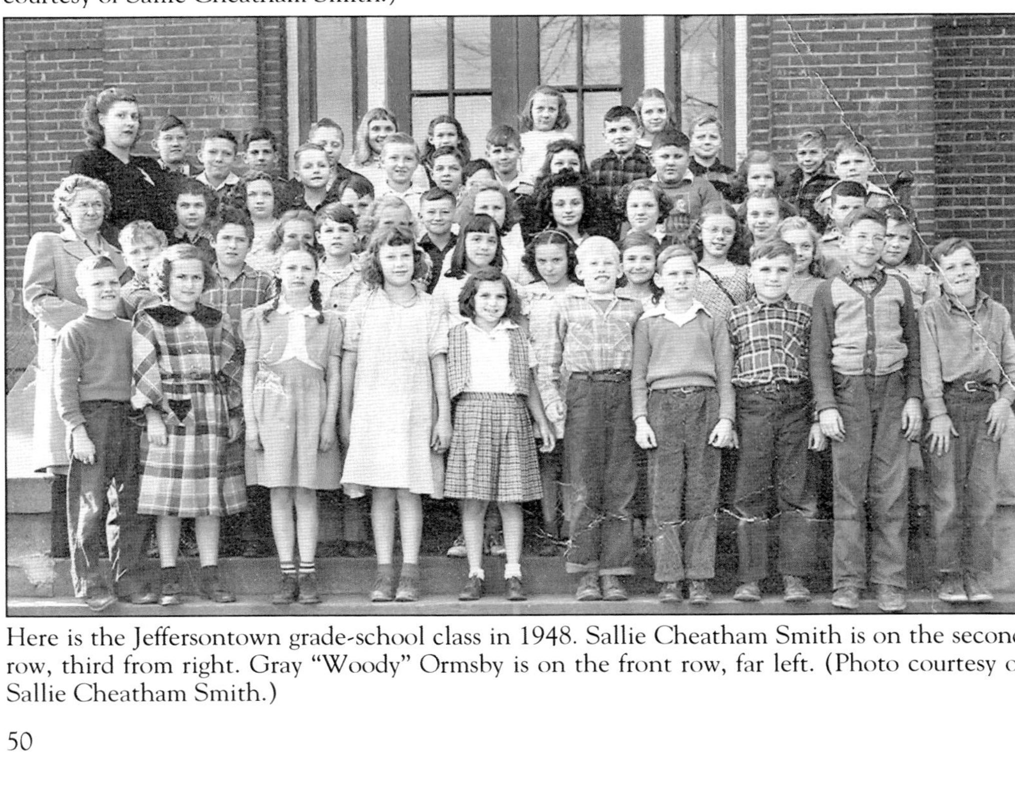

Here is the Jeffersontown grade-school class in 1948. Sallie Cheatham Smith is on the second row, third from right. Gray "Woody" Ormsby is on the front row, far left. (Photo courtesy of Sallie Cheatham Smith.)

This photo shows Mr. Kemp, a teacher at Jeffersontown High School, next to a busload of children. (Photo courtesy of Carole Chambers Davis.)

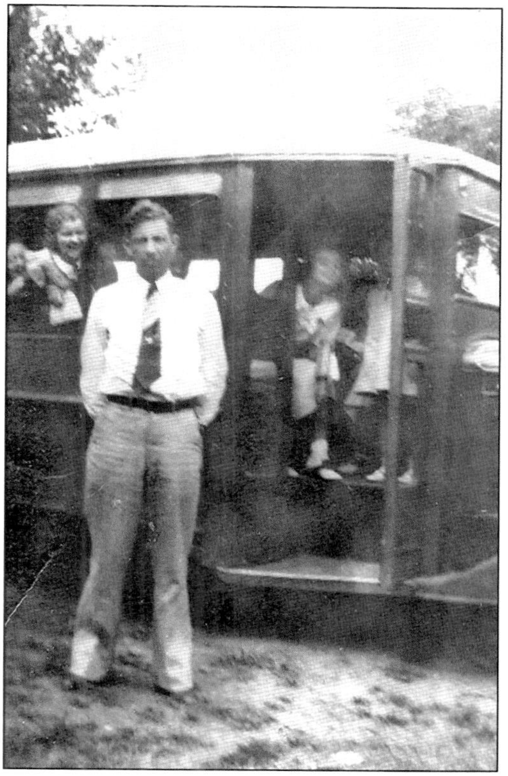

This photo shows Mrs. B.H. Dean and her class. (Photo courtesy of the Jeffersontown Historical Museum.)

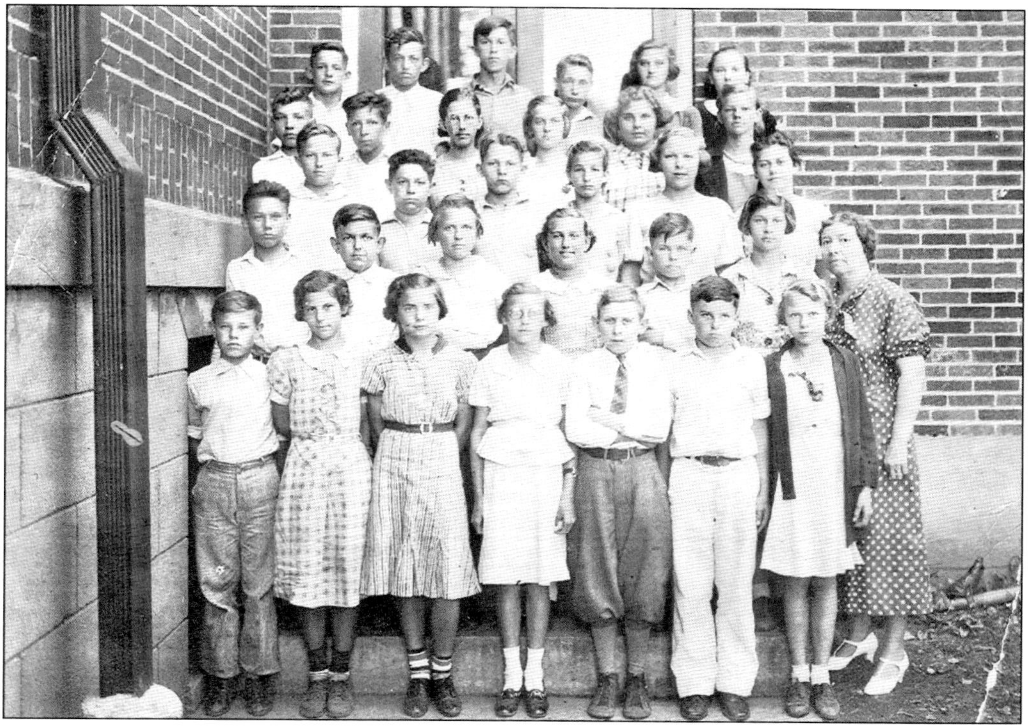

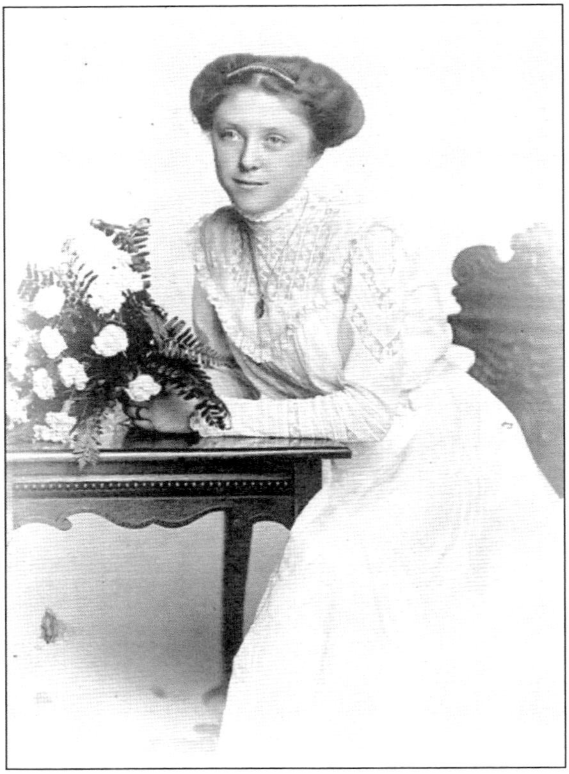

This is an early portrait of Virginia Porter Carrithers, or "Miss Virginia," as she was known to her students at the Jeffersontown School. Virginia was a huge proponent of education. She co-founded the Kentuckiana Center for Education, Health, and Research, which was a school for handicapped children, and, in the 1970s, a middle school was named for her. (Photo courtesy of Sallie Cheatham Smith.)

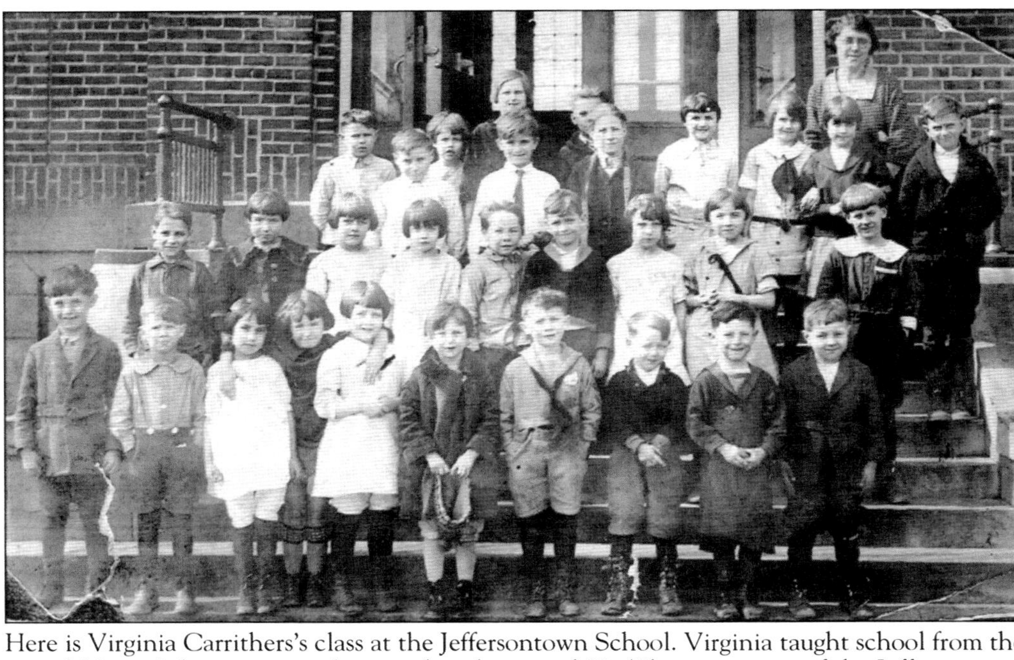

Here is Virginia Carrithers's class at the Jeffersontown School. Virginia taught school from the age of 18 until she permanently retired at the age of 80. (Photo courtesy of the Jeffersontown Historical Museum.)

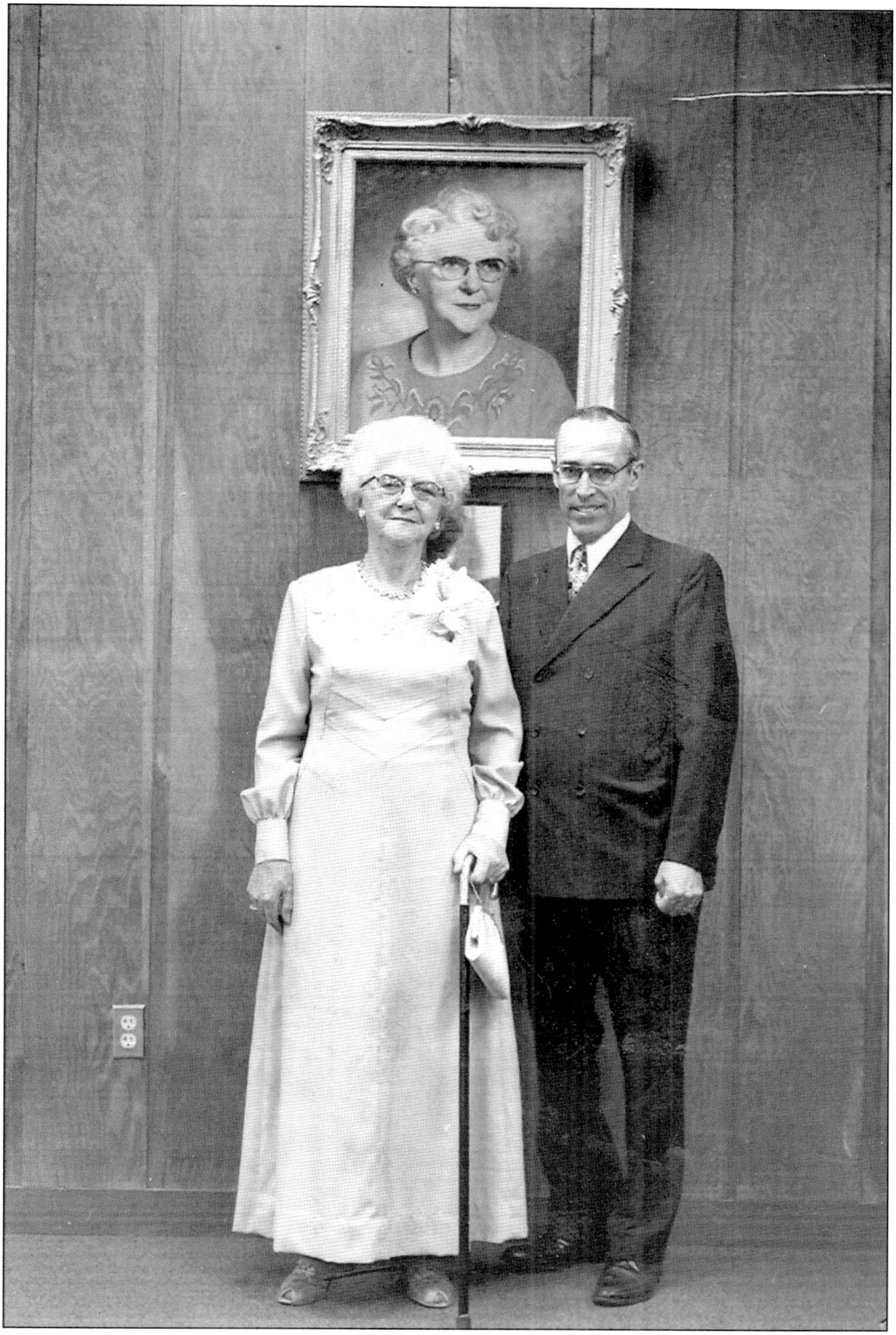

This photo shows Virginia Carrithers in her later years, standing next to George Yankey, then principal of Carrithers Middle School. (Photo courtesy of the Jeffersontown Historical Museum.)

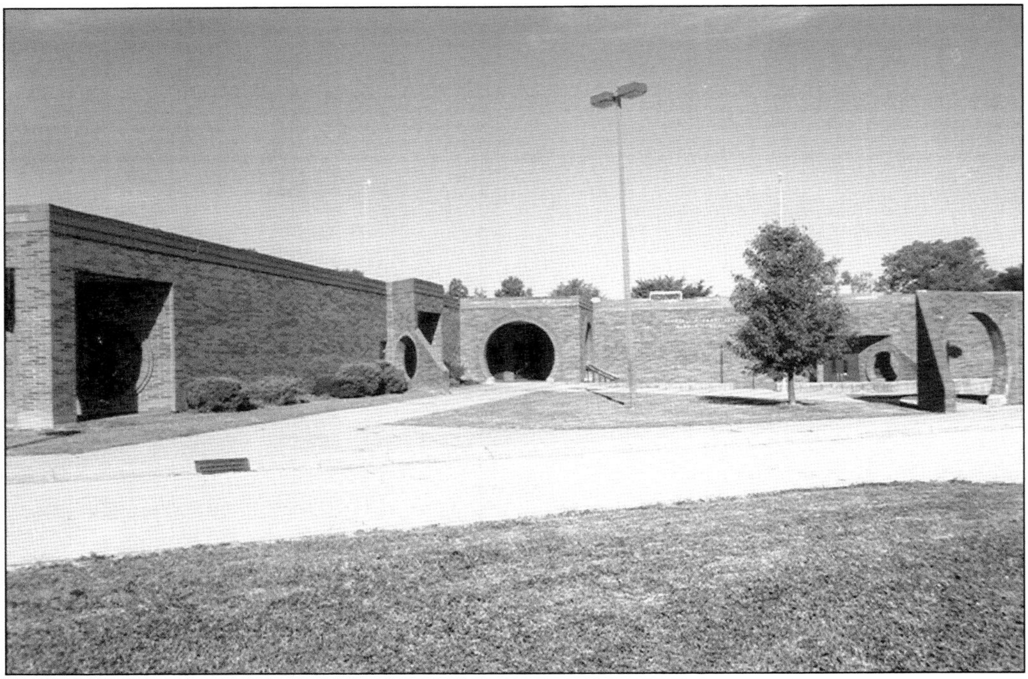

Shown here is Virginia P. Carrithers Middle School on Billtown Road. (Photo courtesy of the Jeffersontown Historical Museum.)

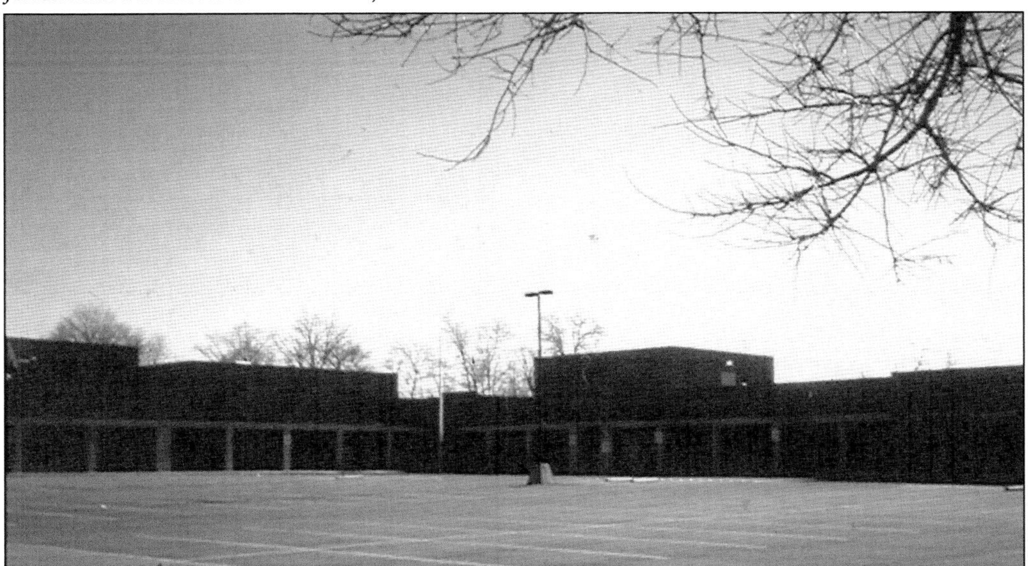

The old Jeffersontown Elementary School was razed in the 1970s. Since it had been erected on land donated purely for educational purposes by developer E.R. Sprowl and his associates in 1911, one of his descendants, Marcia Horton, made an impassioned plea in a 1972 *Voice-Jeffersonian* article that the land continue to be used for its original purpose. Her voice was heard, and Tully Elementary School, pictured here, was built on the same site. (Photo courtesy of Jane Smith.)

Three

Churches and Cemeteries

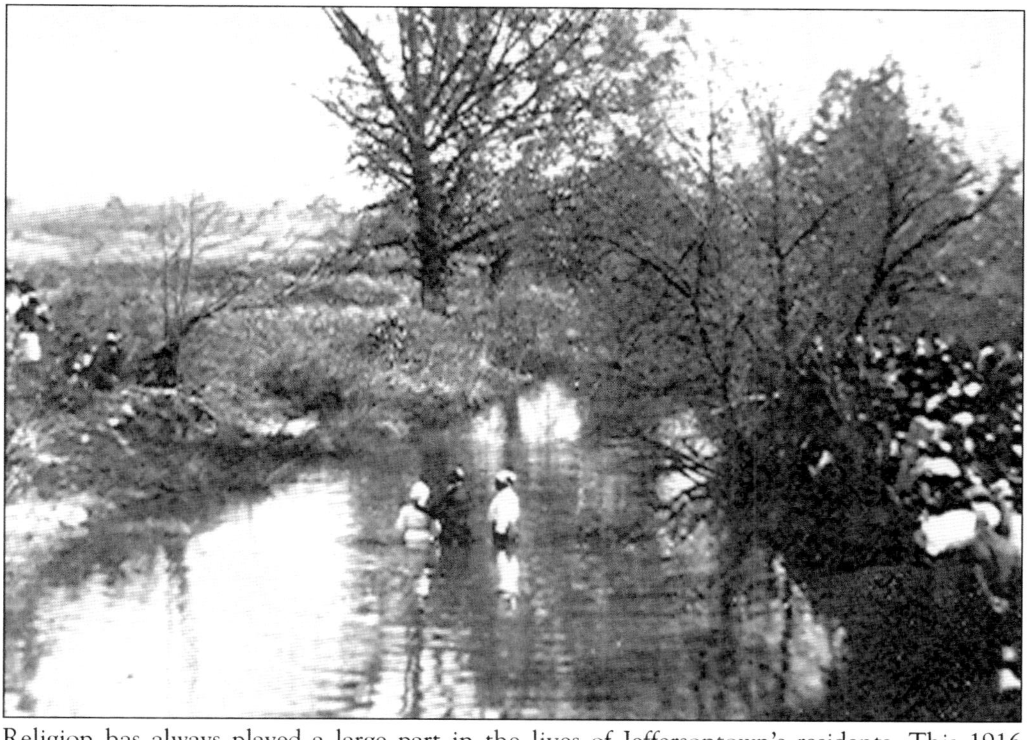

Religion has always played a large part in the lives of Jeffersontown's residents. This 1916 photo shows a baptism held in a wide spot in the creek on Watterson Trail. (Photo courtesy of Julia Smith.)

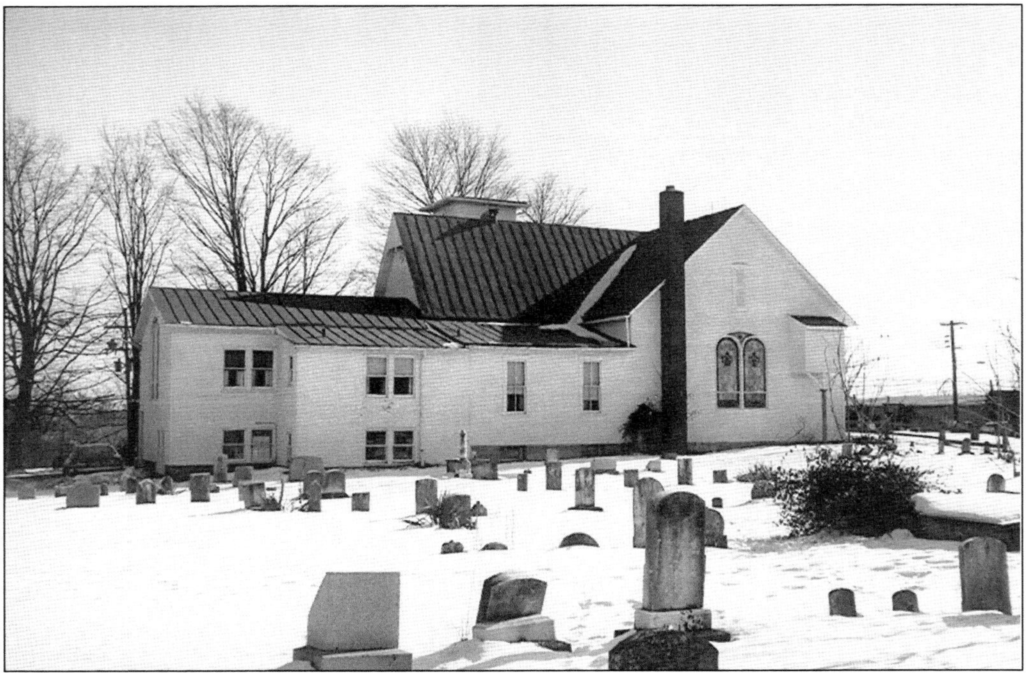

This is the site of the Old Lutheran Church and cemetery on the corner of Watterson Trail and Shelby Street. In the early years of Jeffersontown, a building known as the Union Church was located directly across the street and was shared by four separate congregations, each meeting there one week a month. Eventually, each church raised enough money to construct new buildings, and this one became Christ Lutheran Church. (Photo courtesy of Louisville Metro Historic Landmarks Commission.)

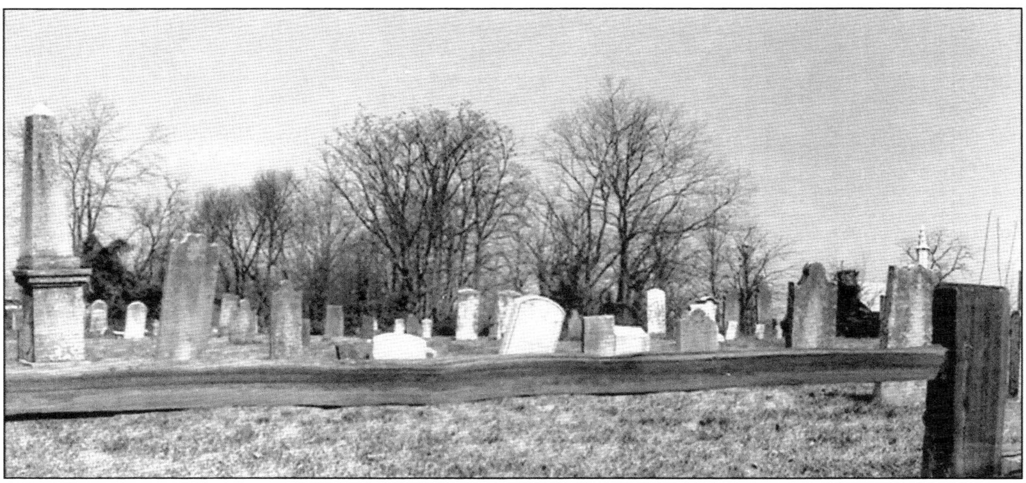

The German Reformed Presbyterian congregation originally purchased lots 26 and 27 on the town square and built a small log church. A cemetery was begun behind the church, and all four congregations from the Union Church across the street buried people there. This graveyard is one of the oldest in Kentucky, its earliest recorded burial being that of Barbara Hoke in 1814. (Photo courtesy of Lt. Col. Robert C. Jobson.)

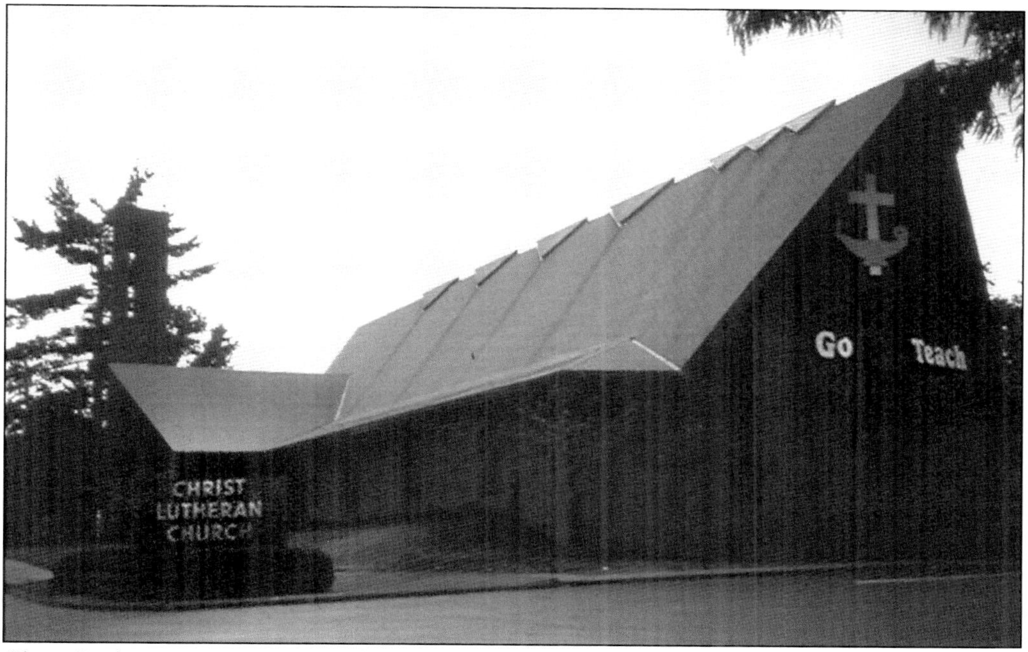

Christ Lutheran's congregation dates back to 1789, and in 1833, they built their first church on the property now owned by Thoroughbred Chorus. The current structure was built in 1895 on the foundation of the original church. The building pictured here is located on Taylorsville Road at Six Mile Lane, where Christ Lutheran's congregation moved in 1957. (Photo courtesy of Jane Smith.)

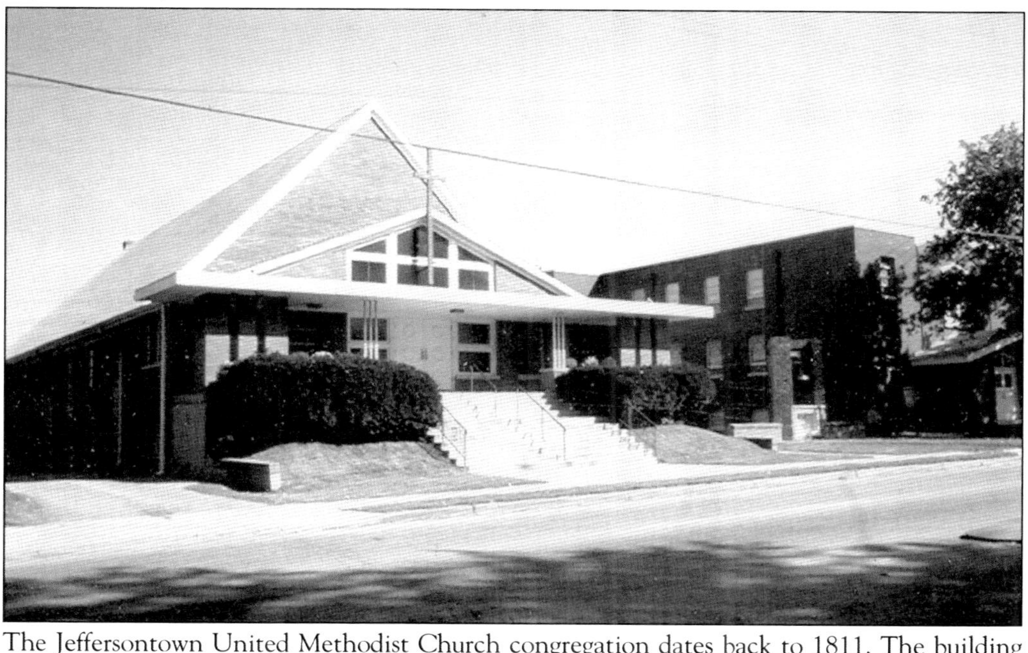

The Jeffersontown United Methodist Church congregation dates back to 1811. The building pictured here is located on Taylorsville Road, not too far from the square. (Photo courtesy of Julia Smith.)

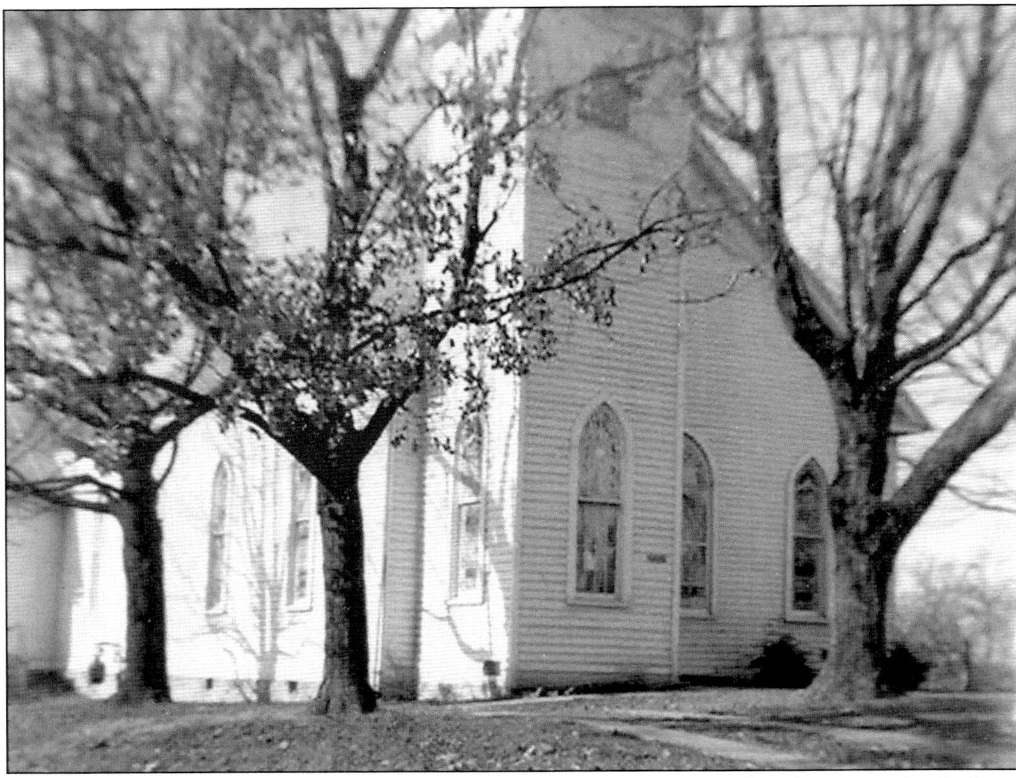

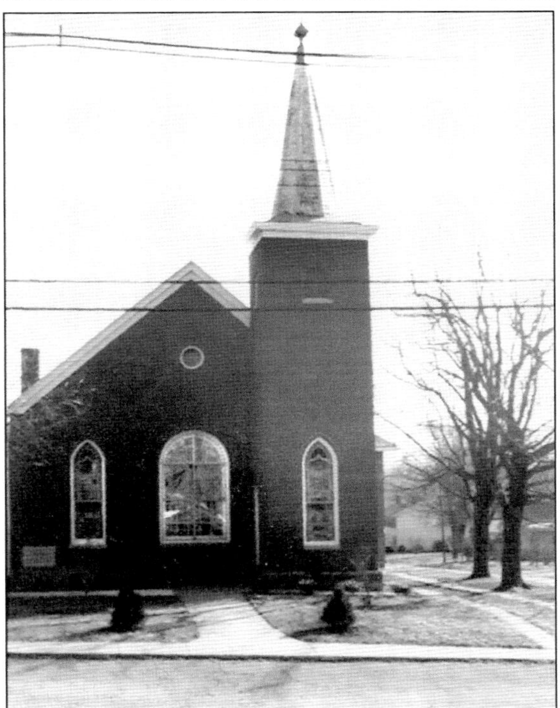

First Baptist Church was established in 1833 by Rev. Henry Adams, who came from Louisville to organize a congregation of black members from the Union Church. Shortly after 1850, they built a log church on the corner of Watterson Trail and Old Taylorsville Road, then replaced it with this frame structure at the turn of the 20th century. (Photo courtesy of Rev. Thurmond Coleman Sr.)

In 1960, during its 127th anniversary celebration, First Baptist Church had a groundbreaking ceremony for a new auditorium. At that time, the exterior of the church was renovated with a covering of brick. (Photo courtesy of Rev. Thurmond Coleman Sr.)

Rev. Thurmond Coleman Sr. was chosen as pastor of First Baptist Church in 1955 and served for 45 years. His resonant sermons were heard and enjoyed by people not only at his church, but also at many events held throughout the city of Jeffersontown. (Photo courtesy of Rev. Thurmond Coleman Sr.)

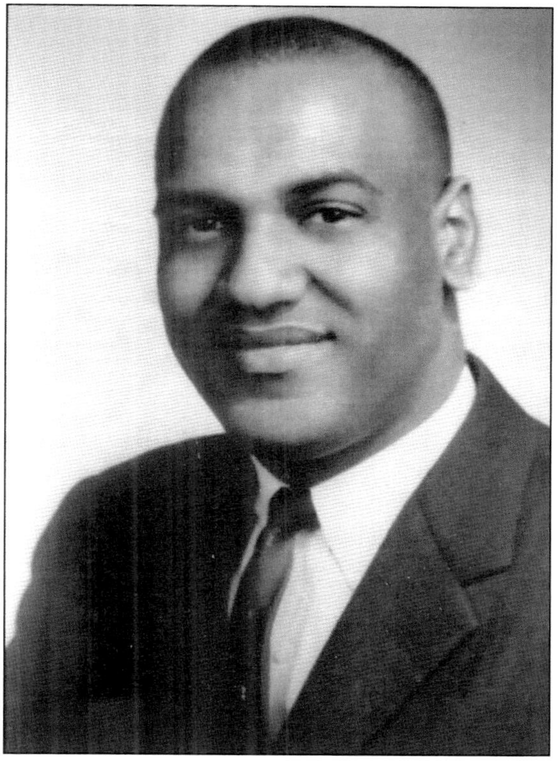

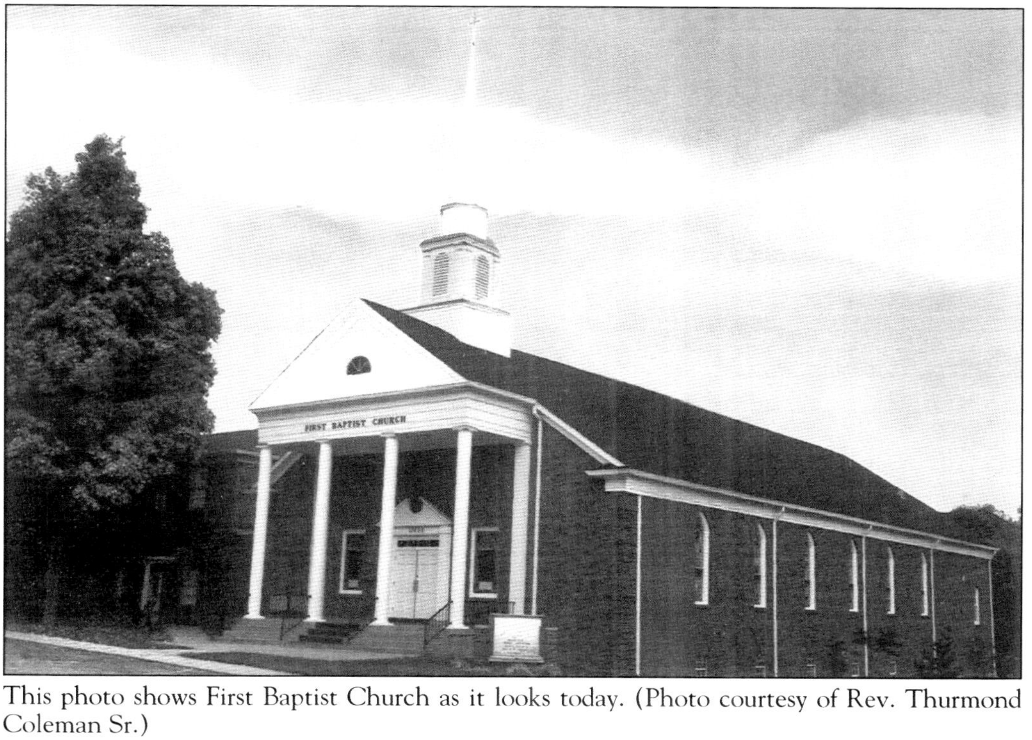

This photo shows First Baptist Church as it looks today. (Photo courtesy of Rev. Thurmond Coleman Sr.)

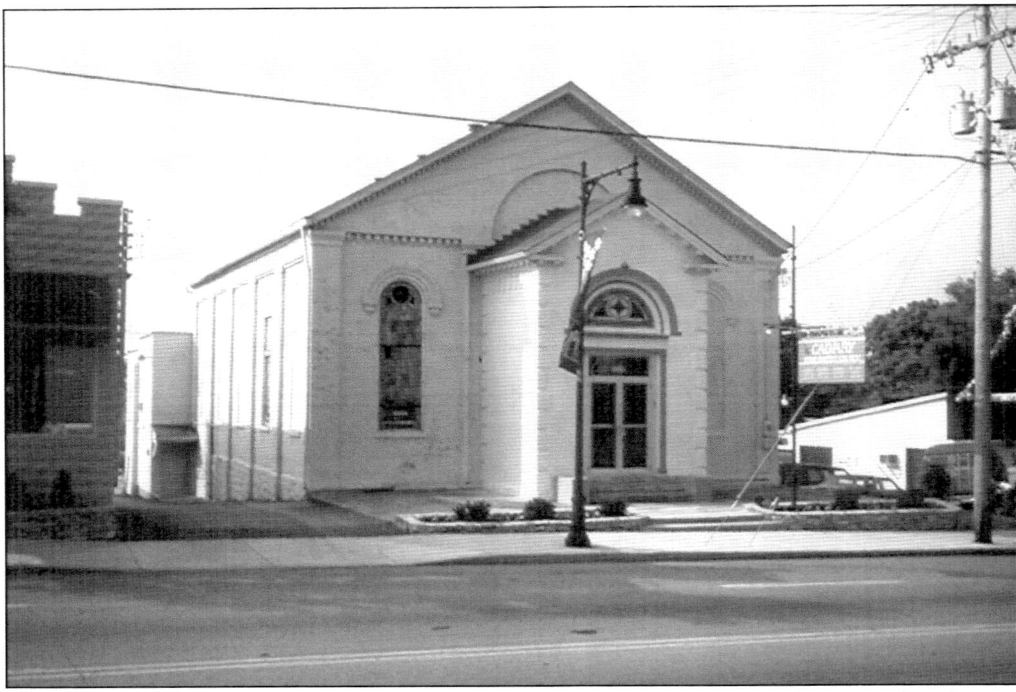

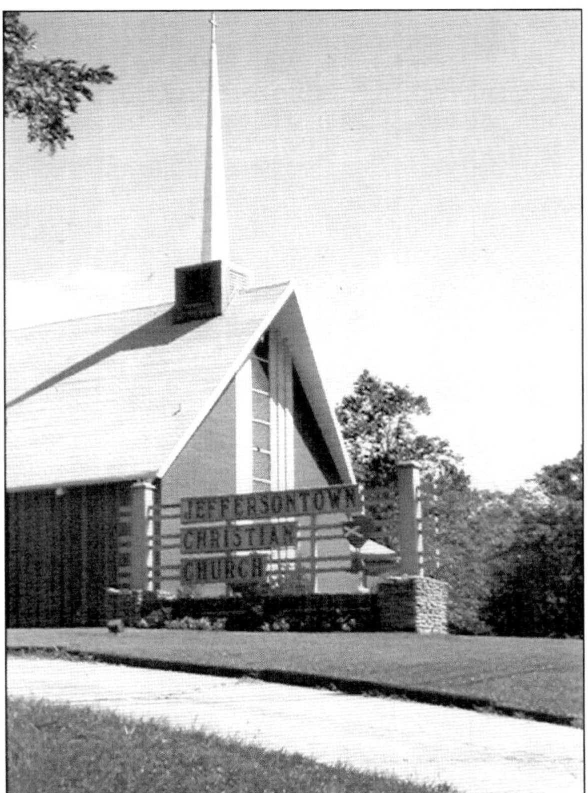

Jeffersontown Christian Church was formed in 1837. The structure pictured here was built in 1878 to replace an 1839 church that burned, and was used to house refugees of the 1937 flood in Louisville. In 1961, this building was sold to the Moose Lodge, and a new church was built on Taylorsville Road. (Photo courtesy of Jane Smith.)

This photo shows the new Jeffersontown Christian Church located on Taylorsville Road. (Photo courtesy of Jane Smith.)

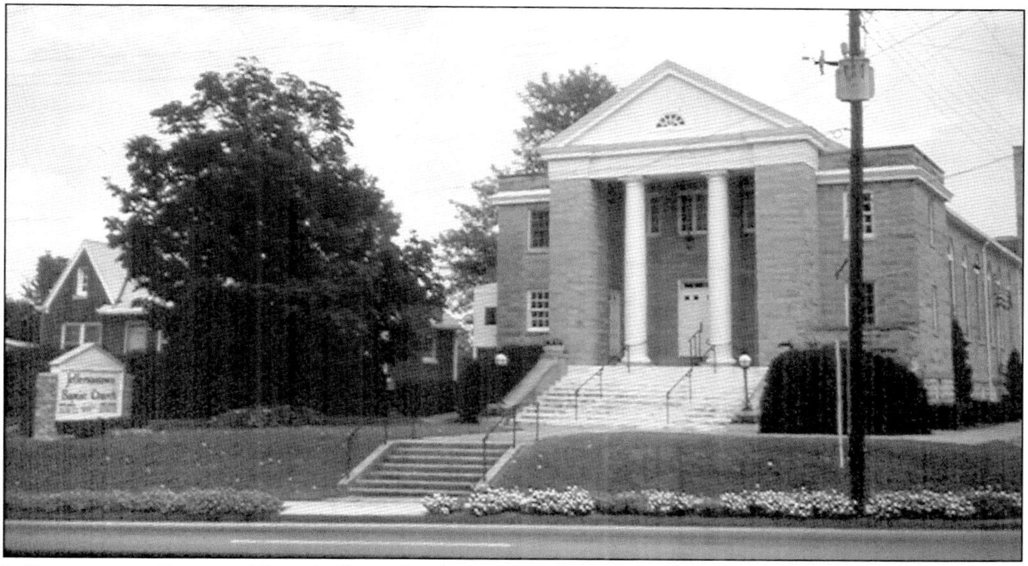

Jeffersontown Baptist Church dates back to 1845. In 1868, the congregation left the Union Church and purchased half of a building owned by the Masonic Lodge. Services were held there until 1925, when the church decided to move to a larger place. Unfortunately, the new church they built burned down after about nine years, so in 1945, the congregation began using the basement auditorium of the building that houses the church today. (Photo courtesy of Jane Smith.)

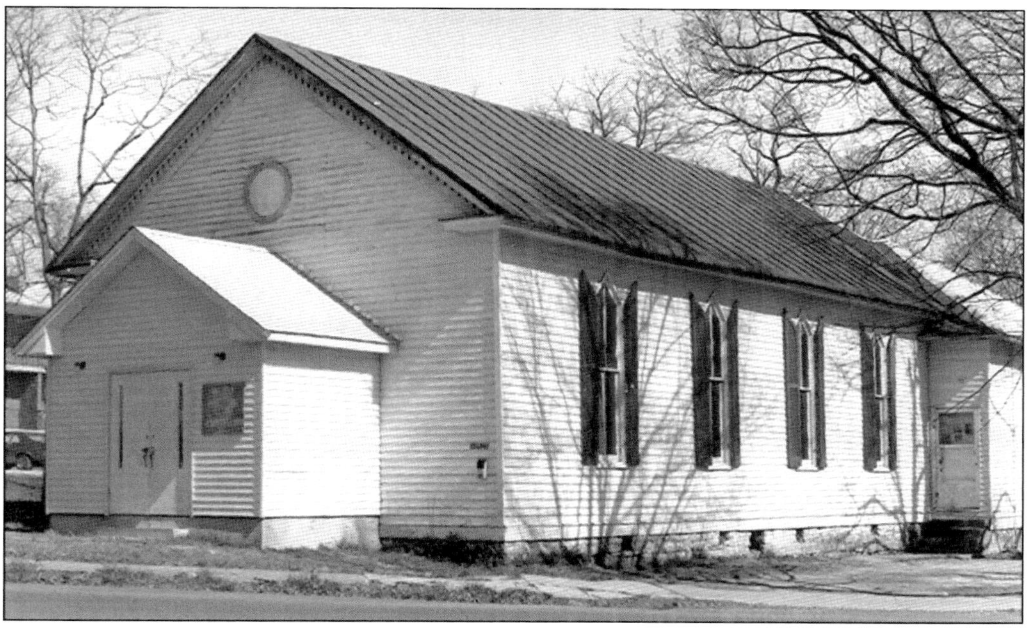

St. Paul's United Methodist Church was founded in 1877. The structure was built on or near the site of the black Union Church, which was still standing in the 1870s, when Rosa Leatherman sold two lots on Old Taylorsville Road for the construction of a church. Only recently did the congregation leave this location for a newer building. (Photo courtesy of Lt. Col. Robert C. Jobson.)

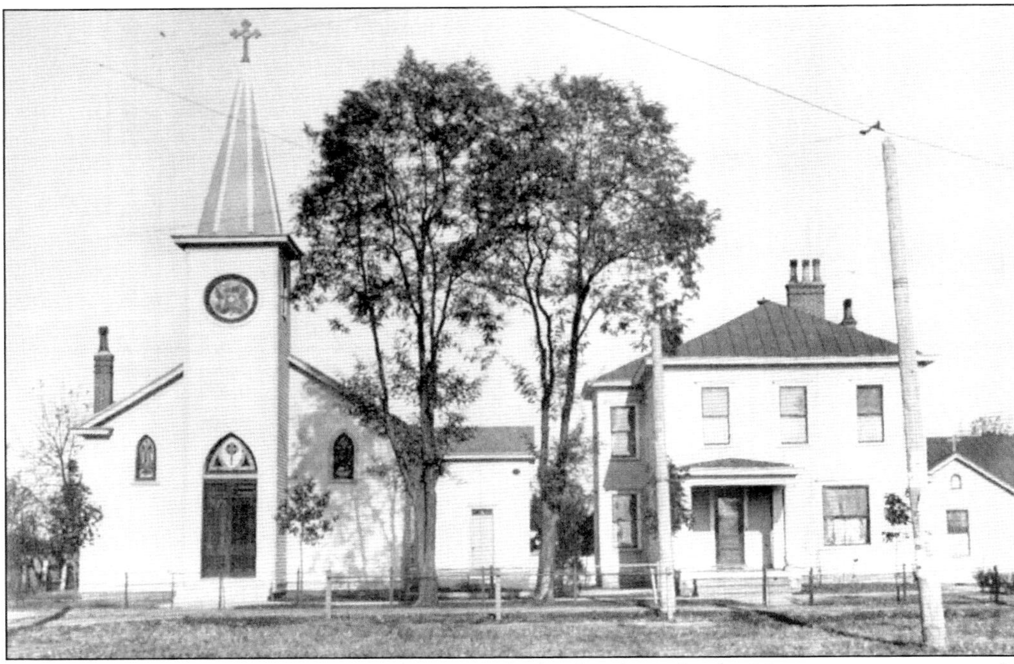

St Edward Parish was built in 1884 by 30 Catholic families who had begun to congregate for mass in 1878. The church, originally called St. Agnes Mission, was located on Watterson Trail, at the southwest corner of the square. A rectory and school were later added to the property. (Photo courtesy of the Jeffersontown Historical Museum.)

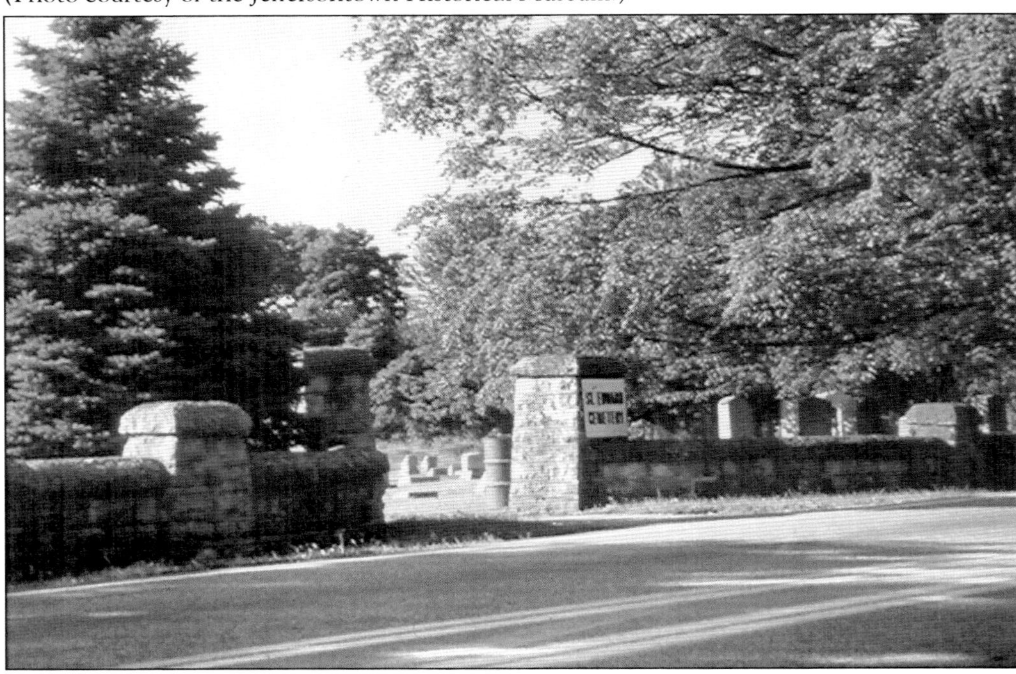

This photo shows the gates of St Edward Cemetery, located on Billtown Road. (Photo courtesy of Jane Smith.)

Rev. Martin Frankenberger was appointed pastor of St. Edward Church in 1937 and served for 19 years. (Photo courtesy of Tillie Meffert, Mary Boring, and Fred Oechslin.)

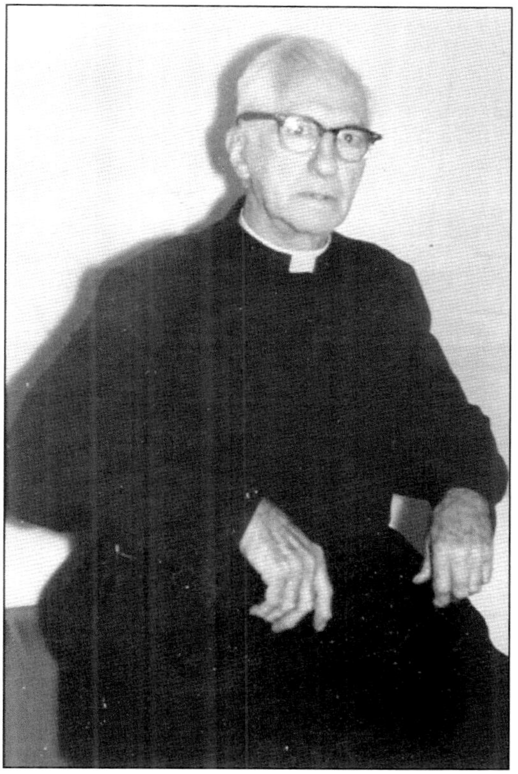

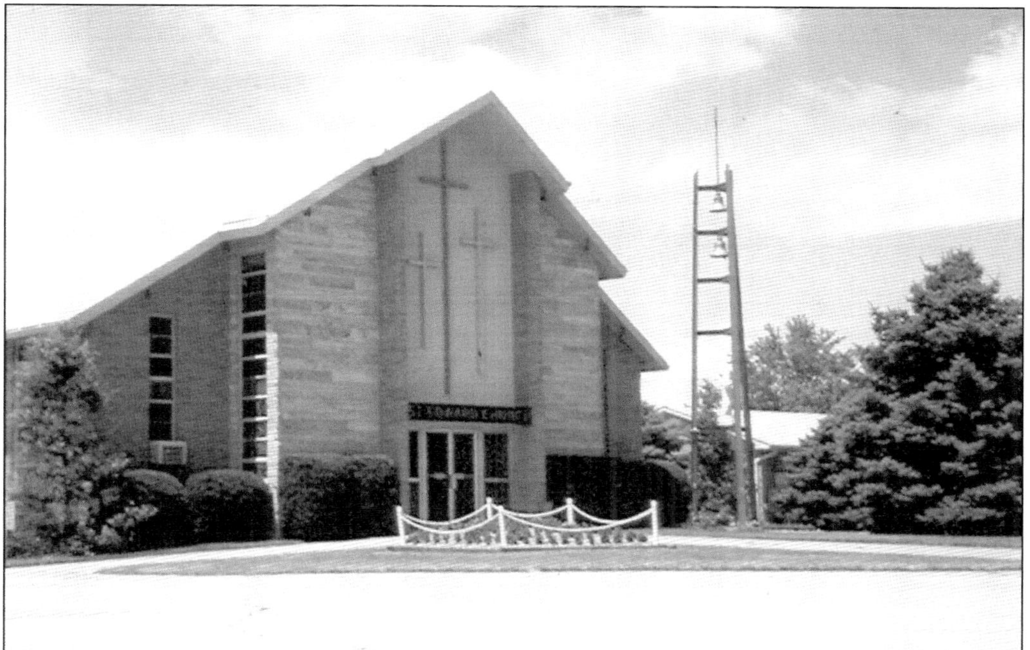

The new St. Edward Church, located on Sue Helen Drive, was dedicated in 1961. The bells out front are from the original church building. (Photo courtesy of Jane Smith.)

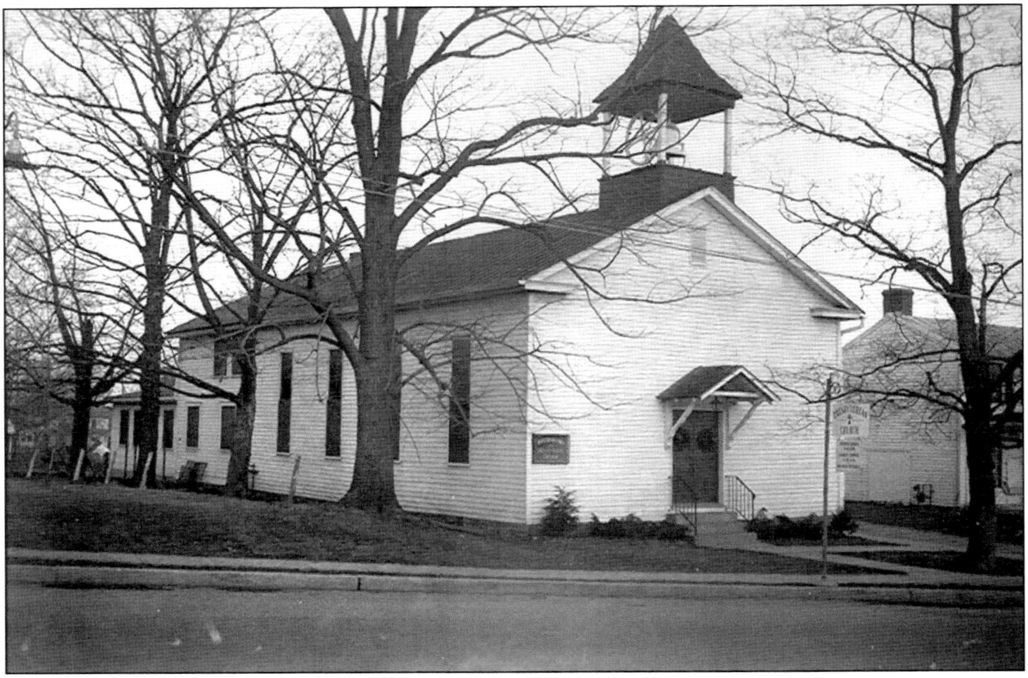

Jeffersontown Presbyterian Church was established in 1861. In 1885, Joseph and Sarah Ann Nunamaker deeded a lot on Taylorsville Road to the congregation so it could build a church there. (Photo courtesy of the Jeffersontown Historical Museum.)

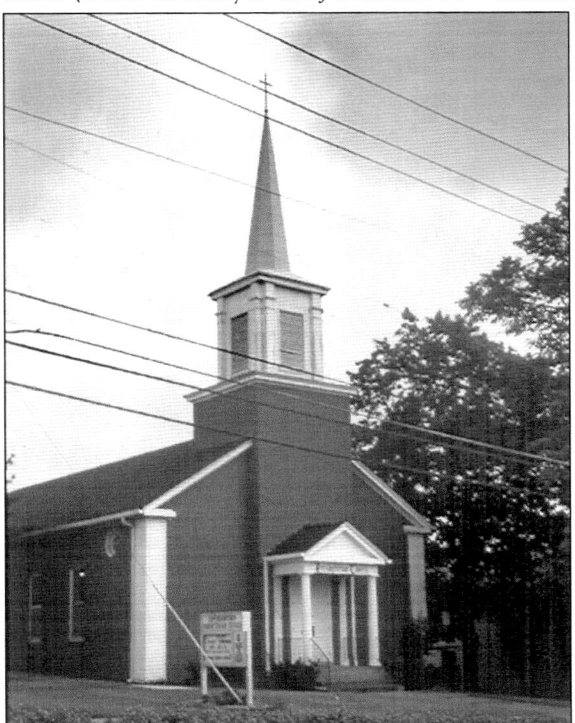

This photo shows the new Presbyterian Church building on Taylorsville Road. (Photo courtesy of Jane Smith.)

Dorothy Sweeney taught Sunday school at the Presbyterian Church. This class photo includes the following, from left to right: (front row) Rita Clark, ? Herr, and LaFon Weller; (back row) Zita Kay McDaniel, Mrs. Sweeney, and John Keeley. (Photo courtesy of the Jeffersontown Historical Museum.)

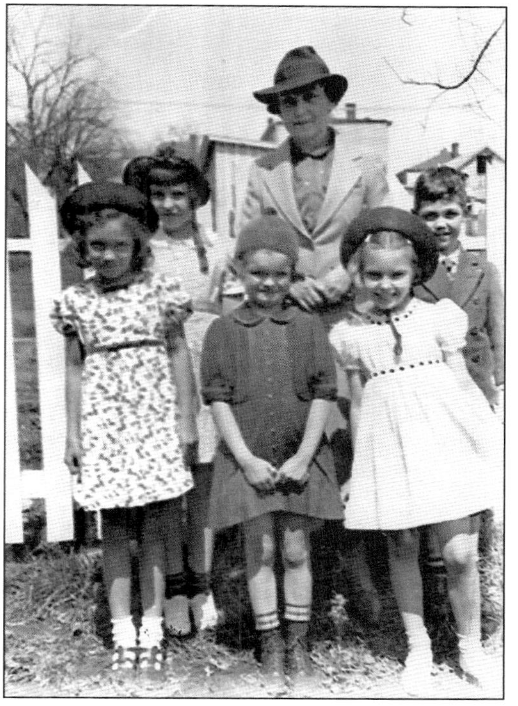

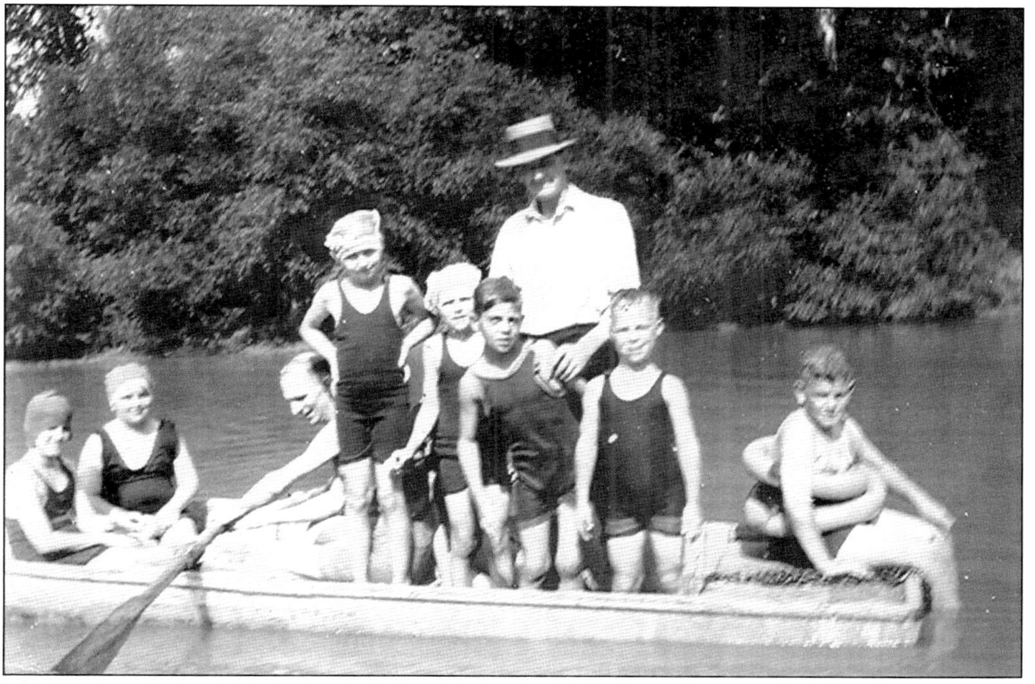

This c. 1925 photo shows members of the Jeffersontown Presbyterian Church on a picnic. Pictured, from left to right, are Elizabeth Miller, Lucille Shacklette, Andrew Hite (rowing), Anna Agee, Marcia Bryan, Bill Spangler, Tom Weller (standing), Billy Hartley, and Ken Davis. (Photo courtesy of Marcia Bryan Horton.)

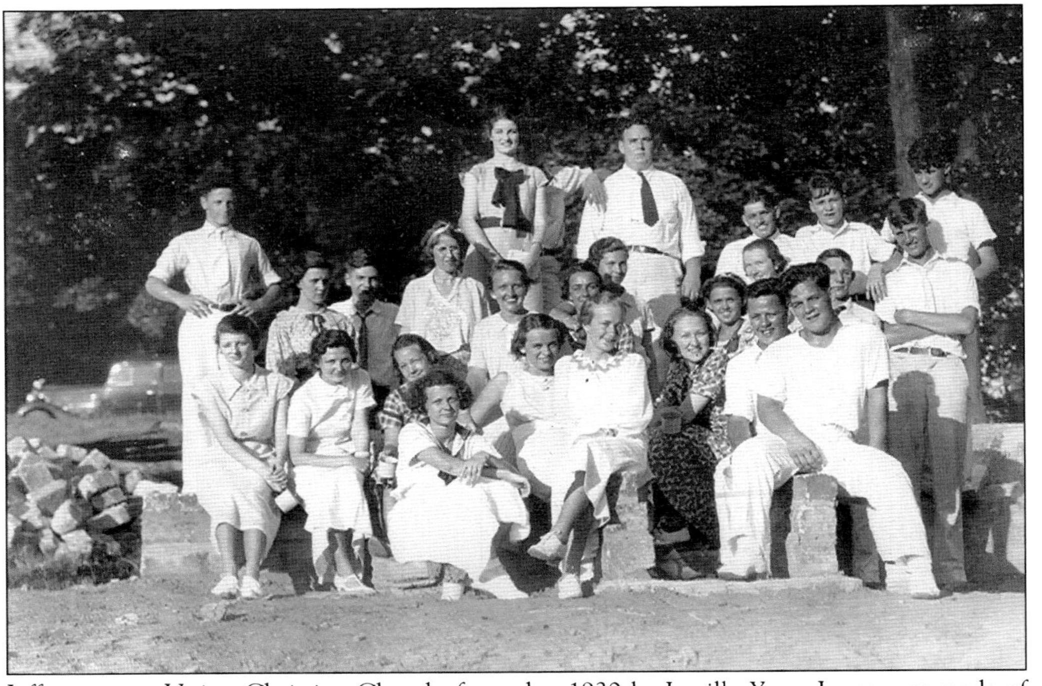

Jeffersontown Union Christian Church, formed c. 1930 by Lucille Yann Jones, was made of members from the Christian, Lutheran, Presbyterian, and Methodist churches. This photo was taken at the Jeffersontown Union Christian Endeavor Picnic held at Iroquois Park in the summer of 1937. (Photo courtesy of Marcia Bryan Horton.)

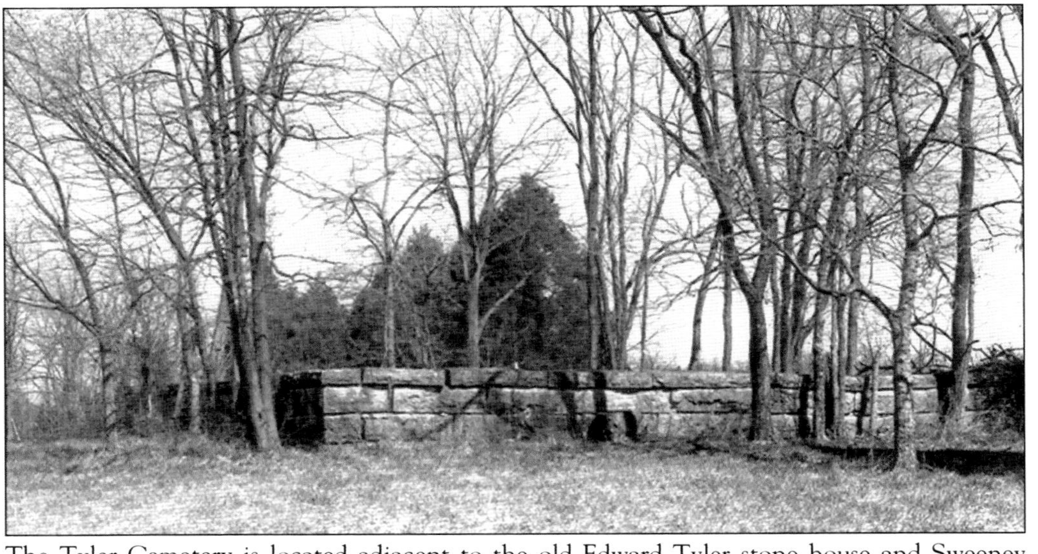

The Tyler Cemetery is located adjacent to the old Edward Tyler stone house and Sweeney Ranch. It was established in 1802, at the time of Edward Tyler Sr.'s death. (Photo courtesy of Lt. Col. Robert C. Jobson.)

In 1904, the Daughters of the Confederacy placed this tombstone in the Jeffersontown Cemetery in honor of four men they felt were unjustly executed during the Civil War. Two of the men still lie buried here, while family members reinterred the other two elsewhere. (Photo courtesy of Jane Smith.)

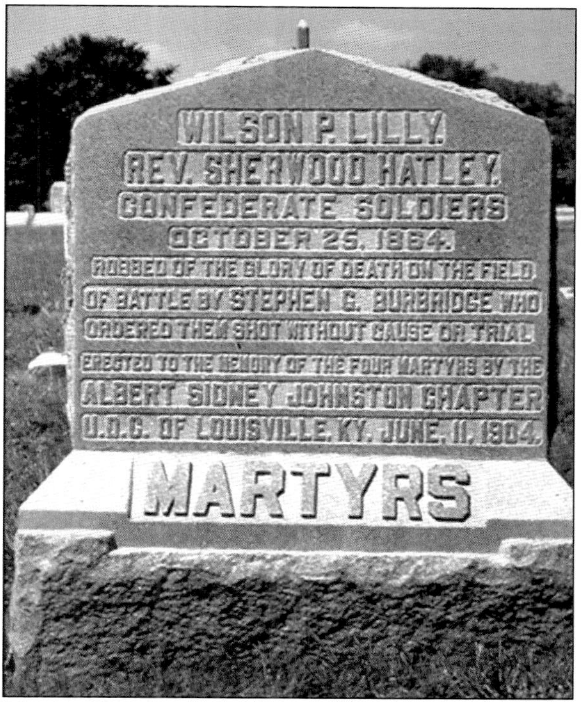

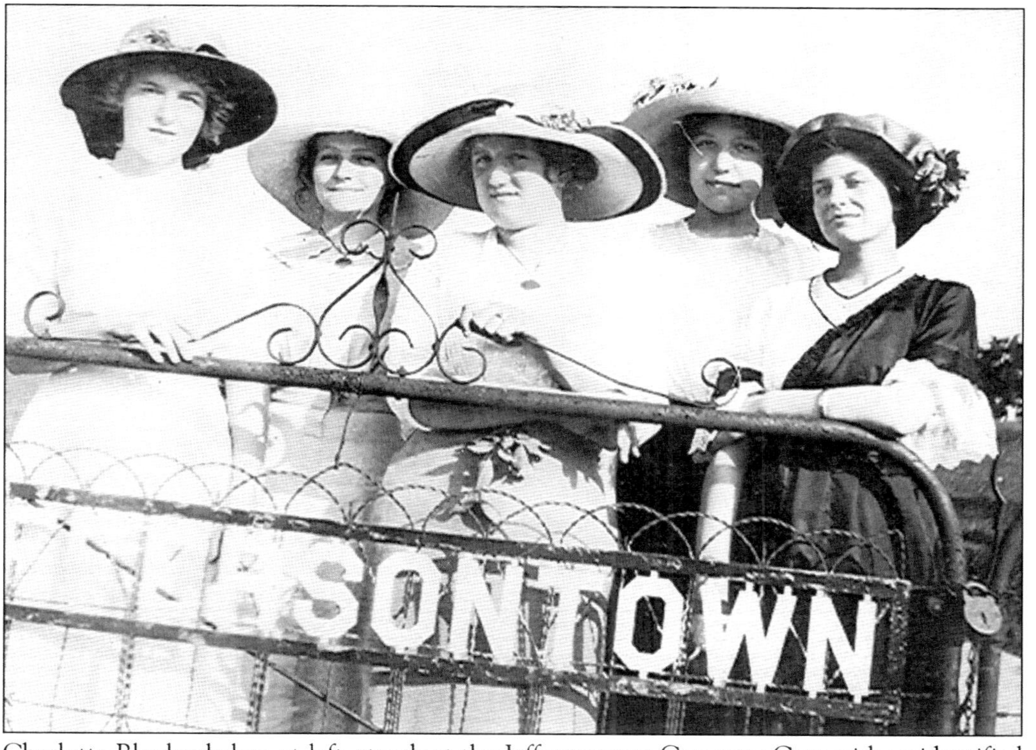

Charlotte Blankenbaker, at left, stands at the Jeffersontown Cemetery Gate with unidentified friends in this c. 1916 photo. (Photo courtesy of Tom Lovett.)

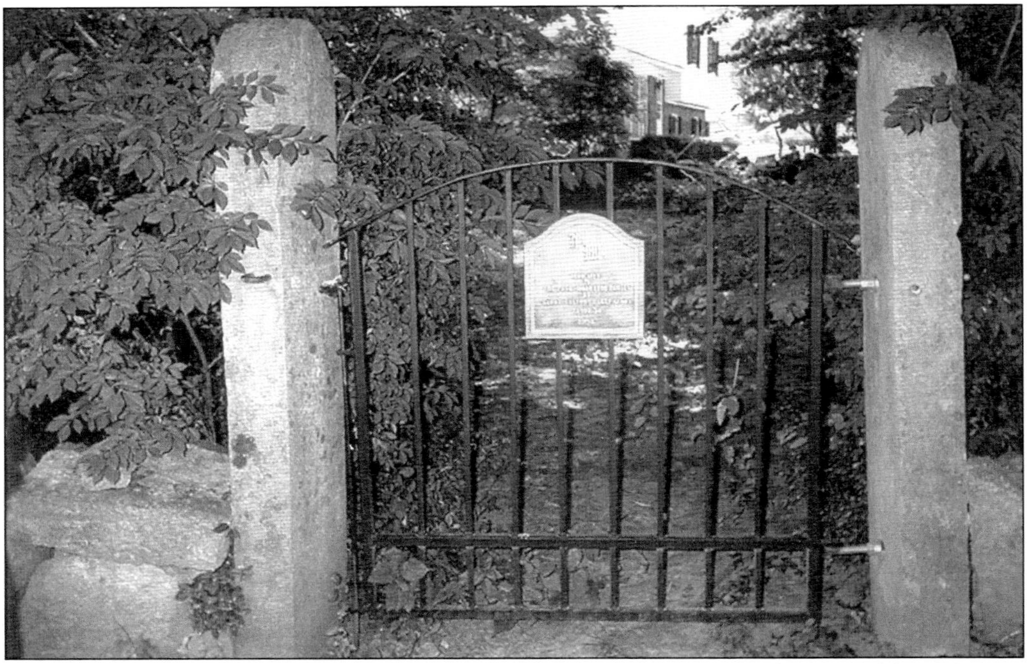

The Funk-Morrison Cemetery is the resting place of Peter Funk and some of his relatives who resided at the home he named Avon, located near the corner of Taylorsville Road and Hurstbourne Lane. (Photo courtesy of the Jeffersontown Historical Museum.)

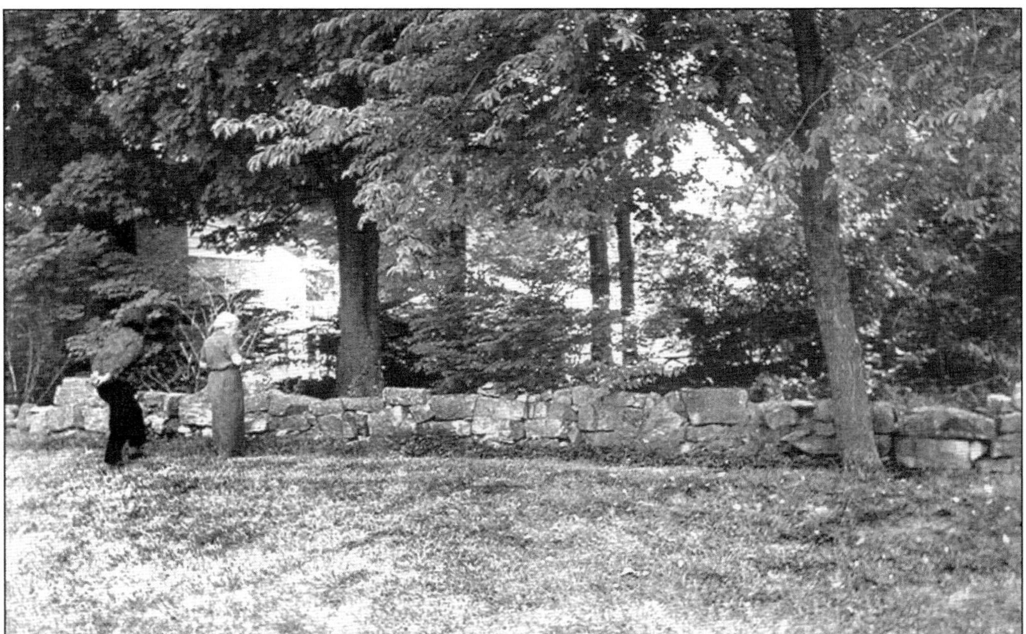

This view shows the low rock wall surrounding the Funk-Morrison Cemetery. (Photo courtesy of the Jeffersontown Historical Museum.)

Four

People and Places

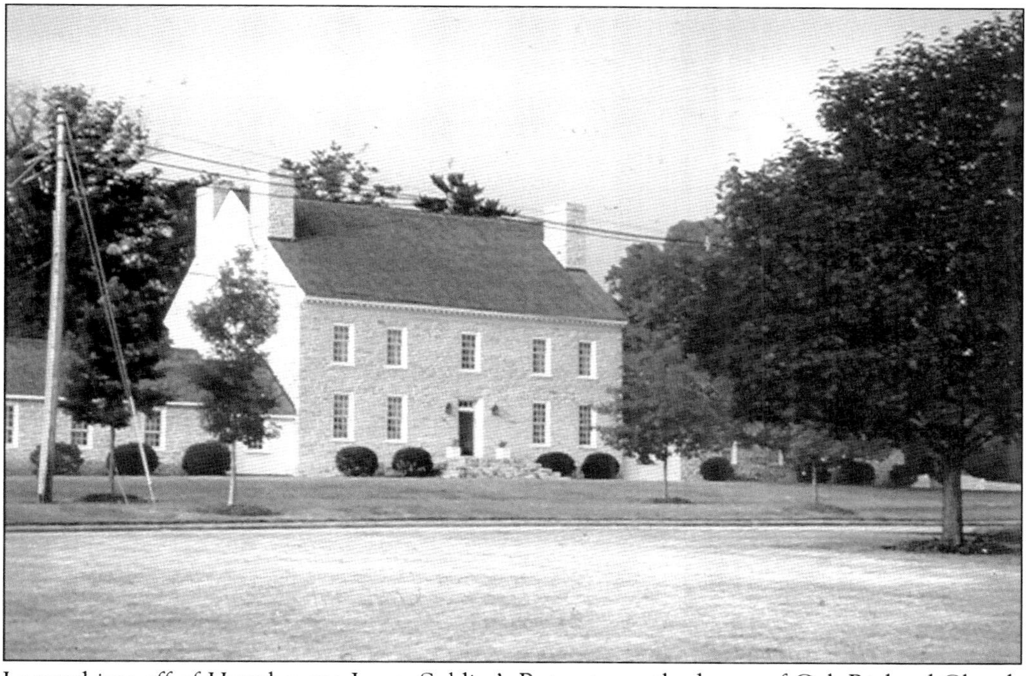

Located just off of Hurstbourne Lane, Soldier's Retreat was the home of Col. Richard Clough Anderson, who was married to Elizabeth Clark, the sister of Gen. George Rogers Clark. For several months, the Andersons took care of the surviving members of the Chenoweth family, after they were massacred by Native Americans at their home in Middletown in 1789. (Photo courtesy of Jane Smith.)

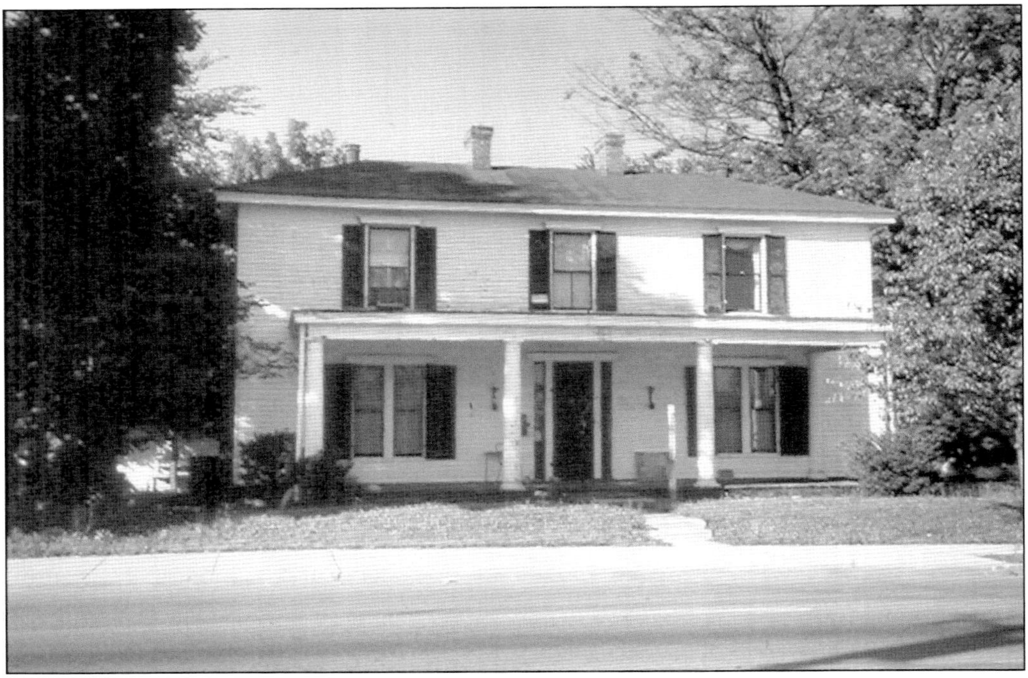

Dr. Leslie A. Blankenbaker practiced medicine in this lovely two-story home, where his family also resided. The house is located on Watterson Trail, across from the Seaton House. (Photo courtesy of Jane Smith.)

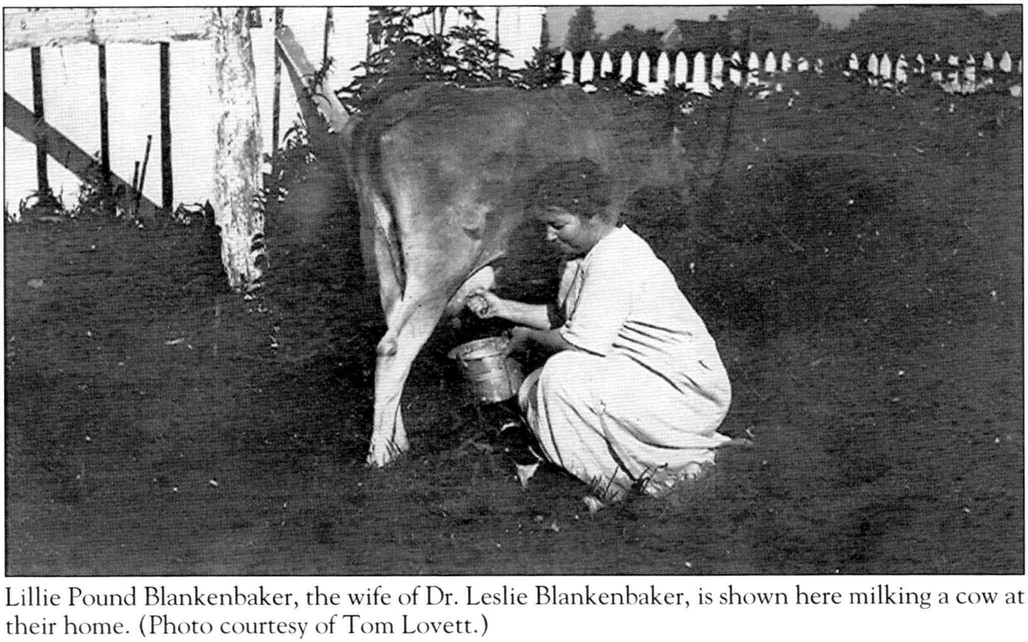

Lillie Pound Blankenbaker, the wife of Dr. Leslie Blankenbaker, is shown here milking a cow at their home. (Photo courtesy of Tom Lovett.)

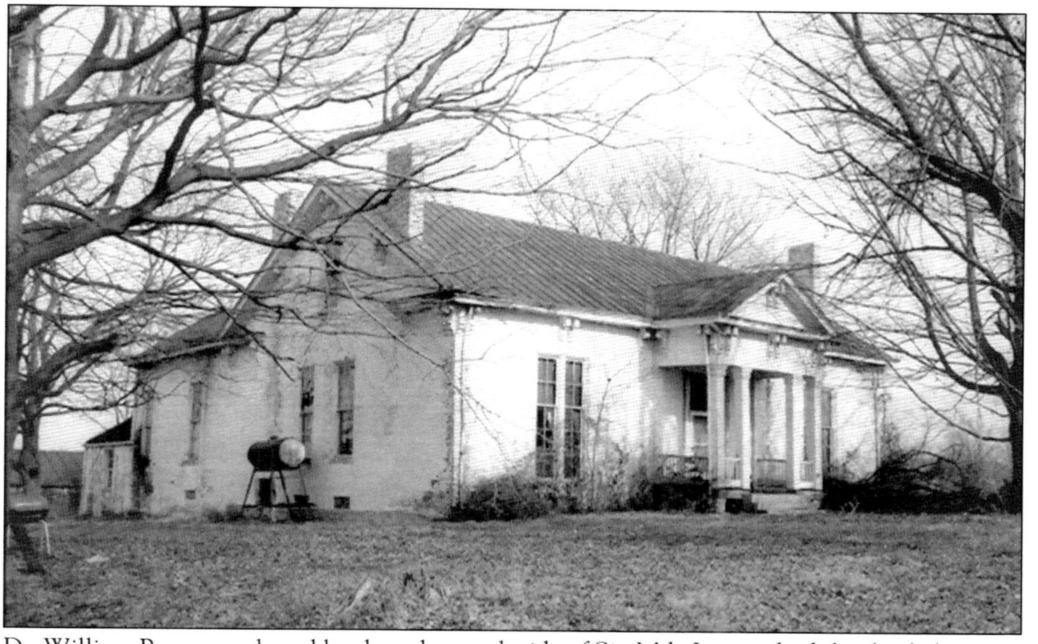

Dr. William Bryan purchased land on the north side of Six Mile Lane, which he deeded over to his son, William F. Bryan. In 1858, William F. Bryan married Fanny Oldham, and they built this one-story home. (Photo courtesy of Louisville Metro Historic Landmarks Commission.)

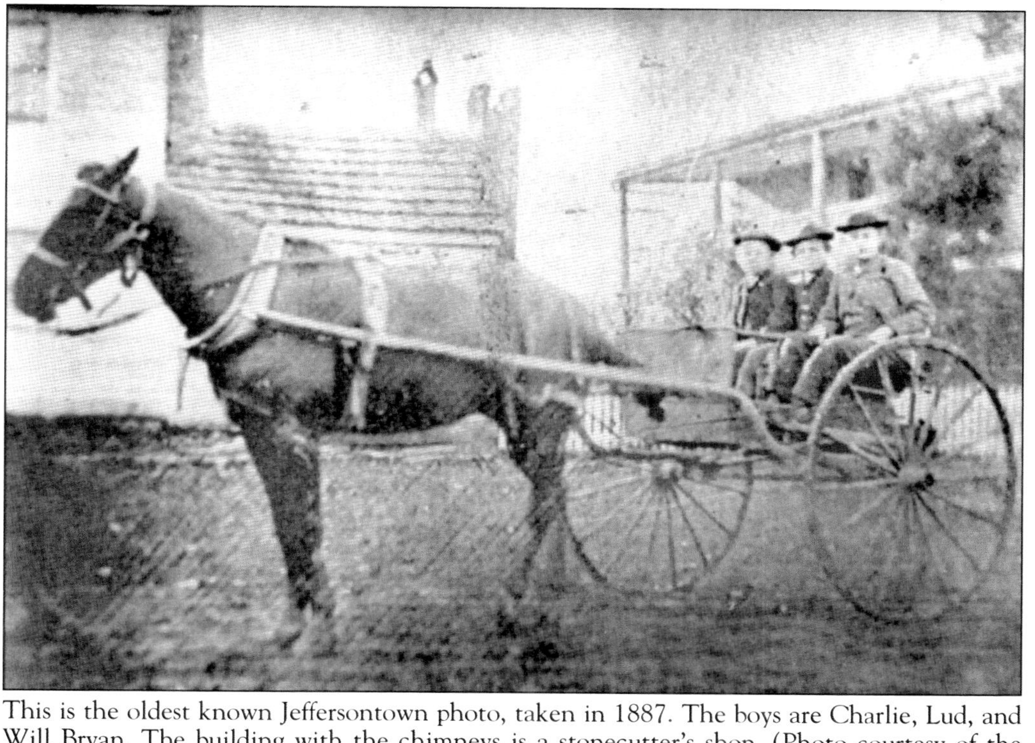

This is the oldest known Jeffersontown photo, taken in 1887. The boys are Charlie, Lud, and Will Bryan. The building with the chimneys is a stonecutter's shop. (Photo courtesy of the Jeffersontown Historical Museum.)

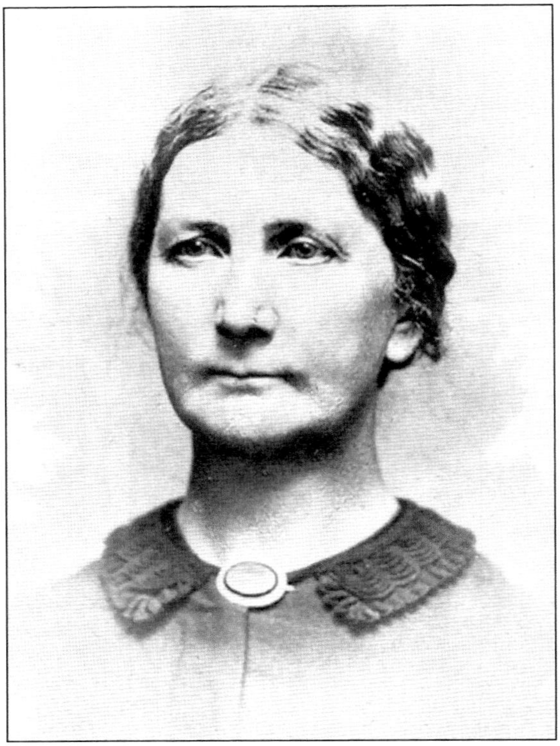

Anna Eliza Hikes Bryan was the daughter of Jacob and Julia Geiger Hikes. She was born in 1811 and married Dr. William Bryan in 1835. (Photo courtesy of Marcia Bryan Horton.)

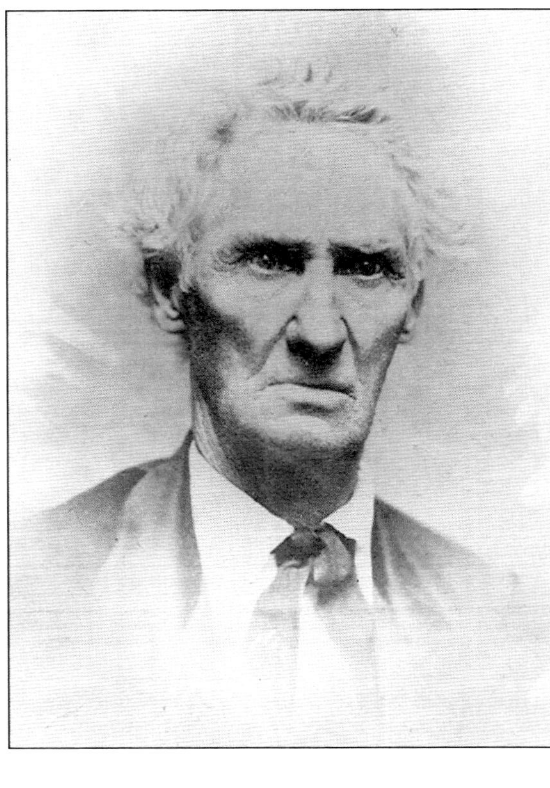

Dr. William Bryan was born in 1791 in Virginia. He began his medical practice about 1819, after he moved to Jeffersontown with his first wife, Margaret. After she died, he married Anna Eliza Hikes and built their new home, called Beechland, in the Six Mile Lane area. Dr. Bryan continued to practice medicine until his death in 1871. (Photo courtesy of Marcia Bryan Horton.)

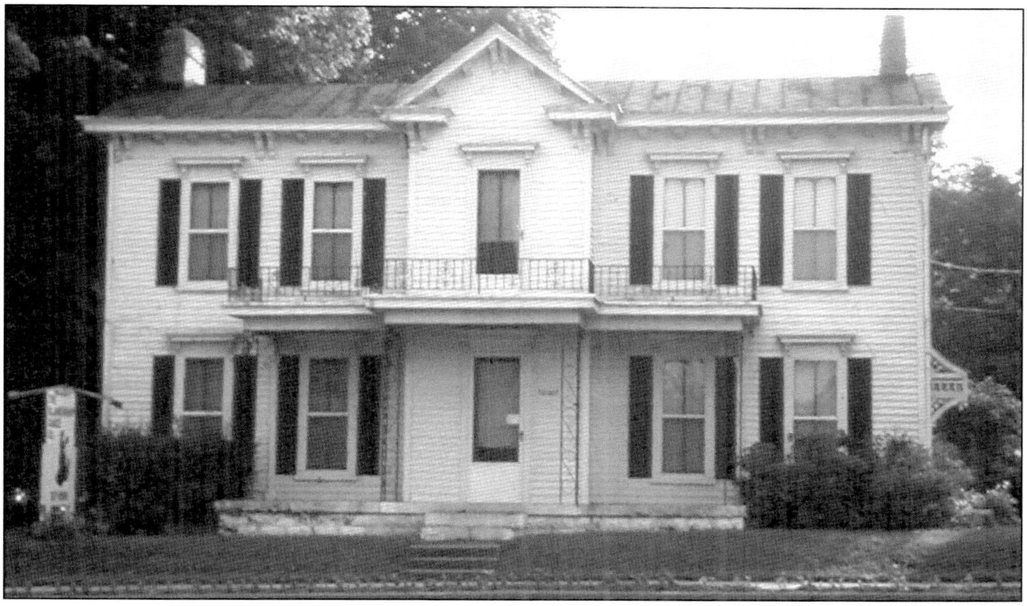

The Buchanan House was built a few years after the Civil War, and was the home of Mr. and Mrs. William Theodore Buchanan, who offered room and board for travelers. In the 1940s, Ida Burdon, who was once mayor of Jeffersontown, resided in this home located on Taylorsville Road across from Sprowl Road. (Photo courtesy of Jane Smith.)

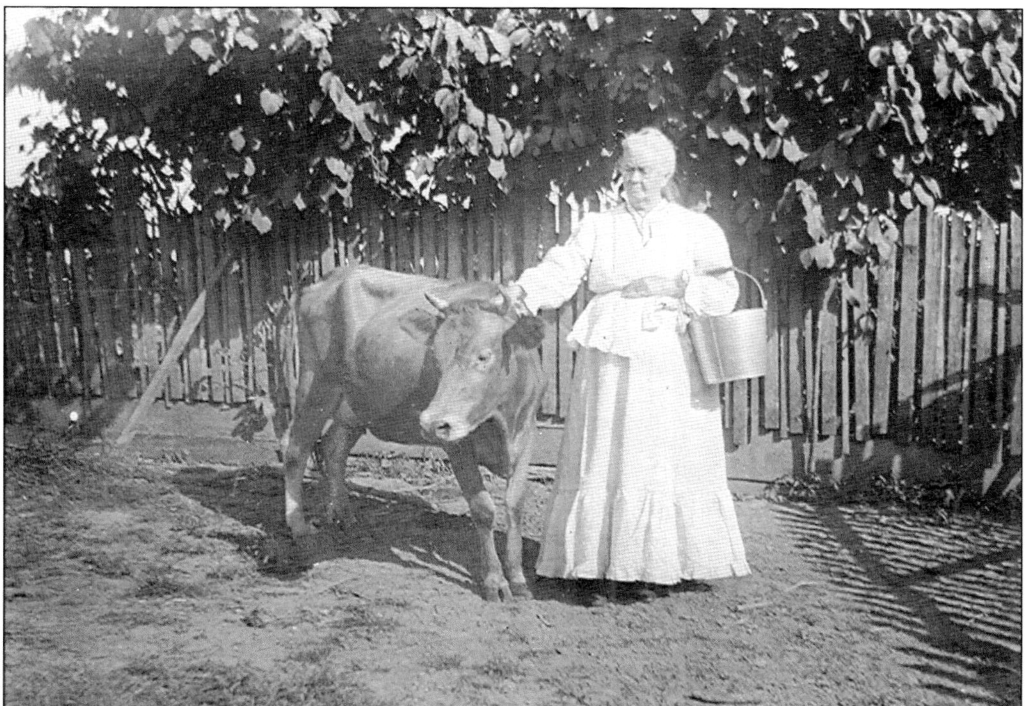

Mary Elizabeth Maddox Buchanan (nicknamed "Mittie") is seen here behind the Buchanan home with one of her cows. (Photo courtesy of Marcia Bryan Horton.)

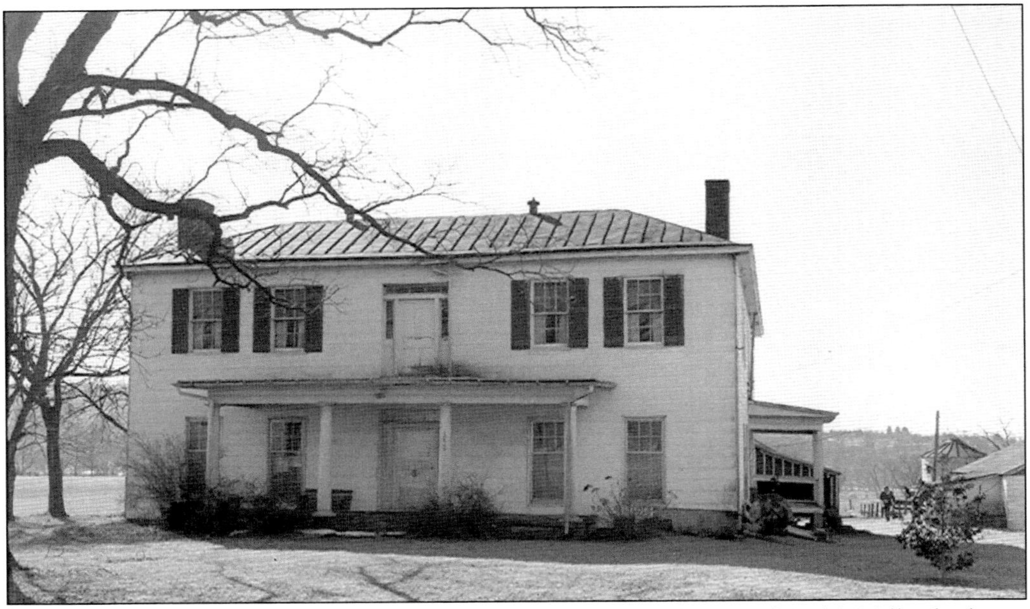

The Abraham Funk House, located on Seatonville Road, was the site of Funk's Mill, which was acquired by the Funk family from John Mundell before 1817. Peter Funk deeded this property to his son Abraham, who married Ellen A. Taylor in 1849. Visitors to the mill traveled there via Funk's Mill Road, which would later become known as Billtown Road. (Photo courtesy of Louisville Metro Historic Landmarks Commission.)

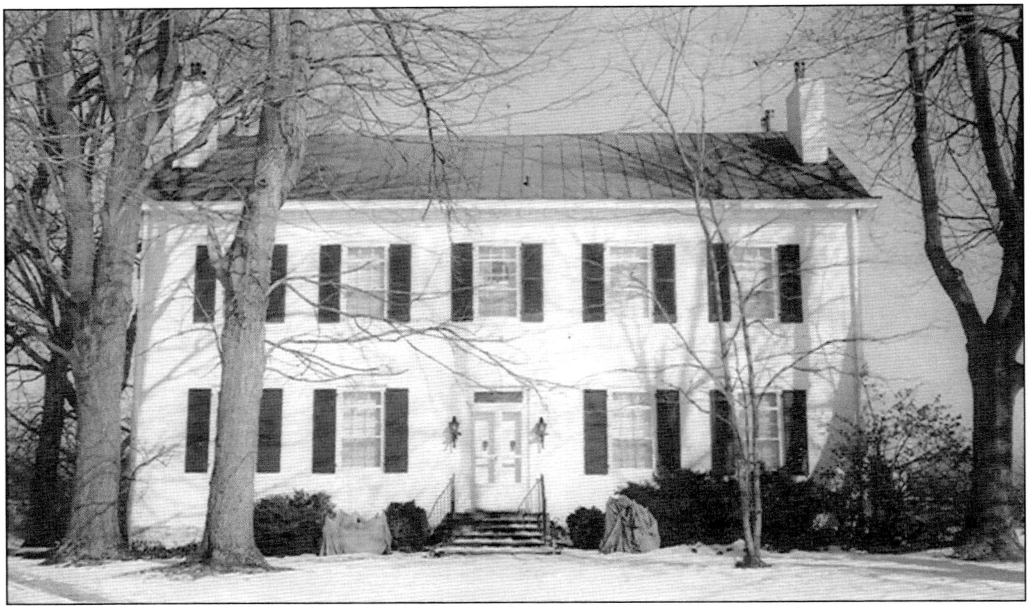

This home, known variously as Funk's Branch, Avon, or Cherry Springs, is located near the intersection of Taylorsville Road and Hurstbourne Lane. It is unclear whether the house was built by John Funk in the 1790s or by his son Peter in the early 1800s. Peter was a very wealthy man, and he saw to it that all of his children were settled comfortably in their own homes. (Photo courtesy of Louisville Metro Historic Landmarks Commission.)

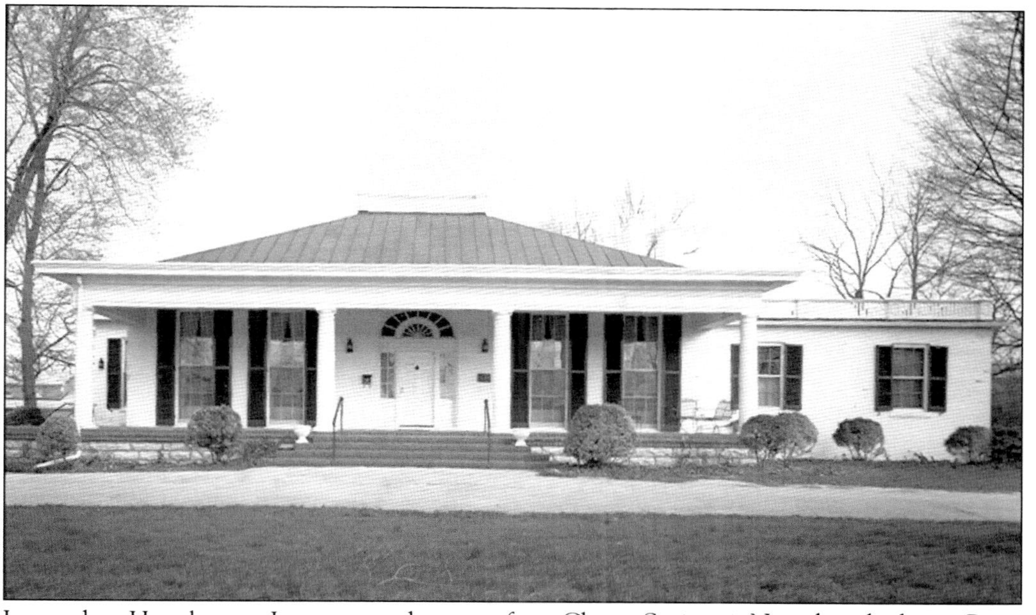

Located on Hurstbourne Lane across the street from Cherry Springs is Nunnlea, the home Peter Funk had built c. 1854 for his daughter, Harriet, after she married Albert Hise (also spelled Hite in some documents). The Beautification League bought Nunnlea and its two surviving outbuildings in 1962, thus providing for the preservation of this lovely home. (Photo courtesy of Louisville Metro Historic Landmarks Commission.)

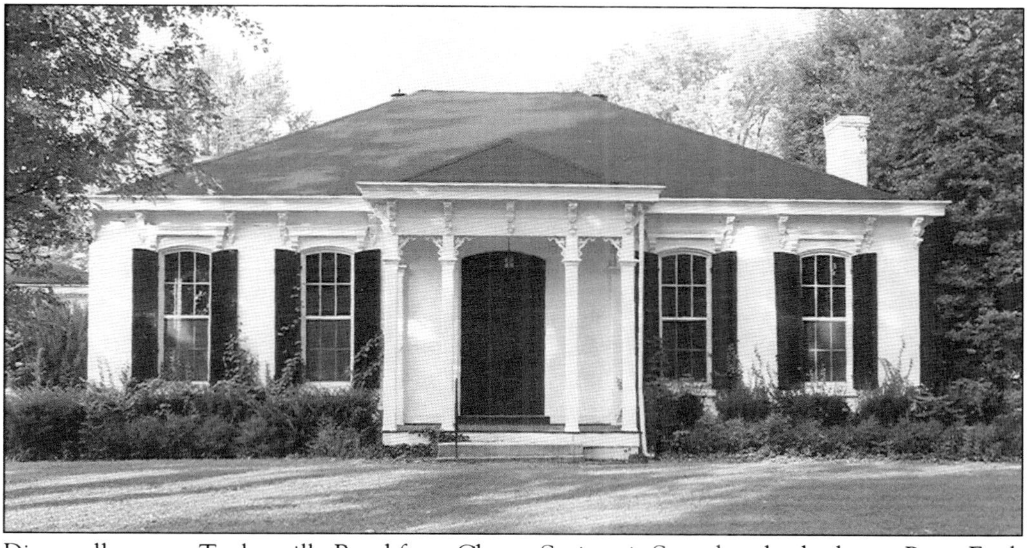

Diagonally across Taylorsville Road from Cherry Springs is Stonybrook, the home Peter Funk had constructed for his son, James Henry, who married Mary A. Yenowine in 1860. Also known as the Bickel Place by local residents, Stonybrook and its conical icehouse were recently moved closer to Taylorsville Road and renovated for commercial use. (Photo courtesy of Louisville Metro Historic Landmarks Commission.)

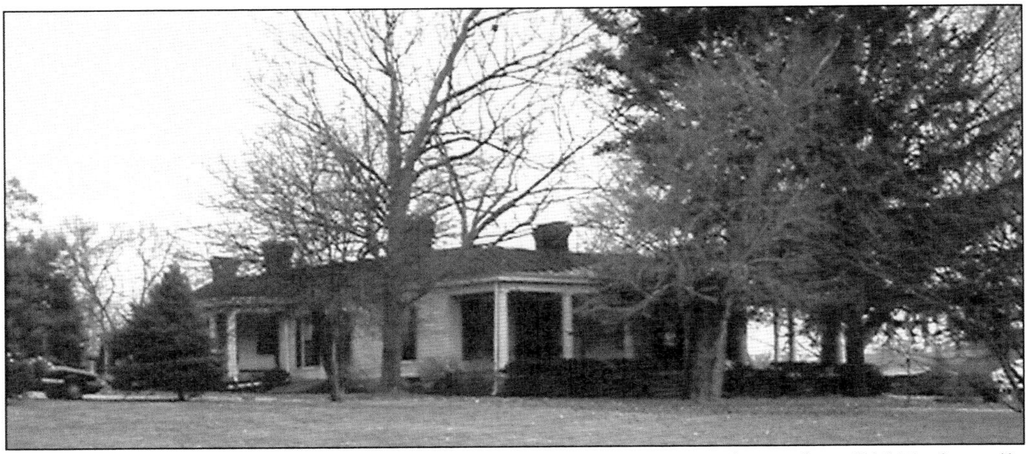

The Greathouse home, supposedly a stagecoach stop at one time, is located on Old Taylorsville Road. It was originally built before the Civil War by saddler John Ward Jean, who was one of Catherine Myers Jean's 10 children. The Catherine Jean House, located on Watterson Trail, was built about 1834 and is probably the oldest remaining frame house from the old section of town. (Photo courtesy of Jane Smith.)

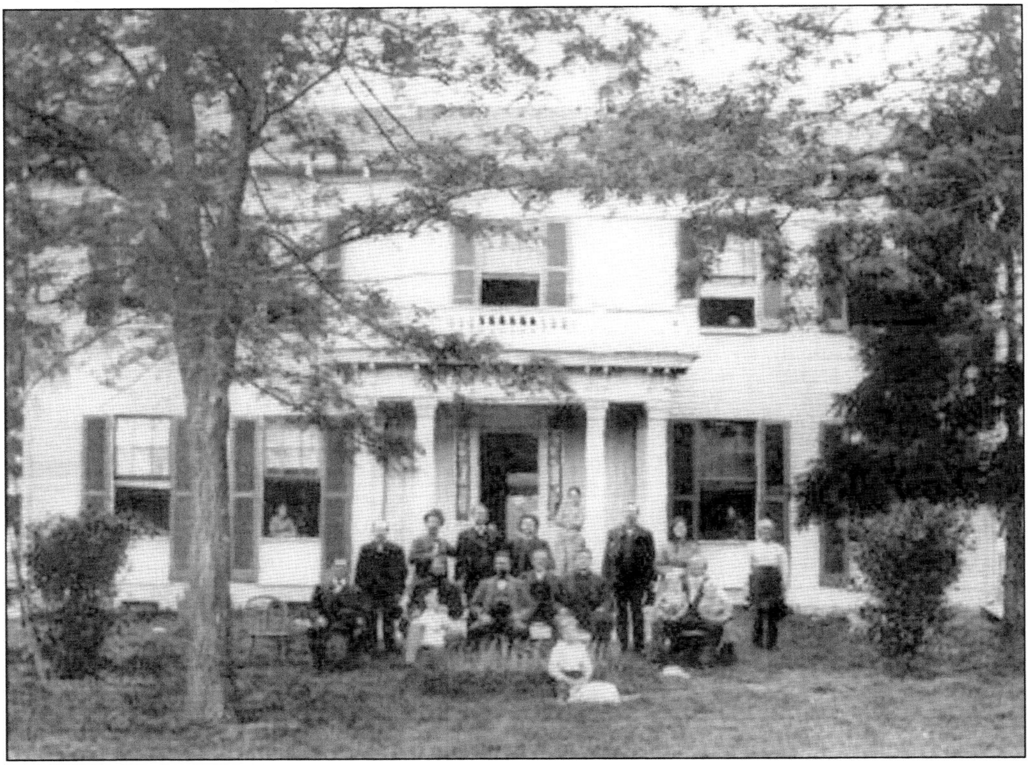

The Maj. Abner Field house, located on Six Mile Lane, was built prior to 1830 for Abner and his wife, Jane Pope Field. Jane was the daughter of Col. William Pope, one of Louisville's early settlers. Abner was already living in the Six Mile Lane area in 1804, and he was appointed surveyor of that vicinity. This photo, taken in 1884, shows the Huber family, who were later owners of the property. (Photo courtesy of Elisabeth W. Salyer.)

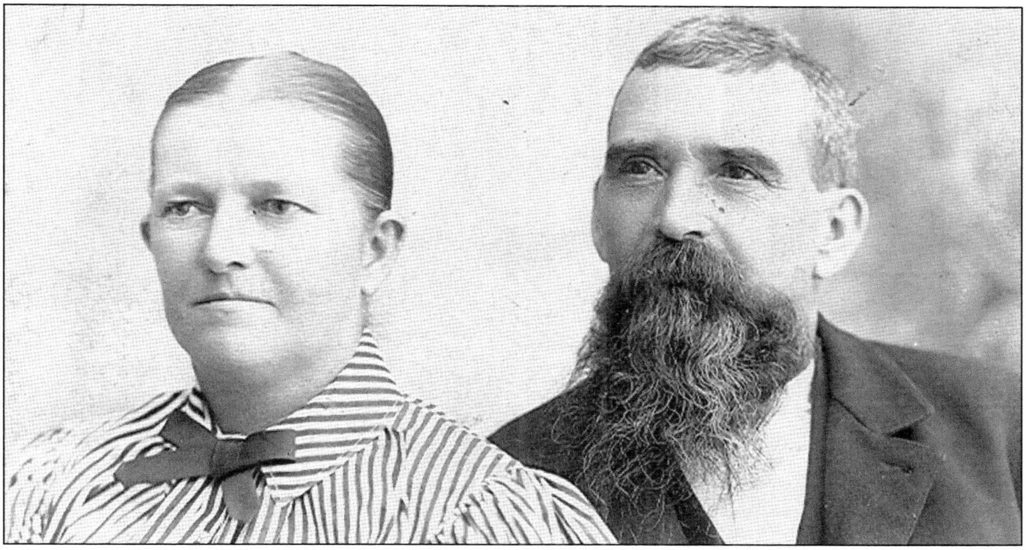

John B. Ford owned a blacksmith shop on the square in Jeffersontown. John and Hallie Tucker Ford were married on February 11, 1868. (Photo courtesy of Betty Ford McClain and Patricia Ford Atchley.)

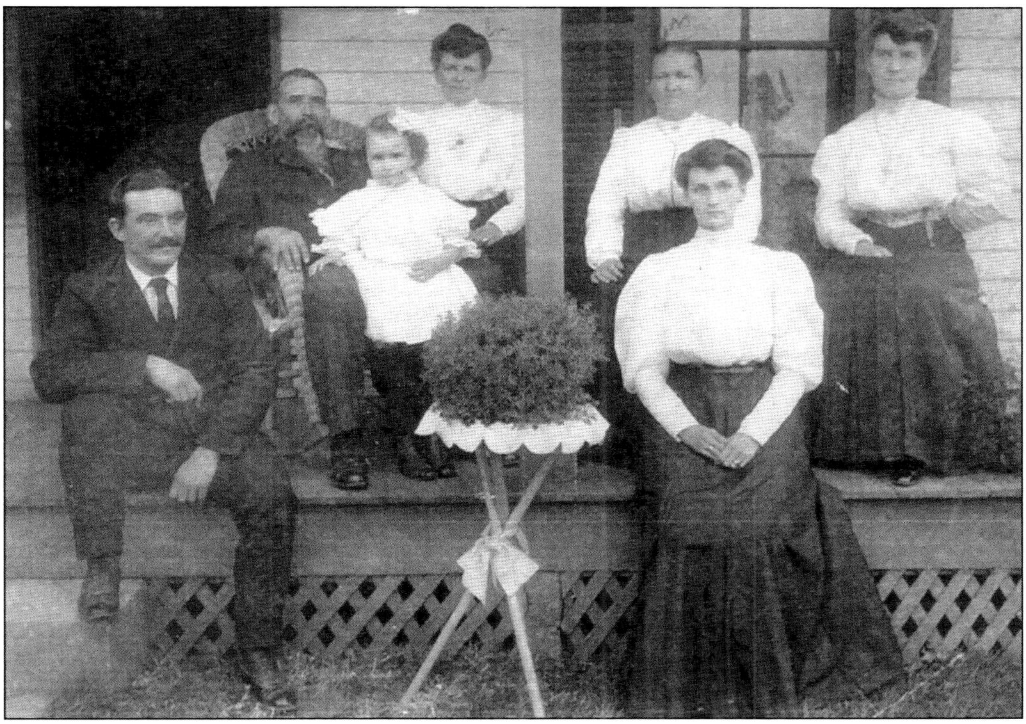

This photo of the Ford family dates to the turn of the 20th century. Pictured from left to right are Lewis Salem Ford; his father, John B. Ford holding his daughter, Geneva Ford; his sister, Emma Ford Gill; his mother, Hallie Tucker Ford; his sister, Evalena Ford; and his first wife, Jeanette Watkins Ford (seated in front). (Photo courtesy of Betty Ford McClain and Patricia Ford Atchley.)

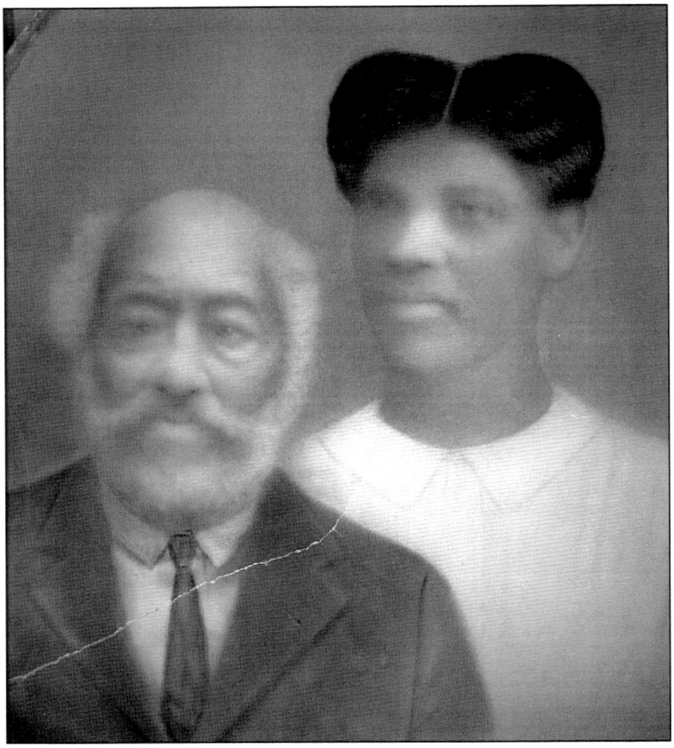

This early photograph is of Jerry Bottoms and his wife, Lucinda. He lived in a Taylorsville Road farmhouse and worked for members of the Hunsinger family in the early 1900s. One of their daughters was Harriet, who married William Drake. Jerry Bottoms died in 1933 at a very old age. (Photo courtesy of Dr. Jewelene Fulton Richards, Ed.D.)

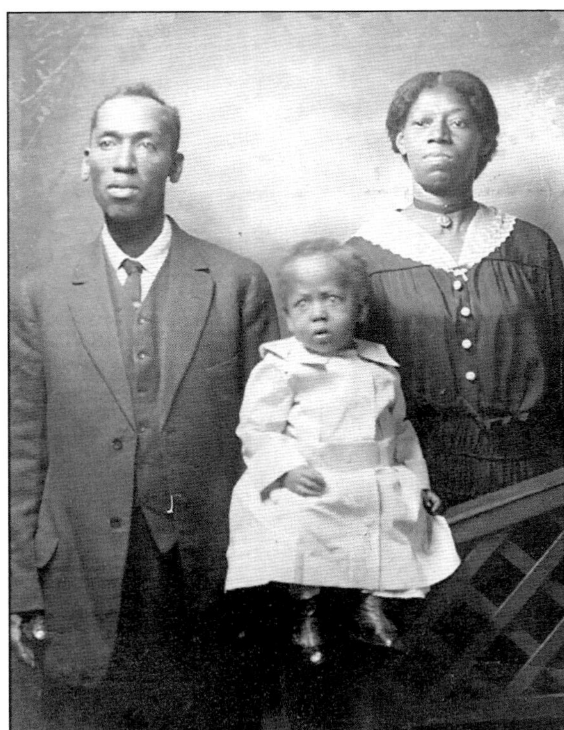

This picture of William (Wilbur), Chester, and Harriet Bottoms Drake was taken around 1915. The Drakes were married from 1909 to 1941. In the late 1930s and early 1940s, they lived on Shelby Street next to the Colored School. Wilbur worked for the Deibel family and other crop growers in Jefferson and Oldham Counties. Their children were Chester and Viola. After the death of Harriet, Wilbur married Grace Dugan in 1943, and they lived on Watterson Trail. (Photo courtesy of Dr. Jewelene Fulton Richards, Ed.D.)

William (Will) Fulton's home was on the corner of what is now Electron Drive and Watterson Trail. He was well known throughout the community as the person who fried fish for many of the community fish fries. He married Josie Johnson in 1898. Their children were Theodore (Scut), Florence (Tink), Carrie, Georgia, Carl, Mary Eliza, and Harry Lee. Will died in 1948. (Photo courtesy of Dr. Jewelene Fulton Richards, Ed.D.)

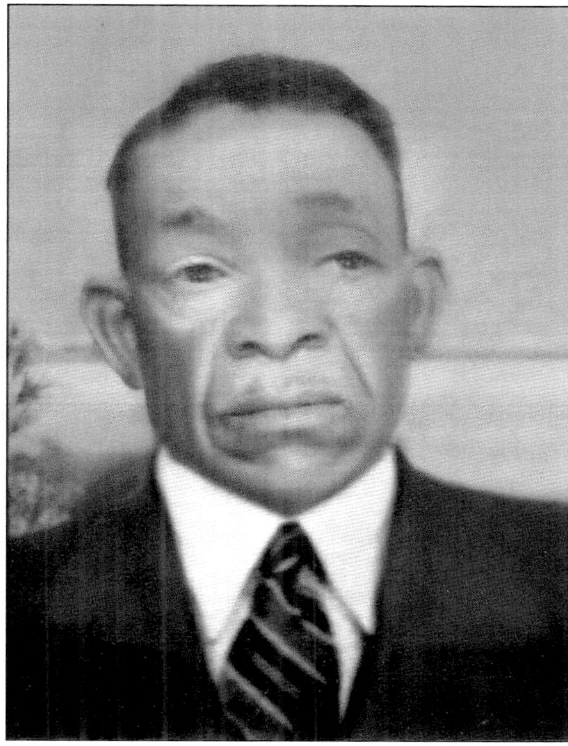

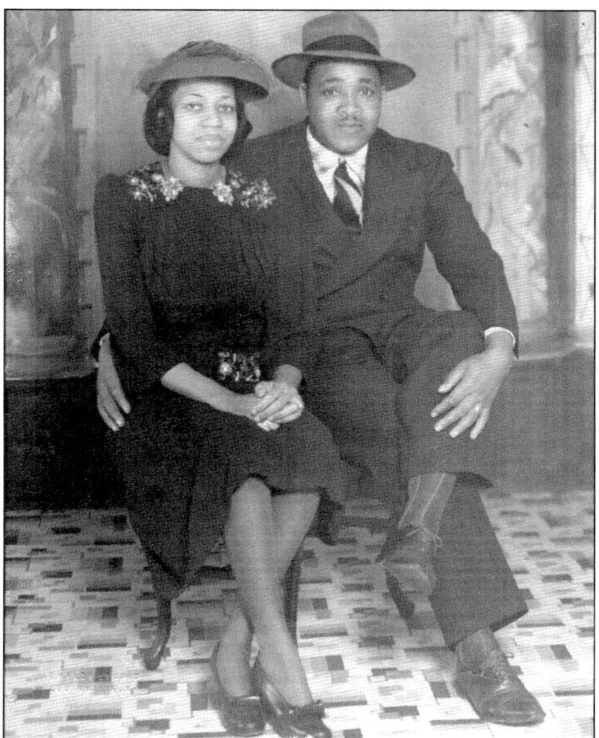

This picture of Carl Nelson and Viola Drake Fulton was taken in the 1940s. They were members of First Baptist Church Jeffersontown. He was also a member of Mt. Calvary Lodge #126 F&AM. She was a member of Primrose Chapter #93 OES. They were the parents of Jewelene, Carl William, Daniel, Sharon, Roderick, and Linda Fulton. (Photo courtesy of Dr. Jewelene Fulton Richards, Ed.D.)

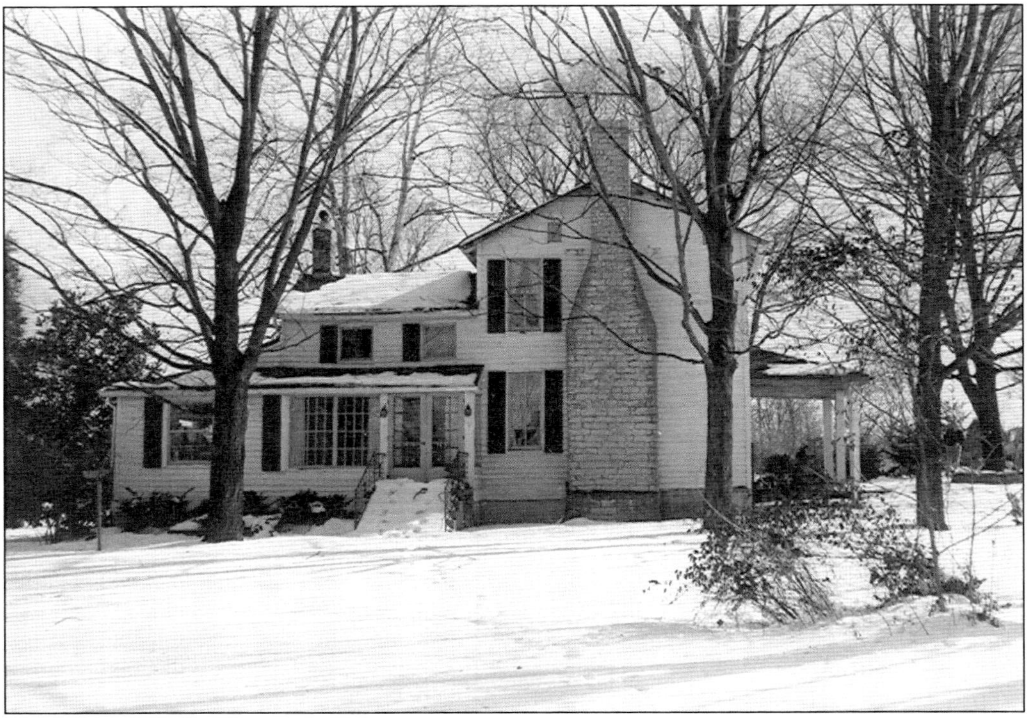

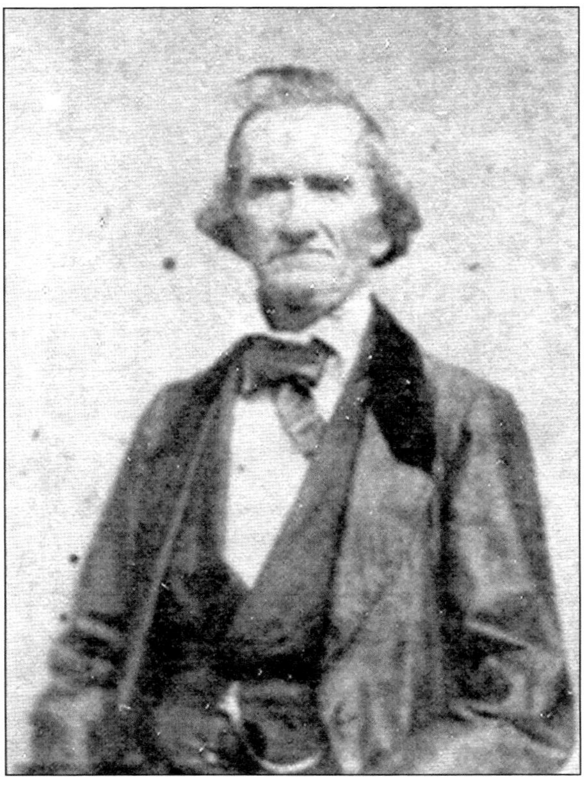

The Goose-Offut House, located on Blankenbaker Road, was built in the mid-19th century, probably by Leonard Goose. The Goose Farm was owned by members of the Goose family until 1918. The fine stone chimney is original to the house. (Photo courtesy of Louisville Metro Historic Landmarks Commission.)

William Goose Jr., the son of William Sr. and Catherine Yenowine Goose, came to Jeffersontown about 1790 and purchased several lots in town, as well as on Rehl Road and Blankenbaker Lane. He married Frances Winand Woolet in 1827 and purchased much of her family's land upon the death of her father. William also helped the Lutheran congregation construct its 1833 church on Watterson Trail. (Photo courtesy of Sallie Cheatham Smith.)

Elizabeth Hummel Goose was the daughter of Jacob Hummel Jr. and Catherine Risinger Hummel. She married Preston Goose in 1857. Their son, Edwin Everett Goose, was one of the organizers of the Jefferson County Bank as well as postmaster at Tucker Station for many years. (Photo courtesy of Sallie Cheatham Smith.)

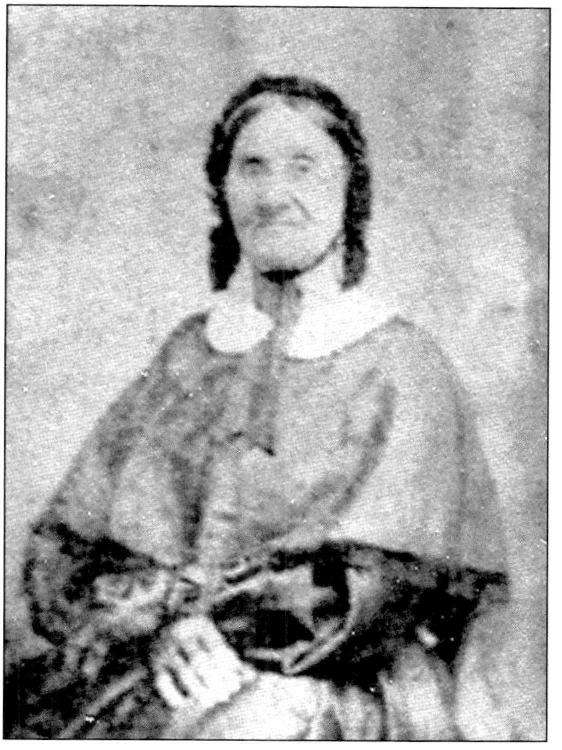

This 1908 photo shows the farmhouse built on Rehl Road by Preston Goose, c. 1857, when he married Elizabeth Hummel. Pictured here, from left to right, are Herbert Goose, Sallie Etta Goose holding baby Irene, and three Swan family daughters, who acted as nurses to Irene. (Photo courtesy of Sallie Cheatham Smith.)

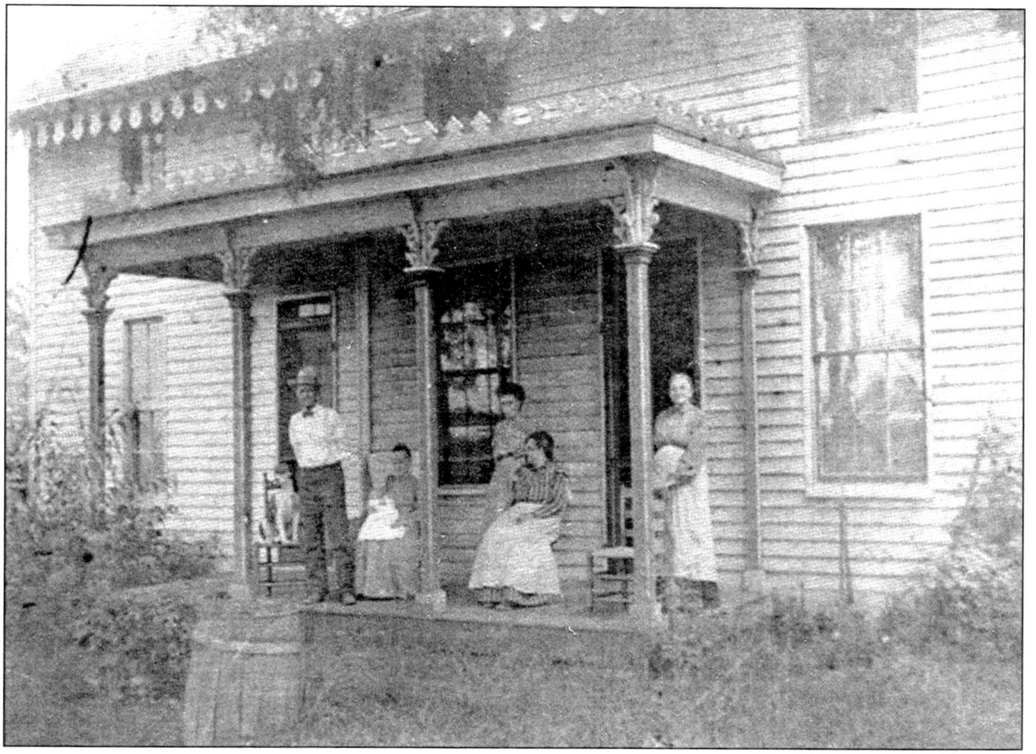

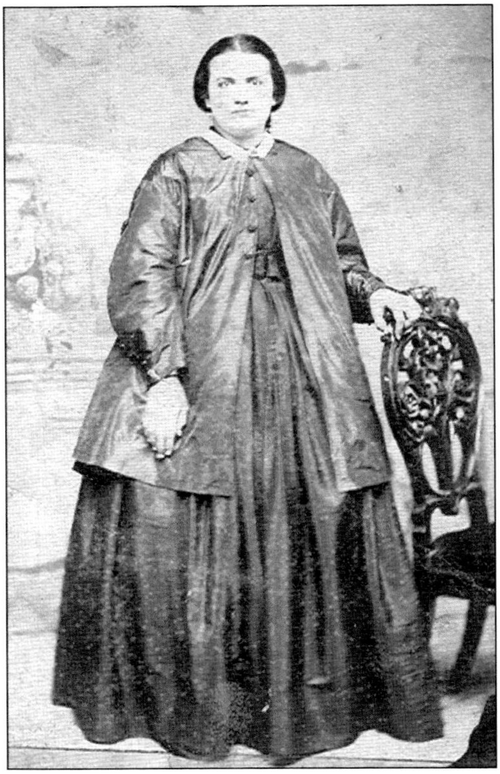

Louise Bence Weller Goose, seen here in a *c.* 1860s photo, was married to John Y. Goose. They were the parents of Herbert Leonard and Myrtle Goose. (Photo courtesy of Sallie Cheatham Smith.)

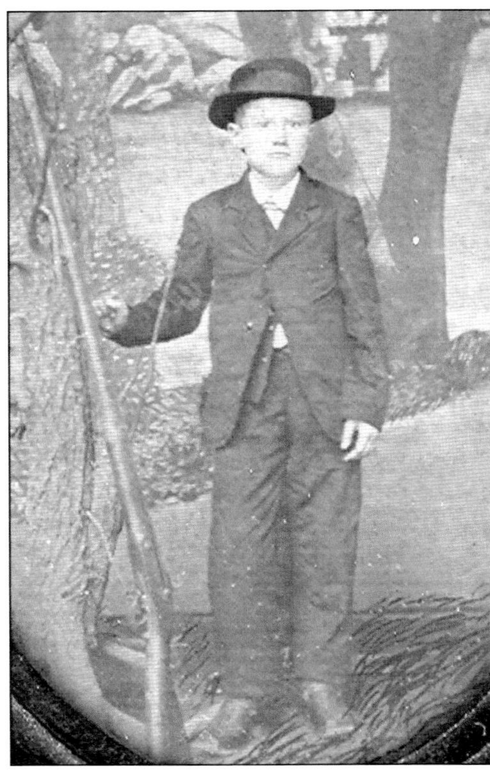

Herbert Leonard Goose as a young man is seen standing next to his rifle, made by a Weller gunsmith. The Wellers were renowned for their finely crafted guns. Herbert Leonard was the son of John Y. and Louise Weller Goose. (Photo courtesy of Sallie Cheatham Smith.)

Myrtle Goose was the daughter of Louise and John Y. Goose. Seen here is one of her children, wearing a lovely hand-made dress with cascades of delicately crocheted lace. Such finely made lace was common to see in the early days, but it was also greatly treasured. The lace on this particular gown has been passed down through many generations of the Goose family. (Photo courtesy of Sallie Cheatham Smith.)

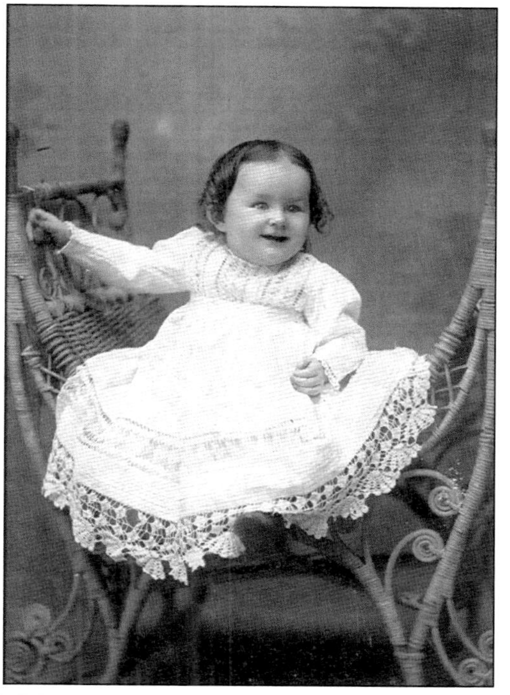

Roscoe Goose (1891–1971), a native of Jeffersontown, rode Donerail to victory in the 1913 Kentucky Derby. Goose tutored many top riders and was the first of 10 men elected to the Kentucky Athletic Hall of Fame in 1957. He was also president of the Kentucky Thoroughbred Breeders Association for three years and a member of the Jockey Club. (Photo courtesy of Churchill Downs, Inc., and Kinetic Corporation.)

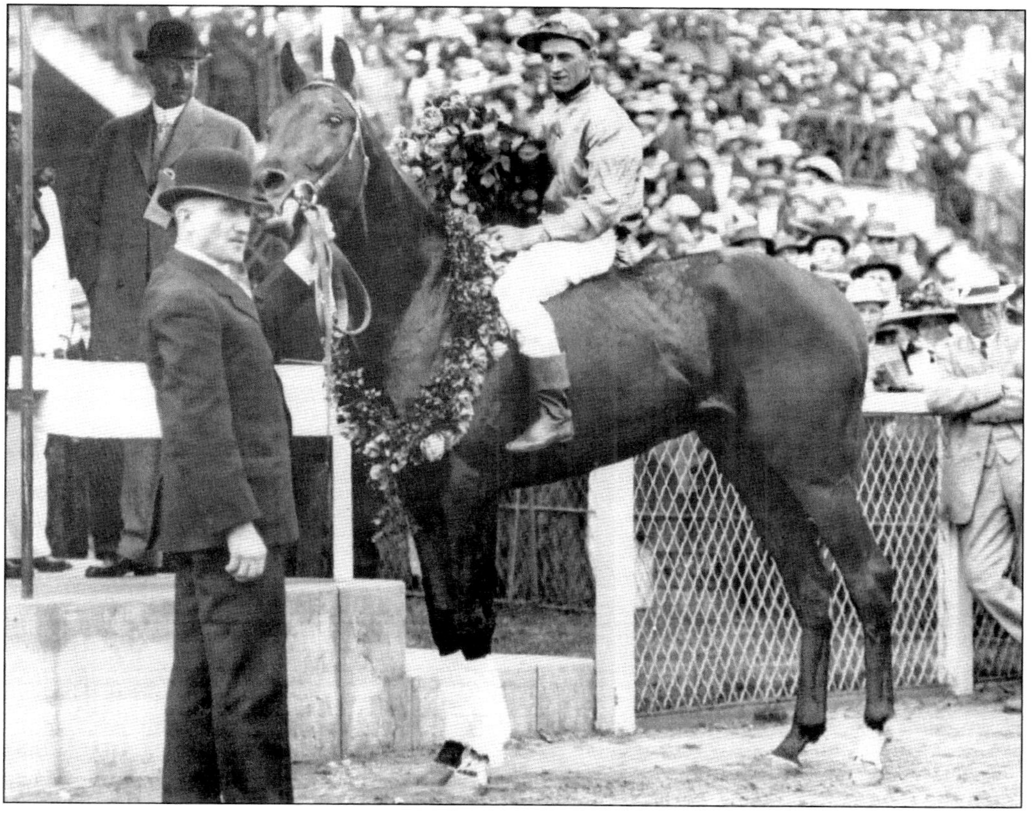

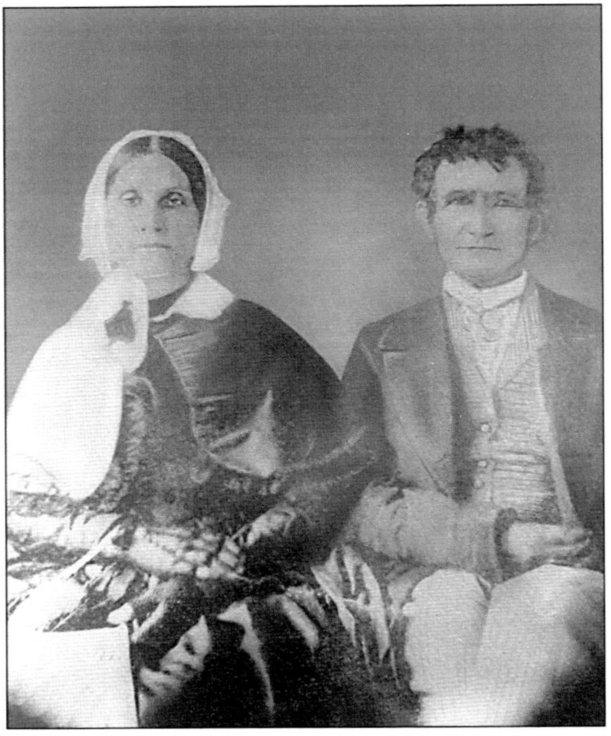

This photo shows George and Elizabeth Jones Hikes, who built the house known as Midlane Farm on Hikes Lane. Although today Hikes Lane is considered outside of the Jeffersontown city limits, when the house was built, the borders of Jeffersontown were much less clear and extended further into areas such as St. Matthews and Fern Creek. (Photo courtesy of Marjorie Hunsinger Weeks Babson.)

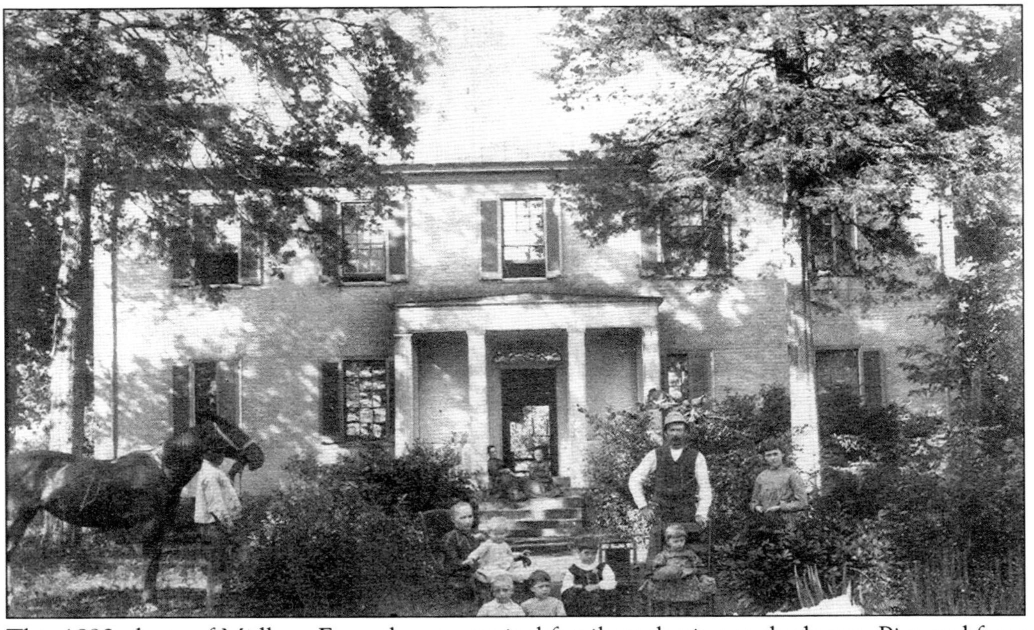

This 1892 photo of Midlane Farm shows a typical family gathering at the home. Pictured from left to right are as follows: (standing) Nat ? standing by Daisy the horse, Lena Hunsinger holding her son Charles, Anna Rose Armstrong, Maud Armstrong, Mary Ellen Hunsinger, John Hikes, and Eugenia Carsons. Sitting on the porch are sisters Mrs. E.J. Hikes and Mrs. J.A. Armstrong. (Photo courtesy of Marjorie Hunsinger Weeks Babson.)

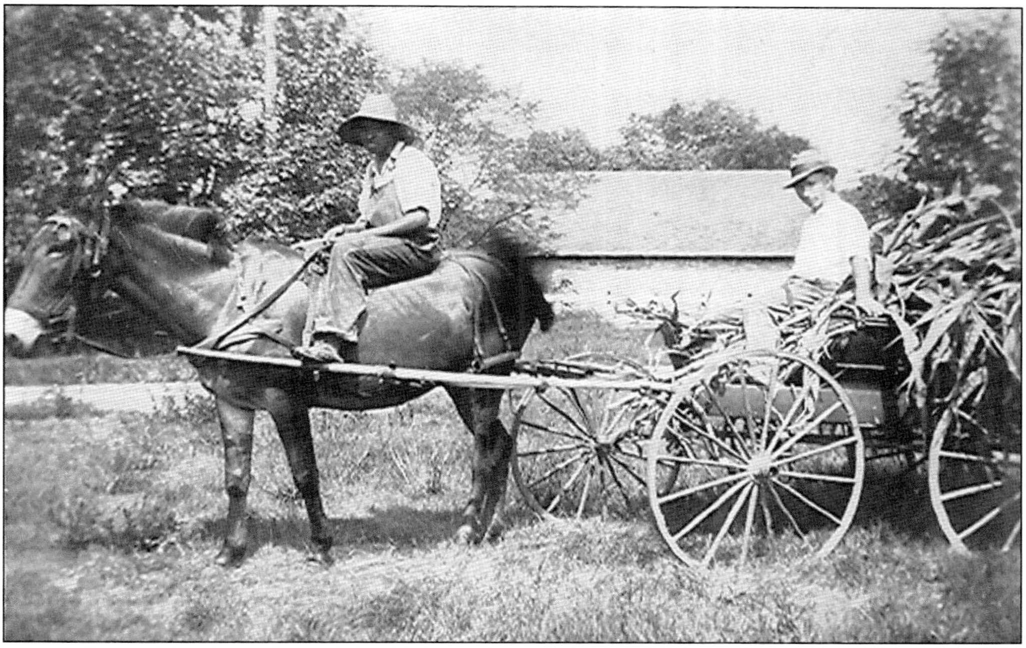

Midlane Farm was on very fertile soil, and many diverse crops were grown and harvested. This photo shows Bill Ender (at left), a tenant who worked the farm with Claude Hunsinger (at right). (Photo courtesy of Marjorie Hunsinger Weeks Babson.)

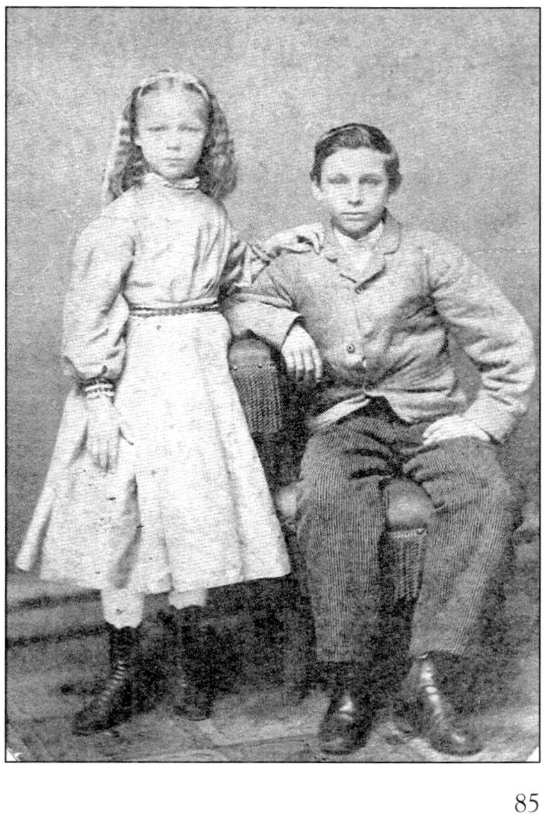

Lena Crawford Hikes (born 1861) and her brother William were the children of Edward Jones Hikes and Paulina Kellar. Edward was the son of George Hikes II, who built Midlane Farm. Lena married Charles Edward Hunsinger in 1881, and they were the parents of Claude Hunsinger (born 1898). (Photo courtesy of Marjorie Hunsinger Weeks Babson.)

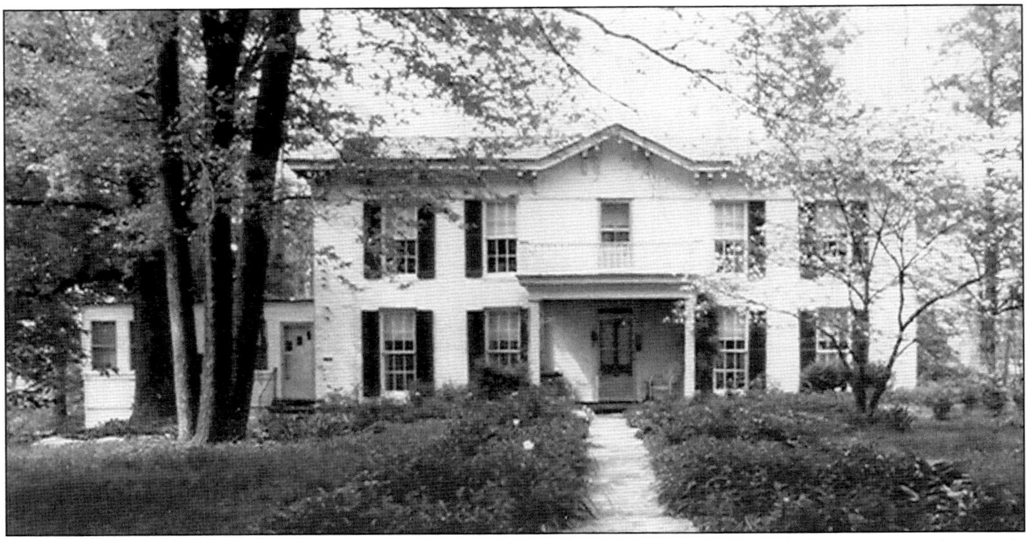

The Joseph Hite house was probably built in the first quarter of the 19th century, although Joseph himself was listed on tax records as early as 1789. In 1837, John Hite sold the farm to William Conrad, who owned a pottery in Jeffersontown. In 1910, Judge Samuel B. Kirby Jr. bought the house, and the adjacent road (Kirby Lane) was named for him. (Photo courtesy of Louisville Metro Historic Landmarks Commission.)

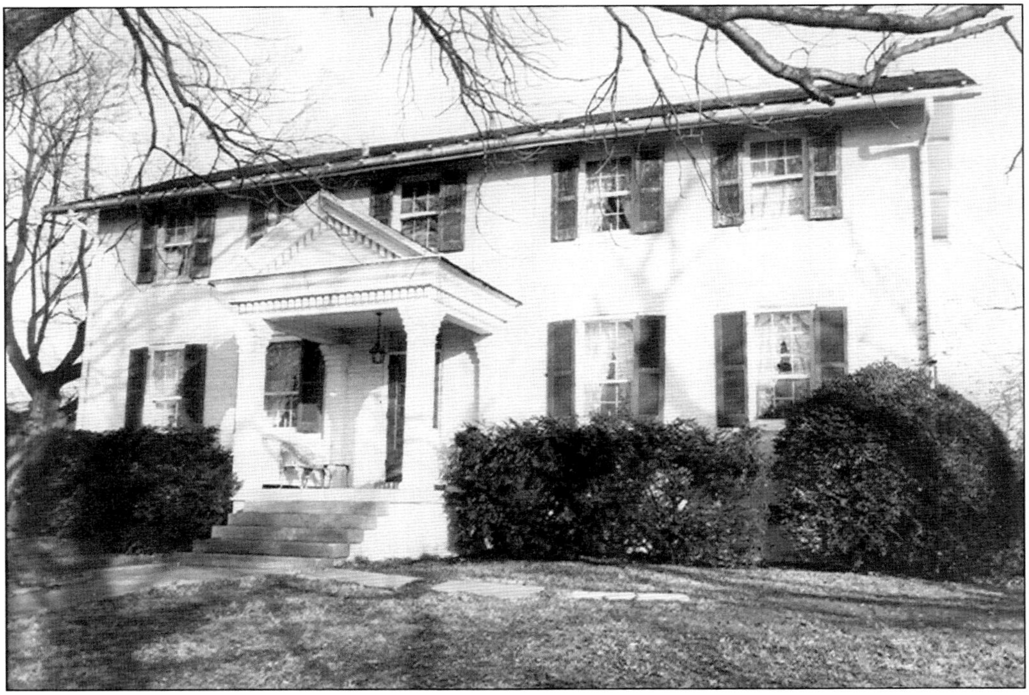

The oldest portion of the Andrew Hoke house on Llandovery Drive was built about 1828 on land owned by Andrew's father, Jacob Hoke. Andrew was a prosperous farmer and one of the founders and directors of the Louisville & Taylorsville Turnpike Company. (Photo courtesy of Louisville Metro Historic Landmarks Commission.)

Catherine Hoffhins of Lancaster County, Pennsylvania, married Adam Hoke in 1786, before settling in Jeffersontown. (Photo courtesy of Marjorie Hunsinger Weeks Babson.)

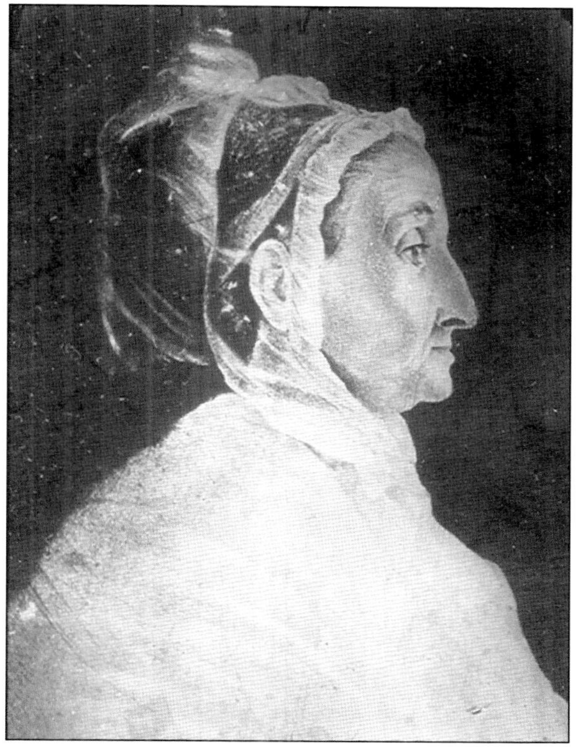

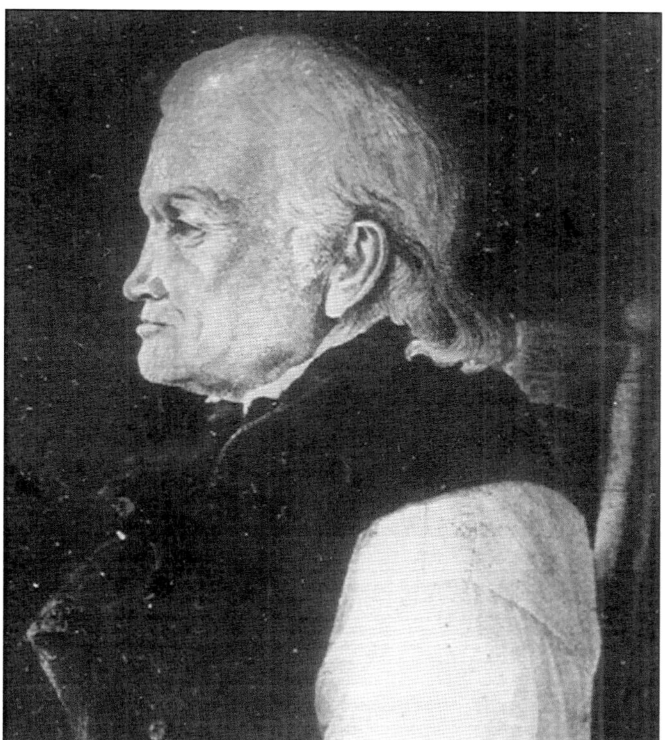

Adam Hoke moved with his parents and family to Jeffersontown in 1795. Adam bought land in the Six Mile Lane area and was very involved in city activities. He was a tobacco merchant, town trustee, and a trustee of the German Presbyterian Church. (Photo courtesy of Marjorie Hunsinger Weeks Babson.)

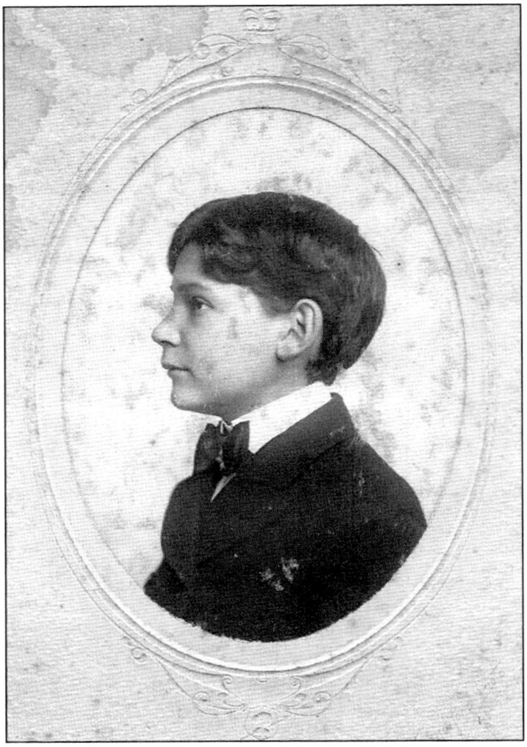

Fred Hunsinger Hoke was born on October 17, 1888, and married Agnes Blackman on March 16, 1916. Fred was the son of Charles W. and Mollie Hunsinger Hoke. (Photo courtesy of Marjorie Hunsinger Weeks Babson.)

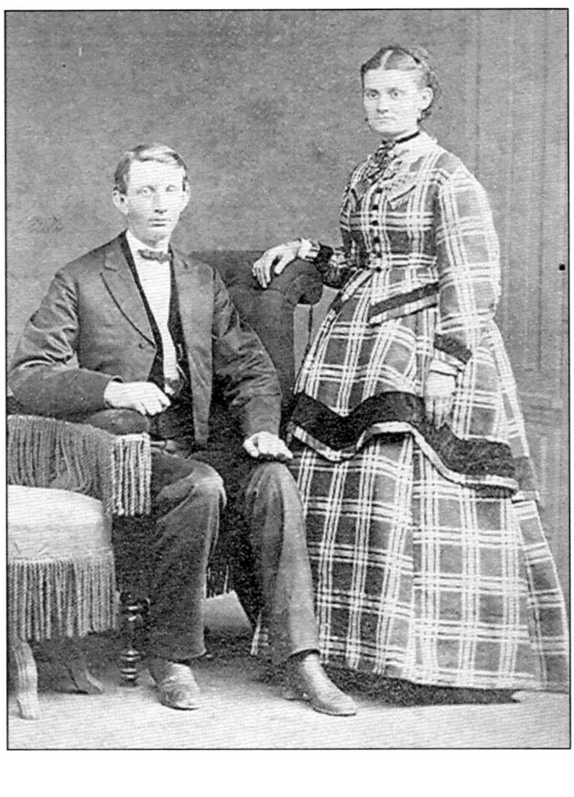

This photo is of William Henry Hummel and Mary Frances (Mollie) Weller, who were married October 27, 1870. William was one of six children born to Jacob Hummel and Catherine Risinger. (Photo courtesy of Sallie Cheatham Smith.)

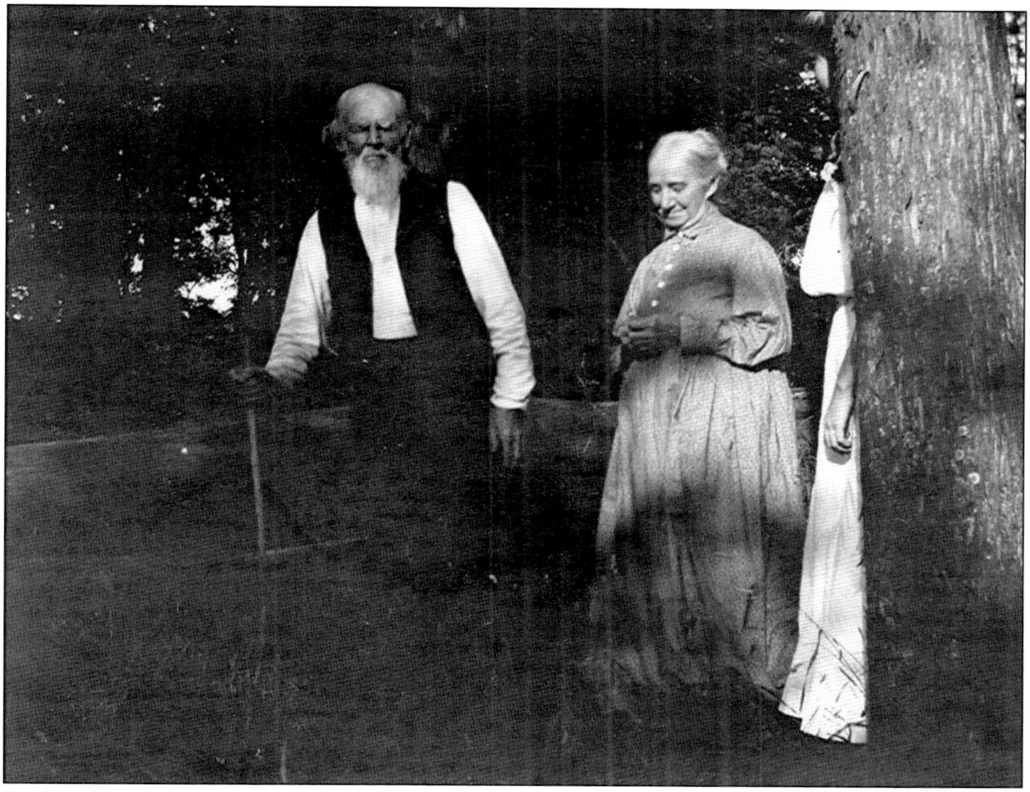

Frederick Hunsinger (1822–1904) married Catherine Elizabeth Winand (1830–1913) on March 19, 1846. This photo was taken c. 1904 at their home on Taylorsville Road at Lowe Road. They had six children: Mary Ellen (Molly), Harriet (Hal), William Frederick (Bud), Houston J., Charles Edward, and Albert S. Hunsinger. (Photo courtesy of Marjorie Hunsinger Weeks Babson.)

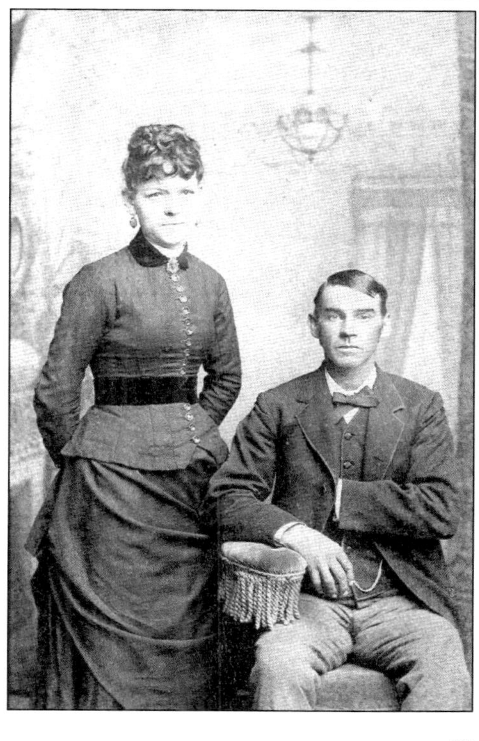

William Frederick (Bud) and Millie Norman Hunsinger were the owners of Nunnlea from the early 1900s until William passed away in 1932. (Photo courtesy of Marjorie Hunsinger Weeks Babson.)

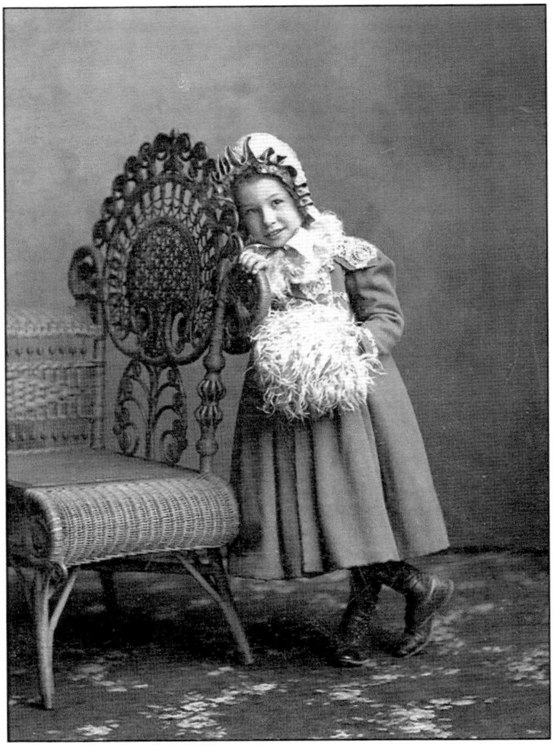

This charming photograph is of Catherine Hunsinger, who later married James Ash. (Photo courtesy of Marjorie Hunsinger Weeks Babson.)

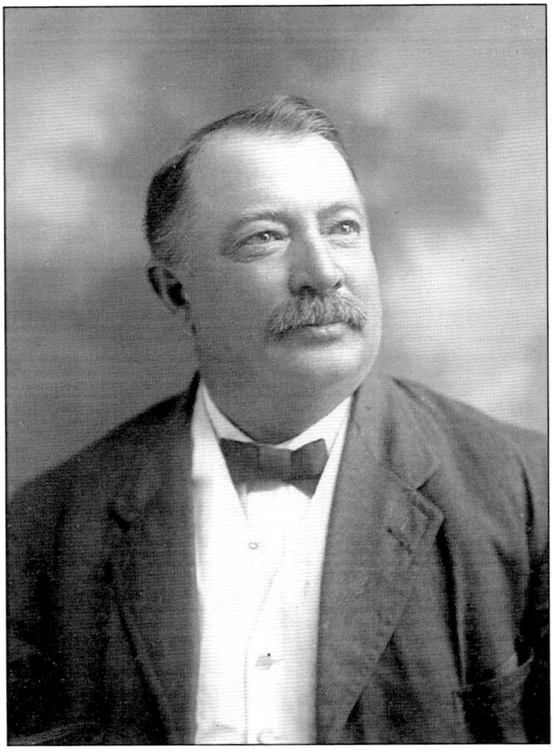

Charles Edward Hunsinger was the son of Charles Fredrick and Catherine Winand Hunsinger. He married Paulina (Lena) Crawford Hikes on December 21, 1881, and they had six children, three of whom died at an early age. Charles lived at Hikes Lane and was a prosperous farmer. (Photo courtesy of Marjorie Hunsinger Weeks Babson.)

Julia Reubelt Hunsinger (born April 24, 1890) was the daughter of Charles Edward and Lena Hikes Hunsinger. Julia Hunsinger was named for Julia Reubelt, the daughter of Jefferson County Bank president H.N. Reubelt. Julia Reubelt was the 1904 founder of the Current Events Club in Jeffersontown. (Photo courtesy of Marjorie Hunsinger Weeks Babson.)

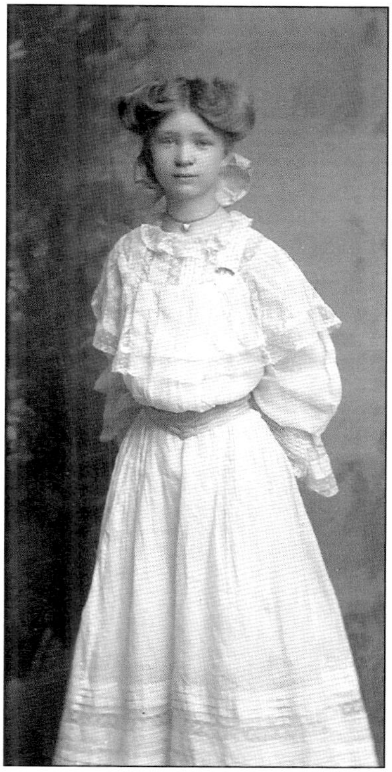

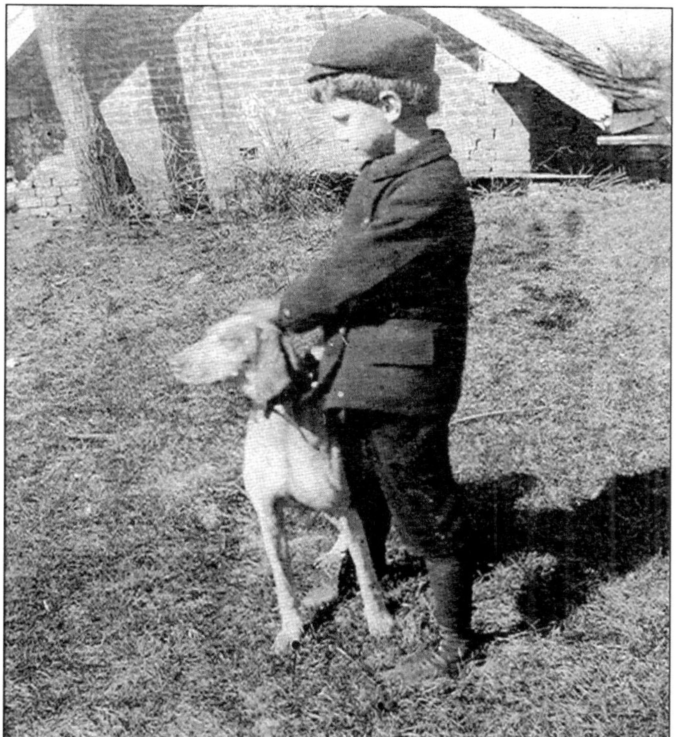

Claude Hobson Hunsinger was the son of Charles Edward and Lena Hikes Hunsinger. Claude was born October 29, 1898. He is seen here in front of a springhouse in the early 1900s. (Photo courtesy of Marjorie Hunsinger Weeks Babson.)

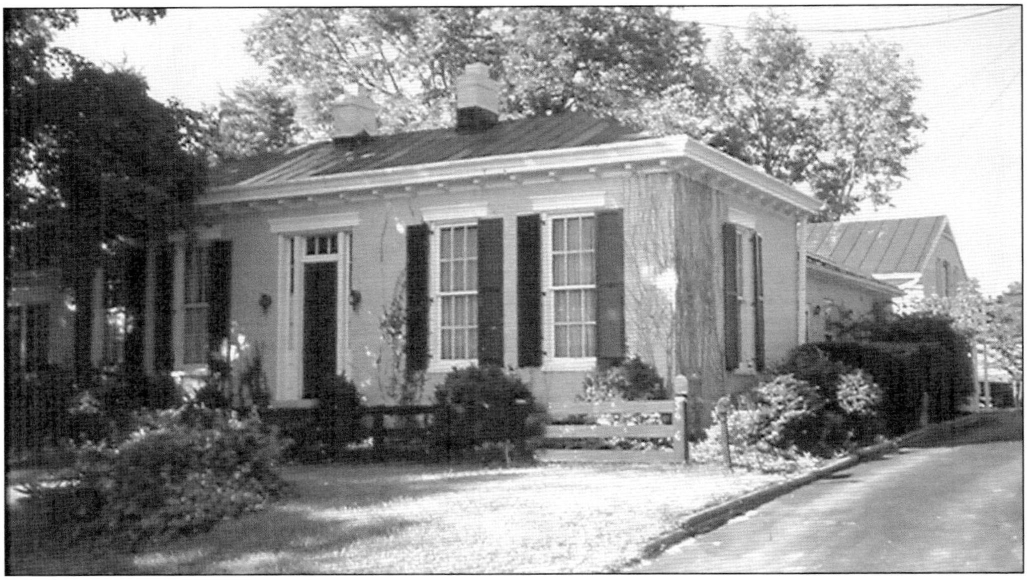

The Leatherman House on College Drive was built *c.* 1860. George W. Leatherman bought the house after its first owner, David L. Wingard, moved to Kansas in 1868. Mr. Leatherman was a town trustee and postmaster. Although he only remained in the house until 1896, it became known by his name. (Photo courtesy of Jane Smith.)

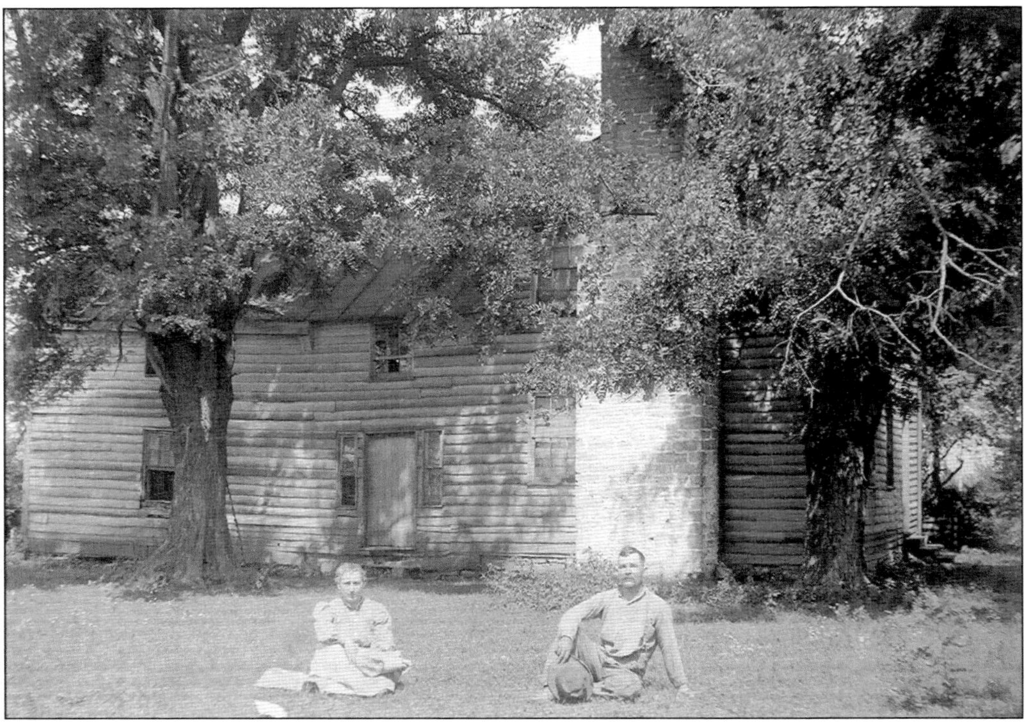

Abraham Lincoln "Linc" Miller and Mary Burkhart Miller are seen here in front of their home in the Billtown Road area. The house was built by Linc's great-grandfather, Windle Kelly Miller, in the early 1800s. (Photo courtesy of Carole Chambers Davis.)

This 1921 photograph shows Galt Miller, seated in front, with (left to right) Lillian Kennedy, Carl Miller, and Isabel Miller. A later generation of the Miller family would own the Sweet Shop that was once located on Taylorsville Road. (Photo courtesy of Carole Chambers Davis.)

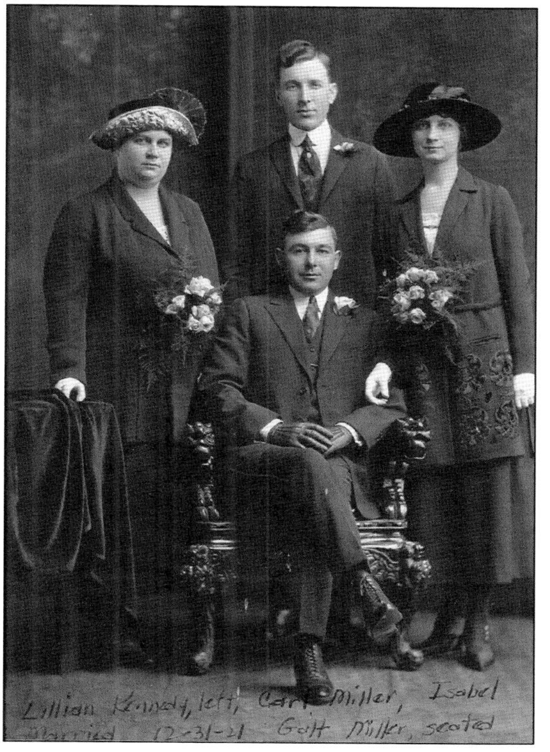

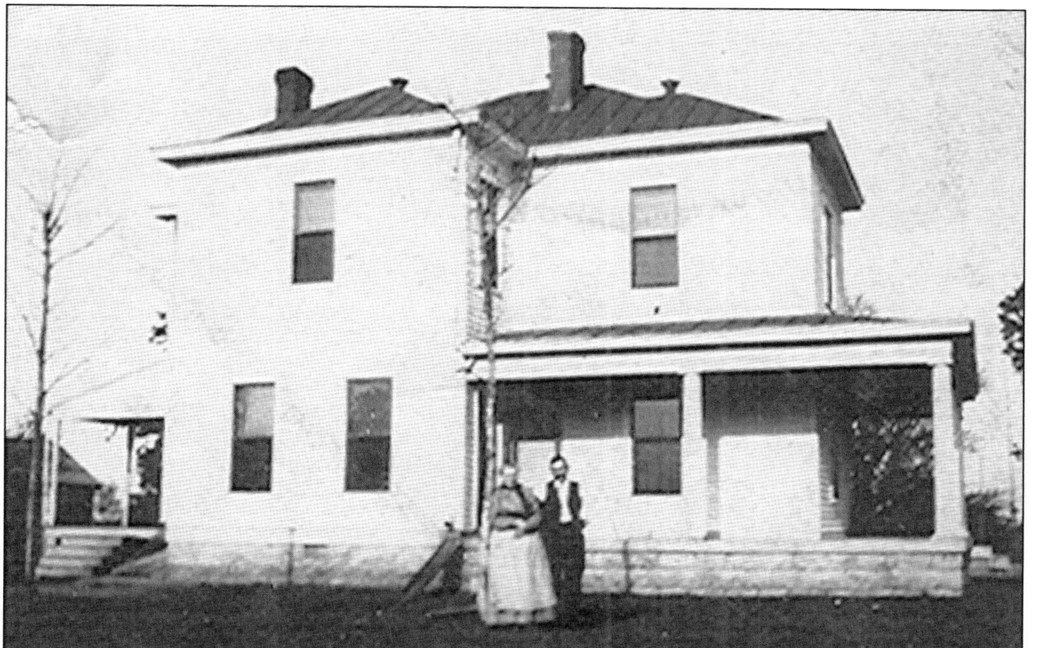

This picture shows a more complete view of the house constructed on Billtown Road by Windle K. Miller. Windle Miller was born April 16, 1799. His great-grandson, "Linc"—seen again with Mary Burkhart Miller—was born June 8, 1862. (Photo courtesy of Carole Chambers Davis.)

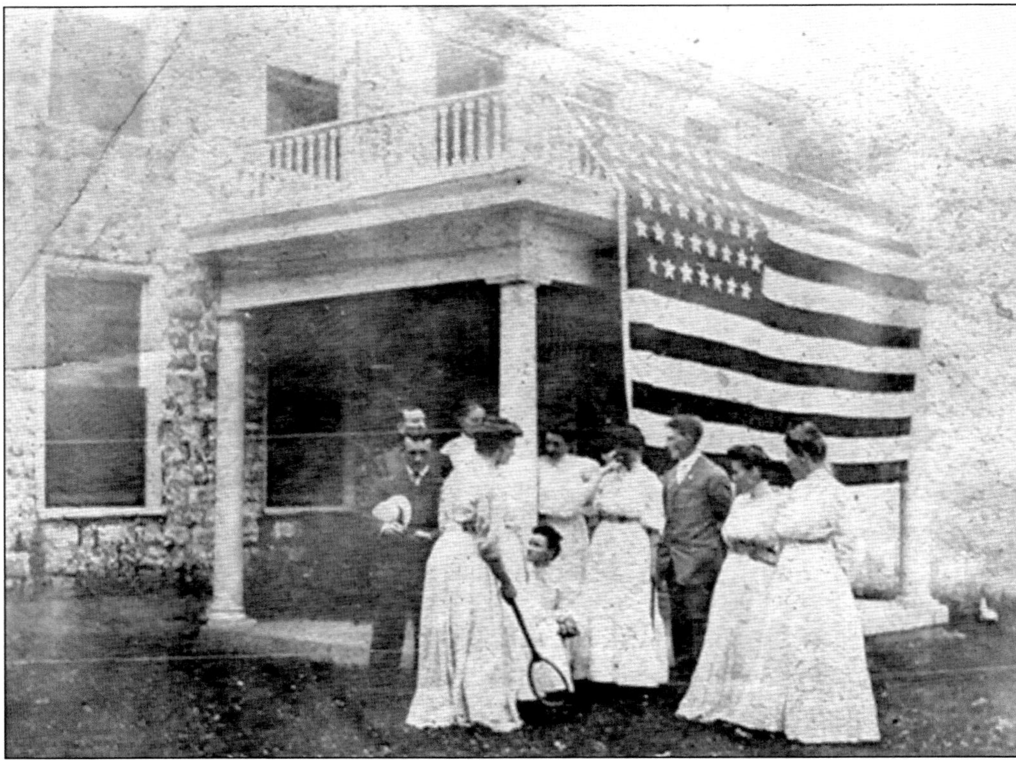

This early 1900s photo shows a gathering at the Mittler home. The Mittlers bought the property in 1905 from the Lutheran Church, and their home became known as "College Heights," since it had previously housed the Jefferson Academy. The property was sold back to the Lutheran Churches of Louisville and Jefferson County in 1925, and it reopened as a home for the elderly in 1927. (Photo courtesy of Jack Mittler.)

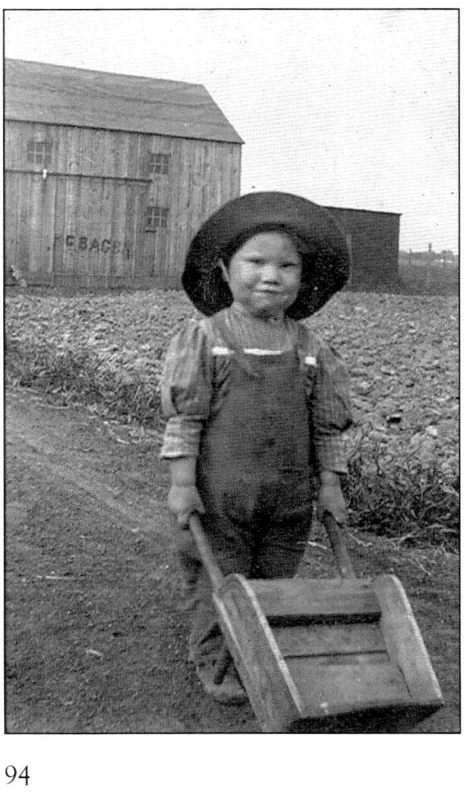

This photo of an unknown Mittler child was taken at the Mittler homestead in the early 1900s. (Photo courtesy of Jack Mittler.)

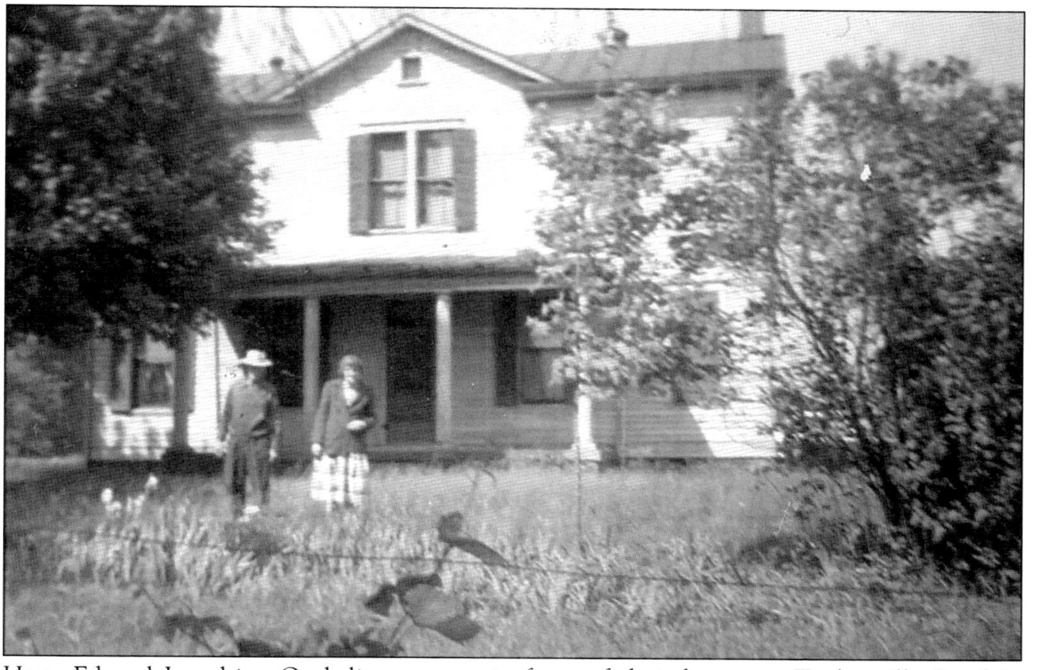

Here, Ed and Josephine Oechslin are seen in front of their home on Taylorsville Road in May 1959. Shortly after that, the property was bought by Jack Durrett, who encouraged the urbanization of Jeffersontown by building the J-Town Shopping Center where the house once stood and creating the subdivision behind it. (Photo courtesy of Tillie Meffert, Mary Boring, and Fred Oechslin.)

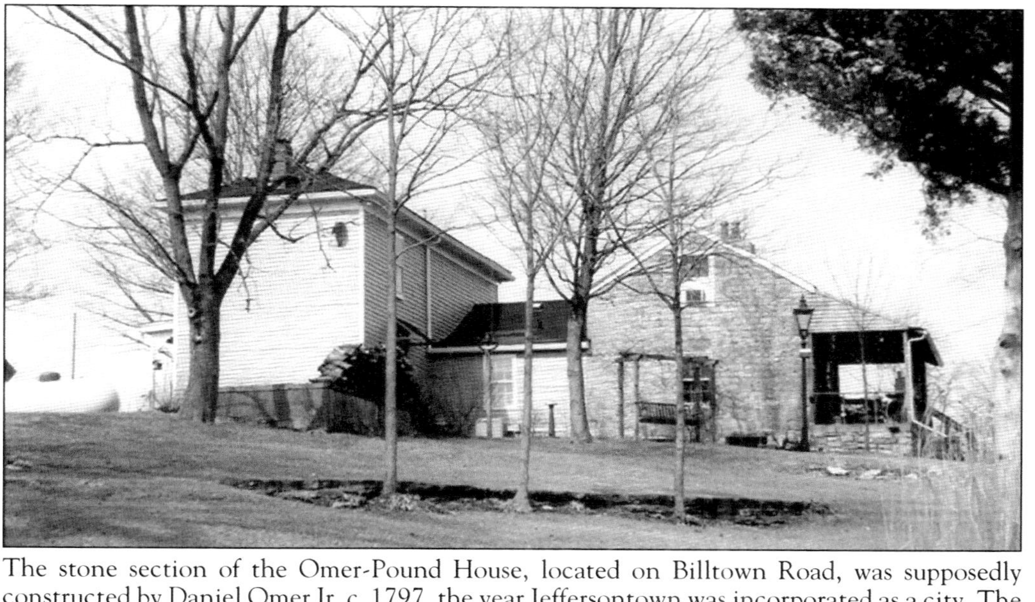

The stone section of the Omer-Pound House, located on Billtown Road, was supposedly constructed by Daniel Omer Jr. *c.* 1797, the year Jeffersontown was incorporated as a city. The Omers (originally spelled Ammer) were Pennsylvanians of German descent who migrated here via the Ohio River by flatboat. (Photo courtesy of Louisville Metro Historic Landmarks Commission.)

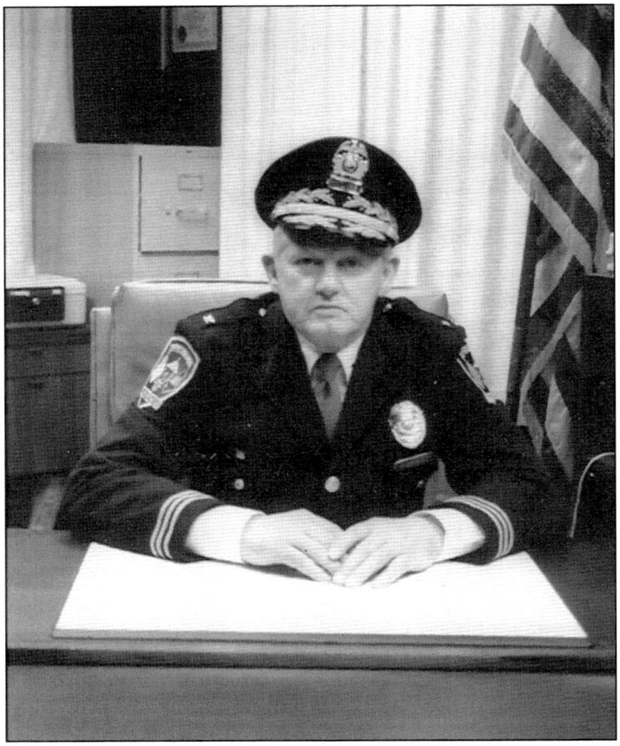

Chief Fred Roemele completed 50 years in law enforcement on October 28, 2004. He began his service with the Jefferson County Police Department in 1954 and worked his way up to assistant chief of police. He started the Narcotic Bureau in Jefferson County in 1961 and the first drug abuse program in the Jefferson County Public School System. He became chief of the Jeffersontown Police Department in January 1982. (Photo courtesy of the Jeffersontown Police Department.)

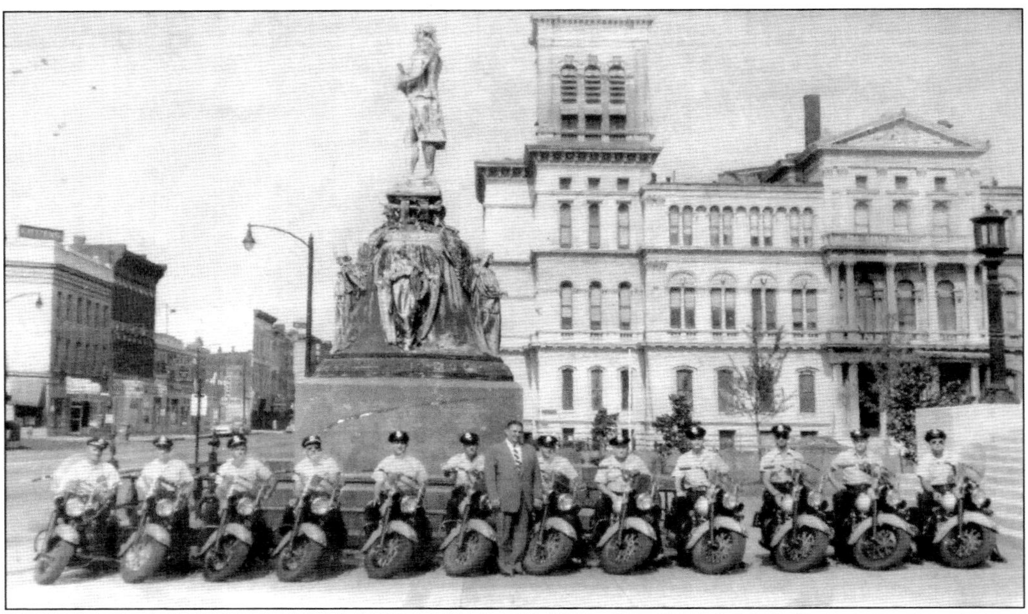

This photo of the 12 motorcycle officers from all three districts of the Jefferson County Police Department was taken in 1958 in front of the Jefferson County Courthouse. Chief Roemele is second from left. He has been the recipient of numerous awards over the years, with a commendation and letter from President Richard Nixon dated November 17, 1972, for disarming a man holding two children hostage at gunpoint. (Photo courtesy of Chief Fred L. Roemele.)

Clarence Garfield Rapson (1881–1931) and his wife, Katie Seitz Rapson, lived in the Hopewell Road area of Jeffersontown. (Photo courtesy of George Rapson.)

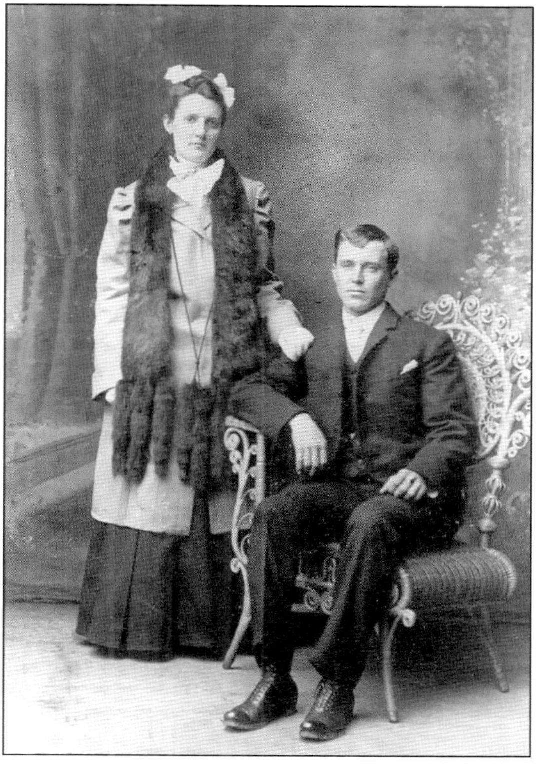

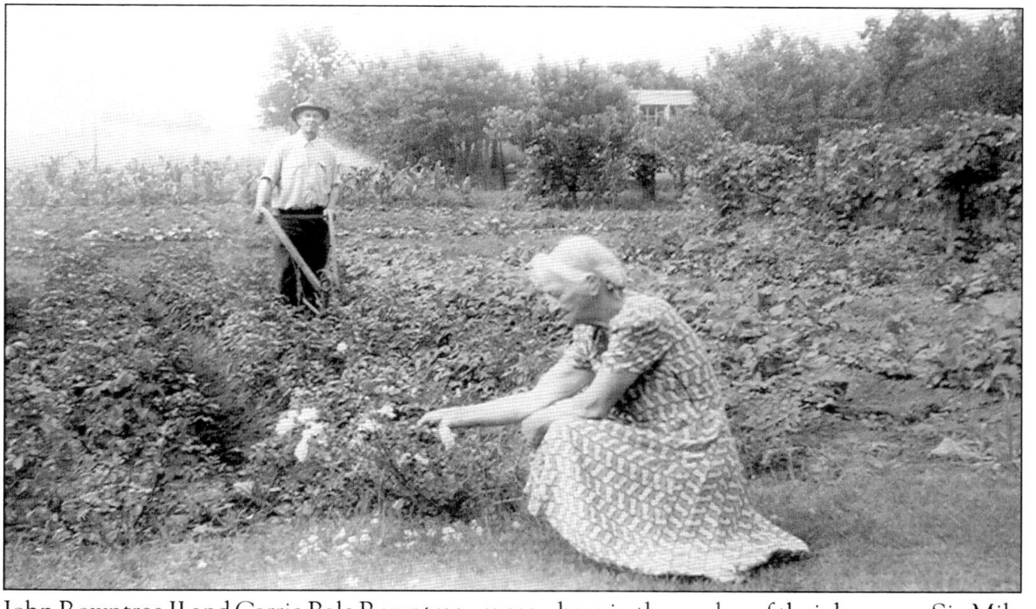

John Rowntree II and Carrie Bale Rowntree are seen here in the garden of their home on Six Mile Lane before Mr. Rowntree gave property to the left of the garden to the City of Jeffersontown to build Rowntree Road. John and Carrie's son, Gradie R. Rowntree, a nationally known physician of public health and occupational medicine, was also health director of Louisville and Jefferson Counties. (Photo courtesy of the Jeffersontown Historical Museum.)

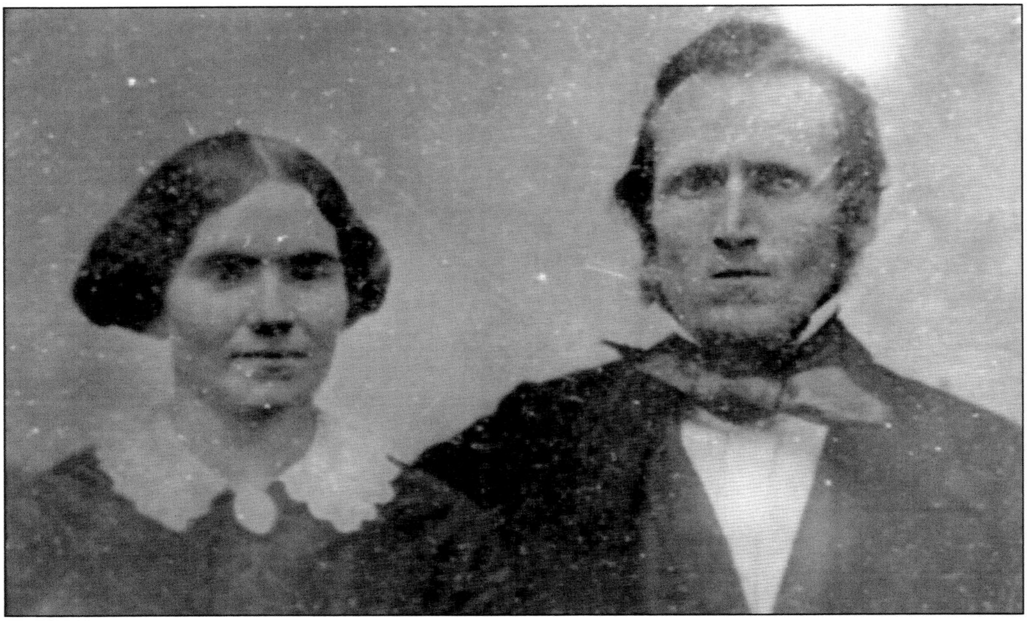

Dr. Robert Vance Sprowl (1820–1876) and Mary Ruthann Vance Sprowl (1825–1859) were the parents of Edwin Ruth Sprowl, Clarence Kennedy Sprowl, Robert Vance Sprowl Jr., and William Henry Sprowl. Dr. Sprowl was a trustee of the Presbyterian Church in Jeffersontown. (Photo courtesy of Marcia Bryan Horton.)

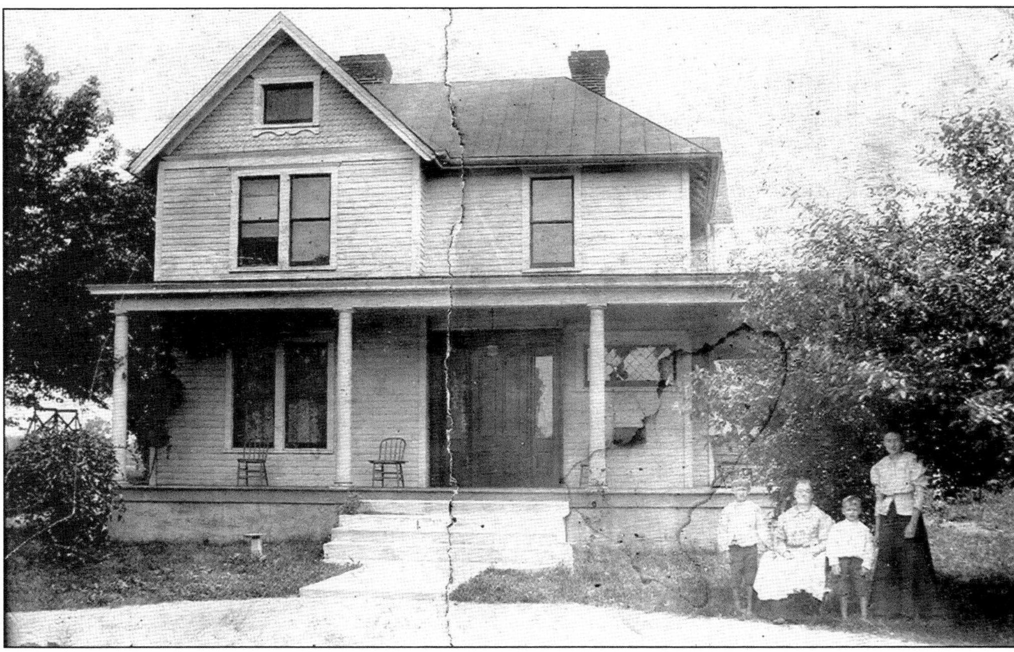

This home on Taylorsville Road was owned by E.R. Sprowl c. 1910. Pictured from left to right are Theodore Shaw Sprowl, Mrs. Eva Beach (Nin) Sprowl, Edwin Vance Sprowl, and Ethel Sprowl. Ethel was the daughter of E.R. Sprowl by his first marriage to Sadie Owings Sprowl. After Sadie's death, Nin took care of Ethel. (Photo courtesy of Marcia Bryan Horton.)

Clarence Kennedy Sprowl was a session clerk for the Jeffersontown Presbyterian Church in the 1890s. His wife, Loulie, died in 1890 after contracting brain fever (bacterial meningitis) at a young age. Loulie was entrusted with the care of her niece, Ethel, just after the death of Sadie Sprowl, and she passed the fever on to six-month-old Ethel, who miraculously recovered. (Photo courtesy of Marcia Bryan Horton.)

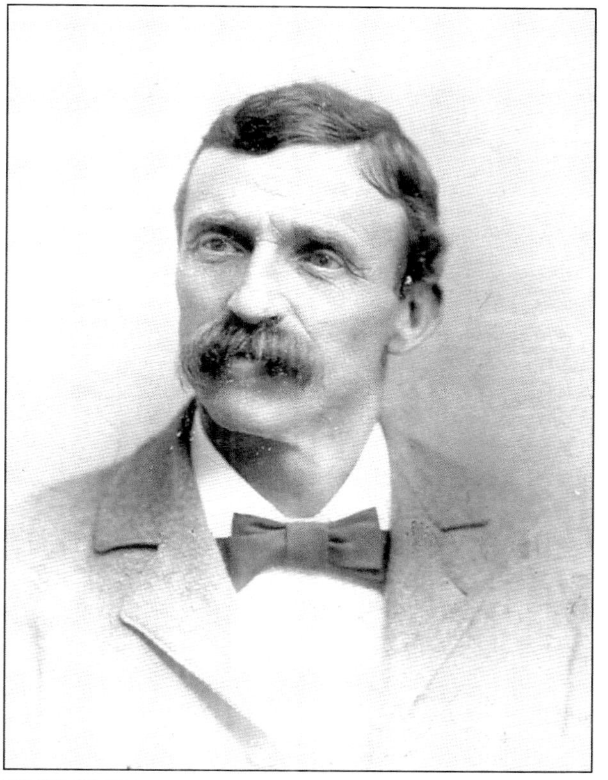

The Clarence K. Kennedy home was located on a lane off Billtown Road opposite Valley Park. Pictured from left to right in this 1895 photo are Mrs. Porter, Mrs. C.K. (Sally Beall Porter) Sprowl, Clarence Kennedy Sprowl, Winn Jean Sprowl, Edgar Sprowl, the maid (standing), and Irvin Sprowl. (Photo courtesy of Marcia Bryan Horton.)

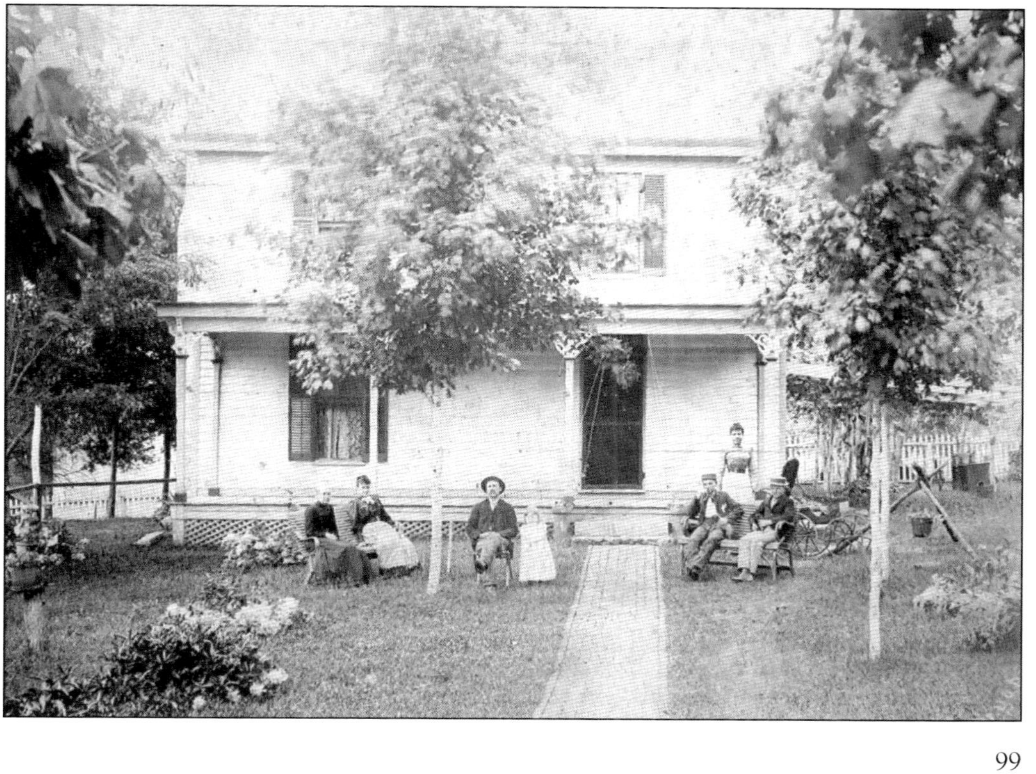

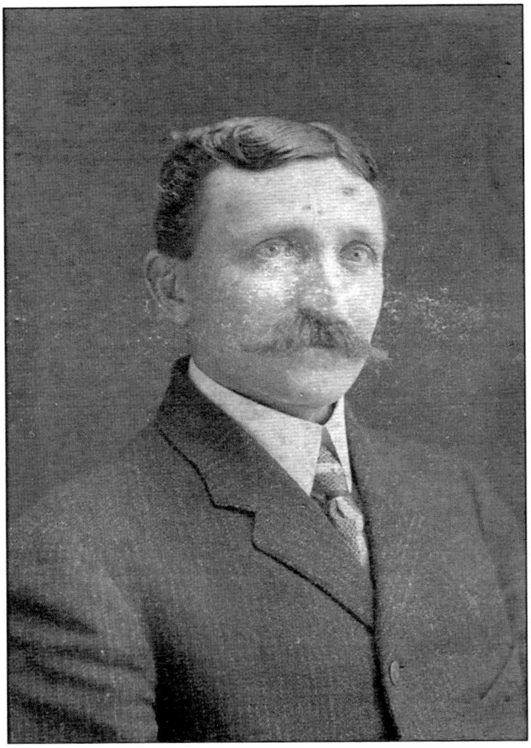

Edwin Ruth Sprowl (1859–1924) was quite an entrepreneur. Early in his career, he sold insurance door to door in Jeffersontown. His business kept him away from home much of the time, but he did get to know his beloved city of Jeffersontown inside and out. In 1908, he published a booklet promoting "Jeffersontown, KY., The Coming Suburb!" which lauded every aspect of "the most fertile acre of land in Christendom." (Photo courtesy of Marcia Bryan Horton.)

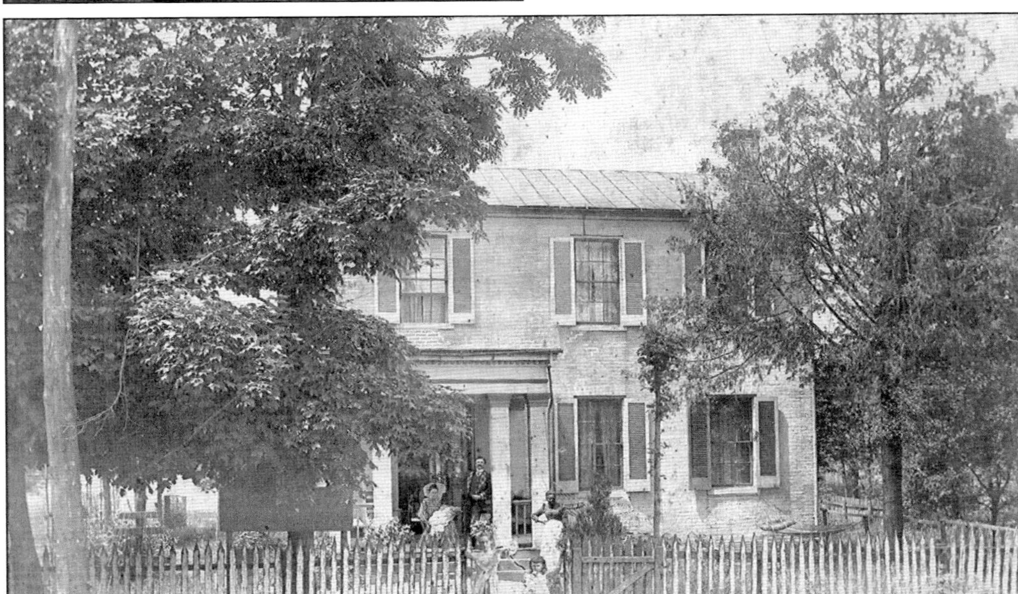

At the time this photo was taken in 1901, E.R. Sprowl was living in the Floore House on Taylorsville Road. Standing at the front gate are Ethel Sprowl and Charlotte Howell. Behind them on the porch are, from left to right, the second Mrs. E.R. Sprowl holding her baby, T.S. Sprowl, Mr. E.R. Sprowl, and the maid, Katie Dorsey. (Photo courtesy of Marcia Bryan Horton.)

Sadie Owings (1866–1889) was the first wife of Edwin Ruth Sprowl. Here, she is seen as a young girl, just after the Civil War. (Photo courtesy of Marcia Bryan Horton.)

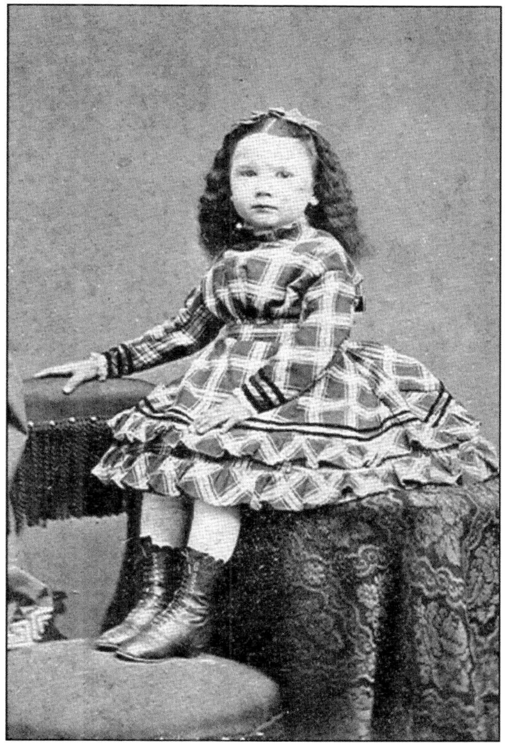

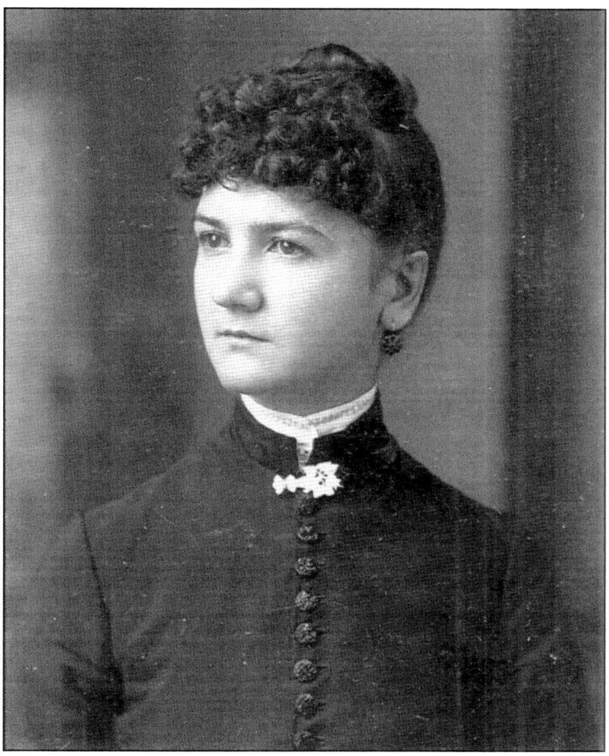

This photo shows Sadie Owings about the time of her marriage to Edwin Ruth Sprowl on February 12, 1889. Just after her marriage, Sadie began making a "log cabin" quilt from silk scraps given to her by a friend who was a seamstress. Unfortunately, Sadie was unable to finish the quilt because she died on December 17, 1889, just 17 days after giving birth to Ethel. Sadie's granddaughter, Marcia Bryan Horton, completed the quilt for her over 100 years later. (Photo courtesy of Marcia Bryan Horton.)

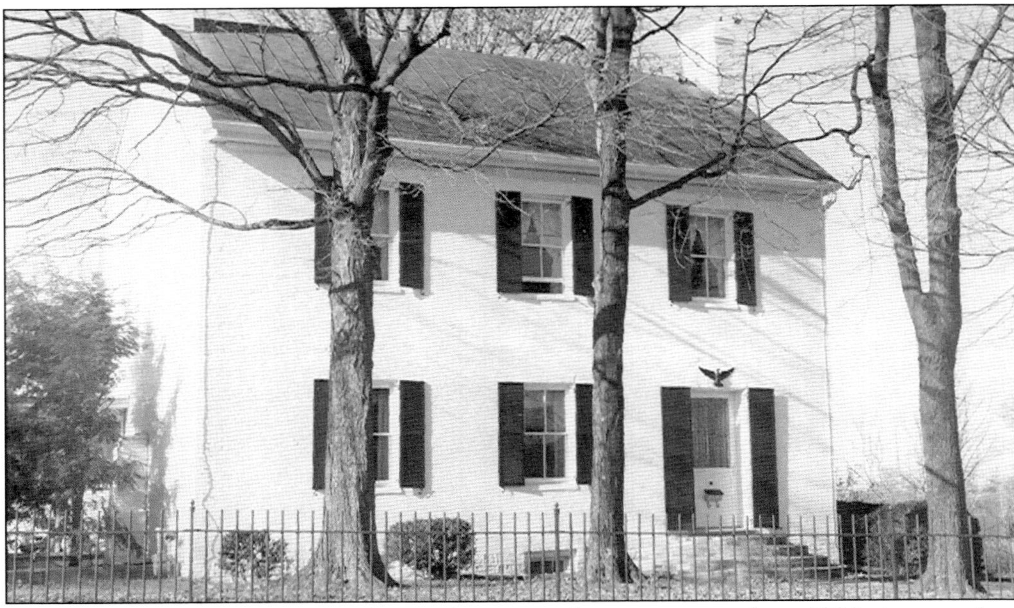

Frederick Stucky opened a tailor shop on lot #38 on the town square about 1820, then set about acquiring property once owned by his grandfather, Martin Stucky. After retiring in about 1840, he built this house on Marlin Drive. (Photo courtesy of Lt. Col. Robert C. Jobson.)

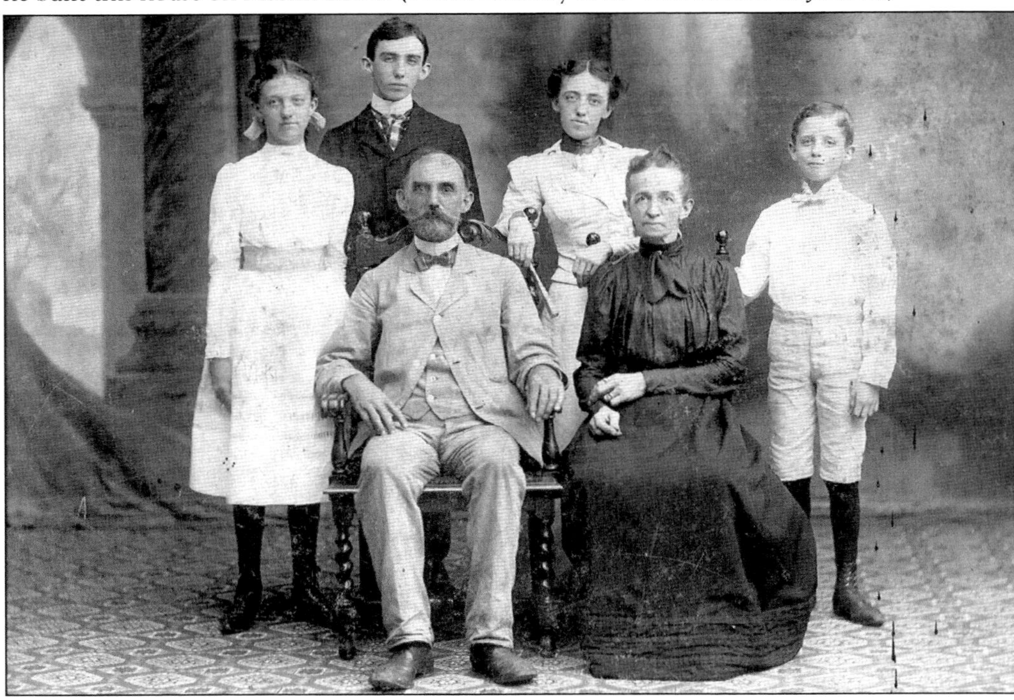

This photo of the Stucky family was taken Saturday, August 5, 1899. Seated in front are Henry Frederick Stucky and his wife, Mary Ellen Cromey Stucky. Standing behind them, from left to right, are their children, Eva Stucky, William Frederick Stucky, Mary Cromey Stucky, and Henry Frederick Stucky Jr. (Photo courtesy of Julia Smith.)

This lovely photo is of Mary Ellen Cromey Stucky (1850–1921), the wife of Henry Frederick Stucky Sr. (Photo courtesy of Julia Smith.)

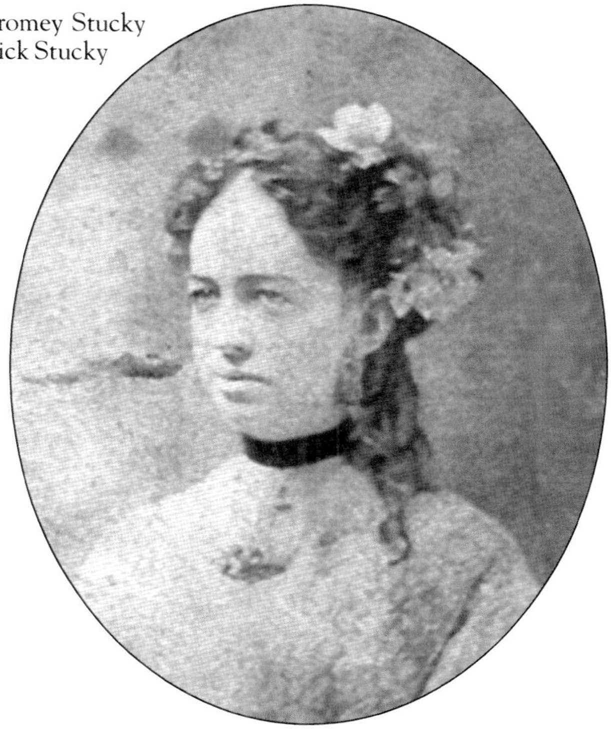

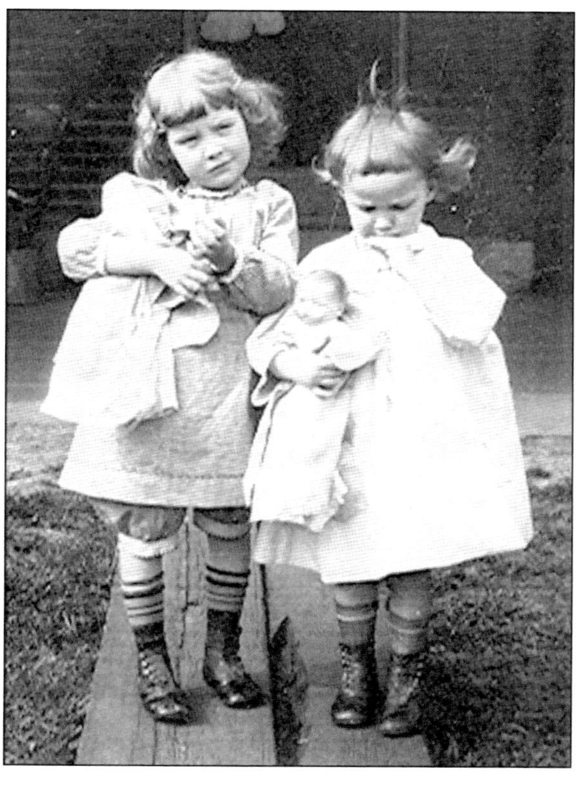

This adorable photograph of Mary Ellen and Julia Smith holding their dolls was taken c. 1925. That same year, their house on Watterson Trail burnt to the ground while they were away visiting relatives. The minister of the Lutheran Church handed Mr. Smith the keys to the Mittler home, which had just been purchased by the Lutherans to make a home for the aged, and told him to move his family in until a new home could be found. (Photo courtesy of Julia Smith.)

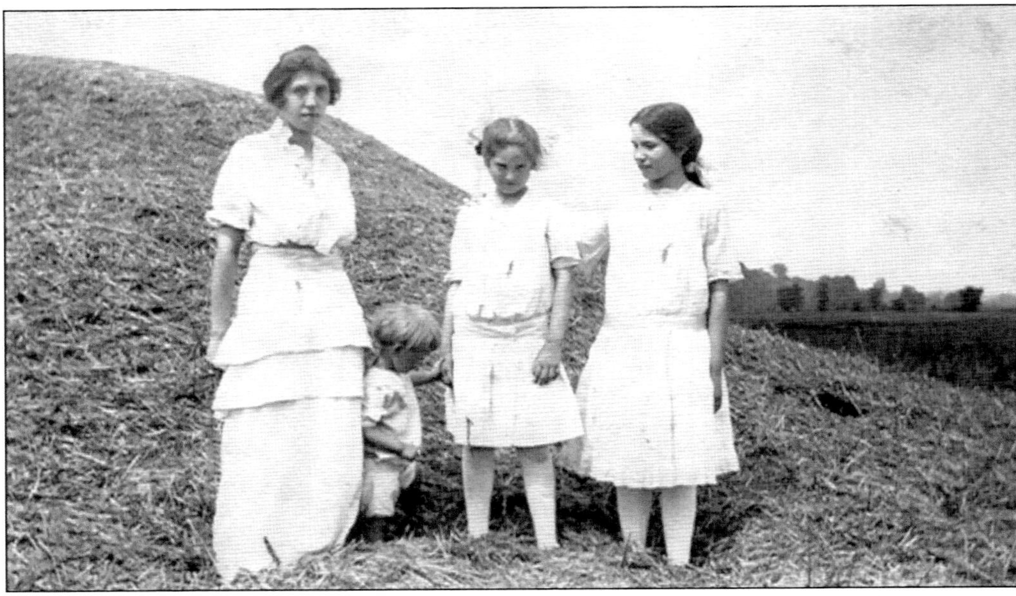

This early 1900s photograph was taken at the Sweeney Ranch on Taylorsville Road. The girl standing at the far right is Dorothy Sweeney; the others are unknown. (Photo courtesy of the Jeffersontown Historical Museum.)

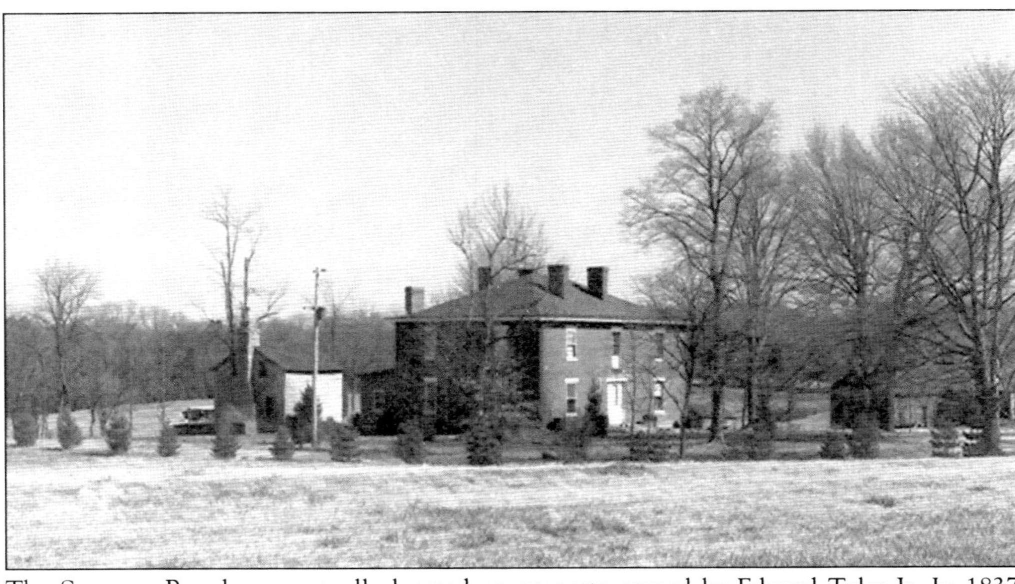

The Sweeney Ranch was actually located on property owned by Edward Tyler Jr. In 1837, he sold the land to Joseph A. Sweeney (1796–1877), who married a great-granddaughter of Edward Tyler Sr. Sweeney was a farmer and Christian church minister. He constructed a brick house in front of the old stone house on the property. (Photo courtesy of Lt. Col. Robert C. Jobson.)

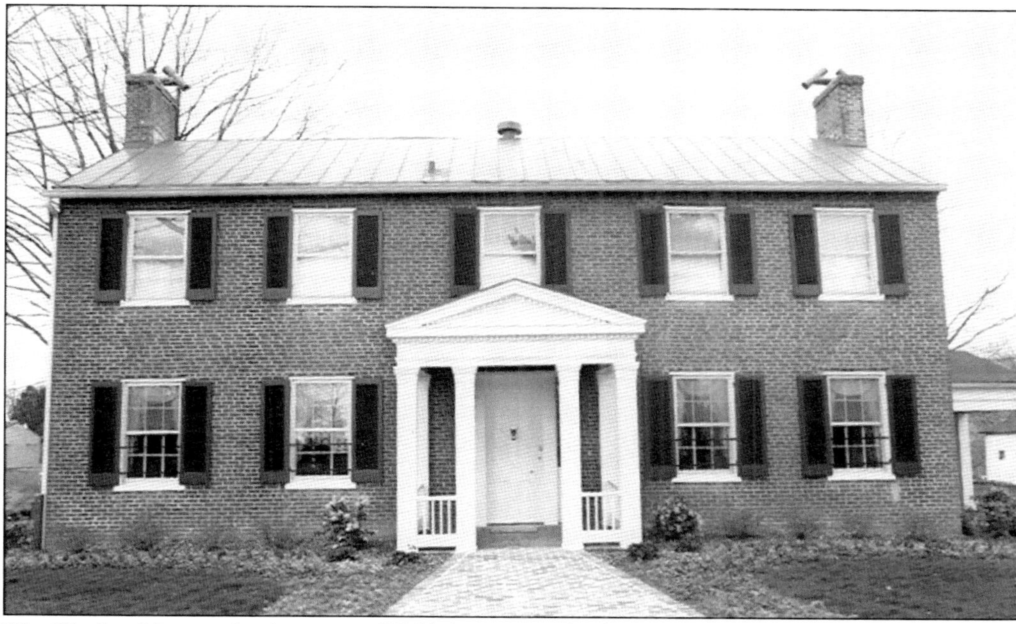

The Tucker House, also known as Wild Acres, was built by Hazael Tucker (1806–1875), who was a farmer and mule trader. The property, located on Tucker Station Road, was purchased by Hazael and his wife, Nancy Jane, in 1839. A year later, they commissioned John Stone to build their federal-style home with solid brick walls, poplar floors, and seven fireplaces. This lovely house is currently a bed and breakfast. (Photo courtesy of Louisville Metro Historic Landmarks Commission.)

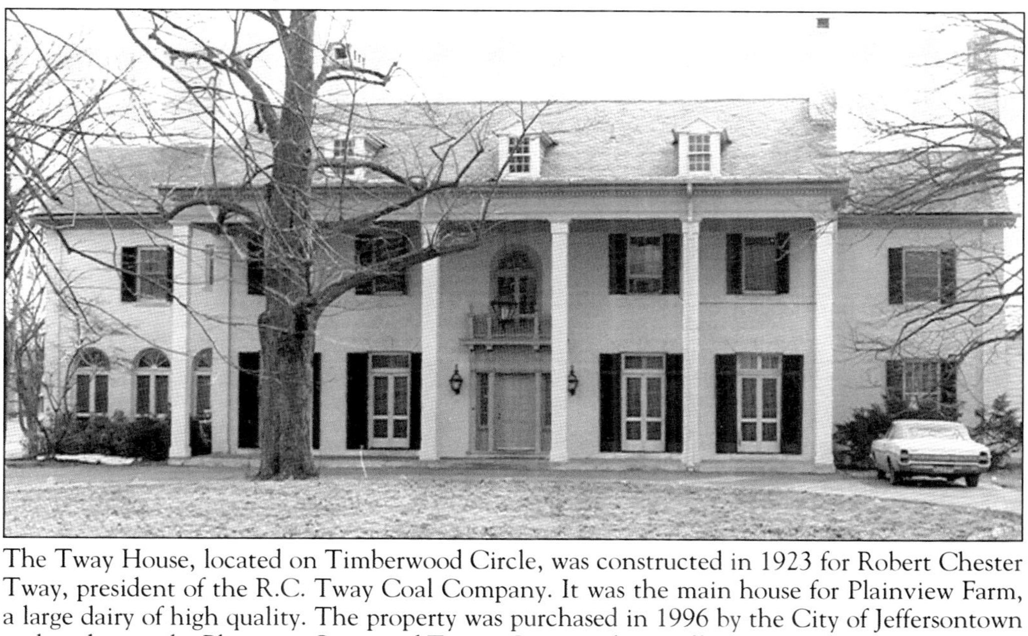

The Tway House, located on Timberwood Circle, was constructed in 1923 for Robert Chester Tway, president of the R.C. Tway Coal Company. It was the main house for Plainview Farm, a large dairy of high quality. The property was purchased in 1996 by the City of Jeffersontown and made into the Plainview Swim and Tennis Center, where Jeffersontown residents can enjoy themselves while relaxing in the shadow of this lovely home. (Photo courtesy of Louisville Metro Historic Landmarks Commission.)

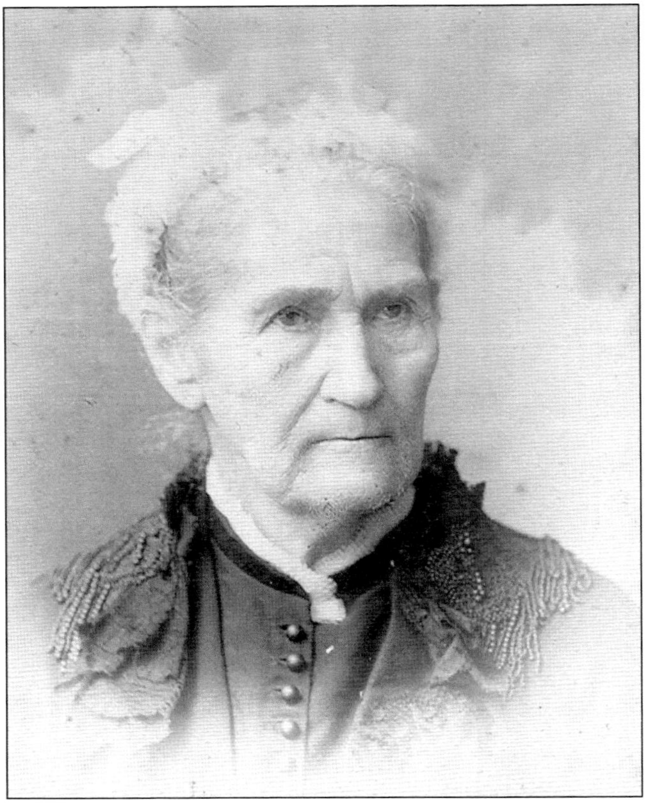

Jane Marmaduke Tyler married Presley Tyler in 1831 and lived with him on his farm until his death in 1879. Catherine Tyler, born in 1832, was the only child of theirs to survive into adulthood. (Photo courtesy of Sallie Cheatham Smith.)

The Presley Tyler Farm, known as Blackacre, was built in 1844 on land he inherited from his parents, Moses and Phoebe Tyler. In 1979, the property was donated as a state nature preserve to be used for the education of the county's schoolchildren. Moses was one of the first settlers in Jeffersontown, so the site, full of houses and other buildings constructed at various times, is a wealth of information on early Jeffersontown life. (Photo courtesy of Jane Smith.)

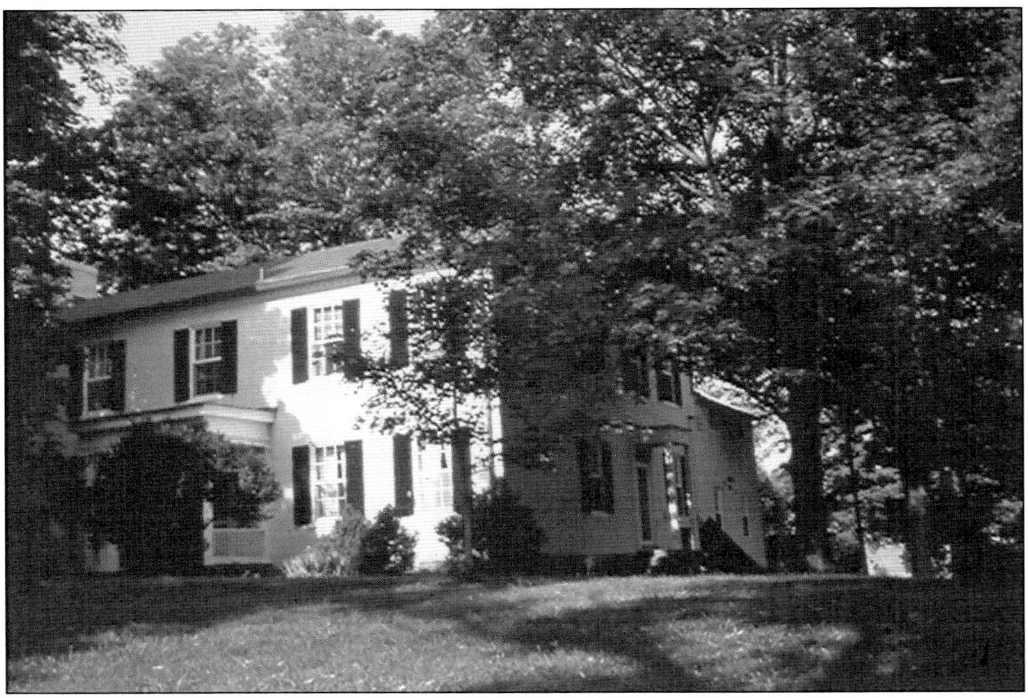

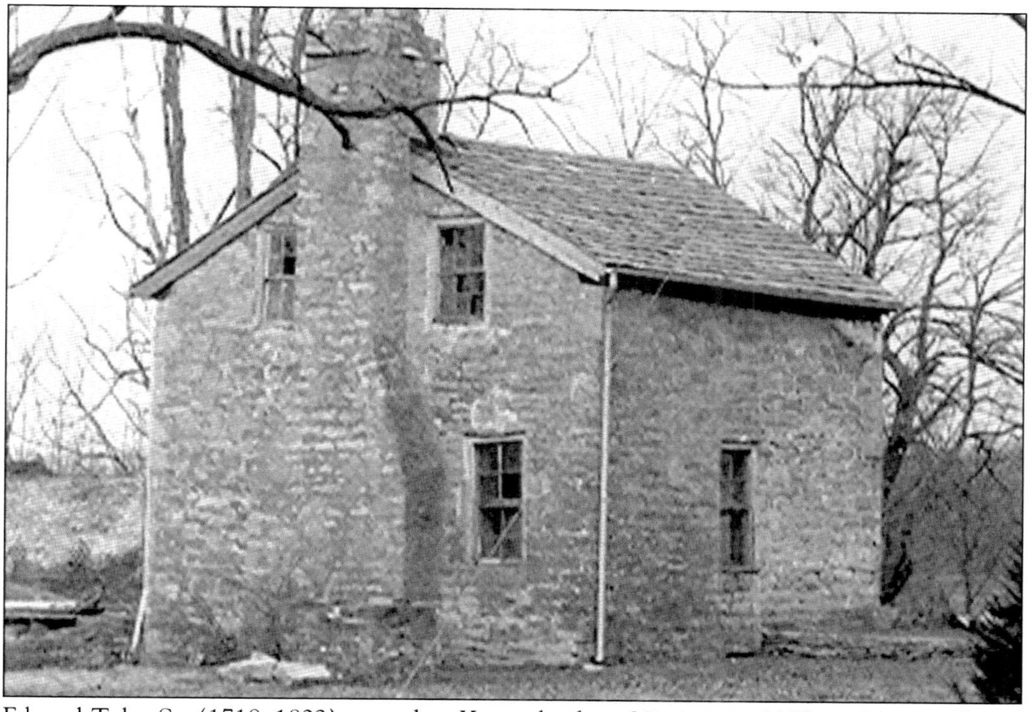

Edward Tyler Sr. (1718–1802) moved to Kentucky from Virginia in 1780, and he purchased two tracts of land between Taylorsville and Rehl Roads in 1782 and 1783. He built a log cabin about 1787, and then joined this stone house to it about 1789. Edward Tyler Sr. was the father of Robert (c. 1751–1840), Moses (1755–1839), William (1755–1836), and Edward Tyler Jr. (1767–1840). (Photo courtesy of Lt. Col. Robert C. Jobson.)

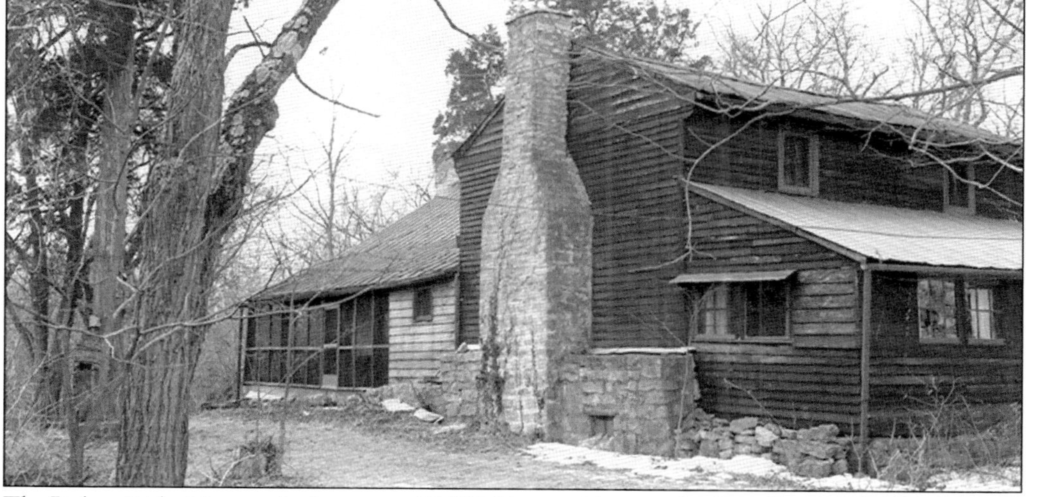

The Robert Tyler House, also known as Old Wilderness Fort, was built to the east of Jeffersontown. Robert, the nephew of Edward Tyler Jr., built a log house on the property first, then had an addition constructed by stone masons who were in the area as early as 1790. The log portion of Robert Tyler's home is believed to be one of the oldest surviving log cabins in the county. (Photo courtesy of Louisville Metro Historic Landmarks Commission.)

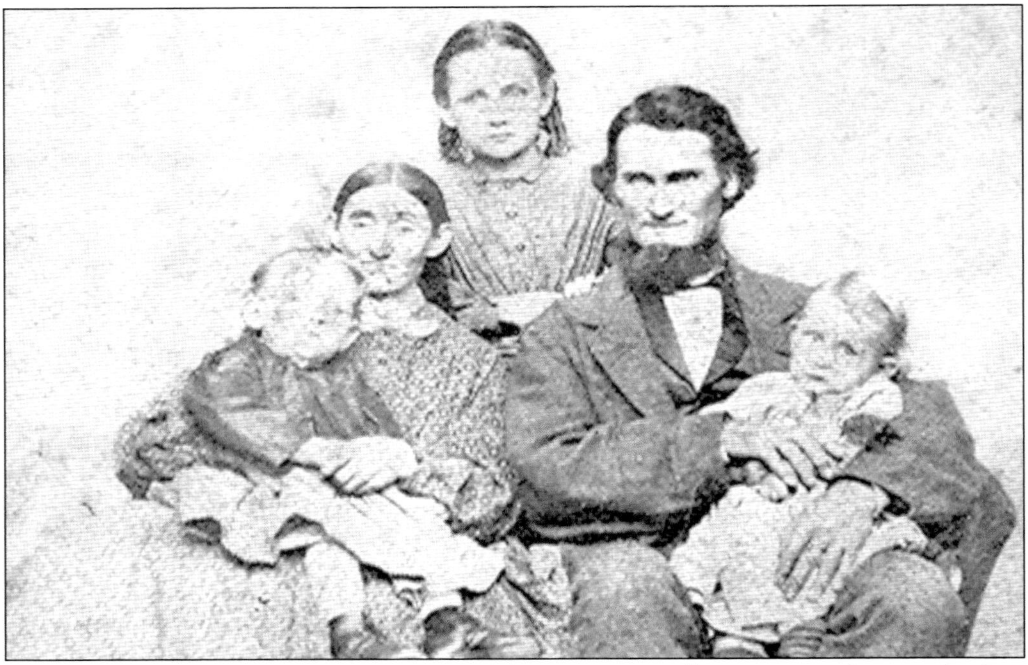

Johnathan Hibbs Weller and his wife, Adeline Goose Weller, are seen here with their three children. The Weller family lived on Billtown Road in the late 1800s. Their property encompassed the area now occupied by Carrithers Middle School, Monticello Place, and the opposite side of the road as well. (Photo courtesy of Sallie Cheatham Smith.)

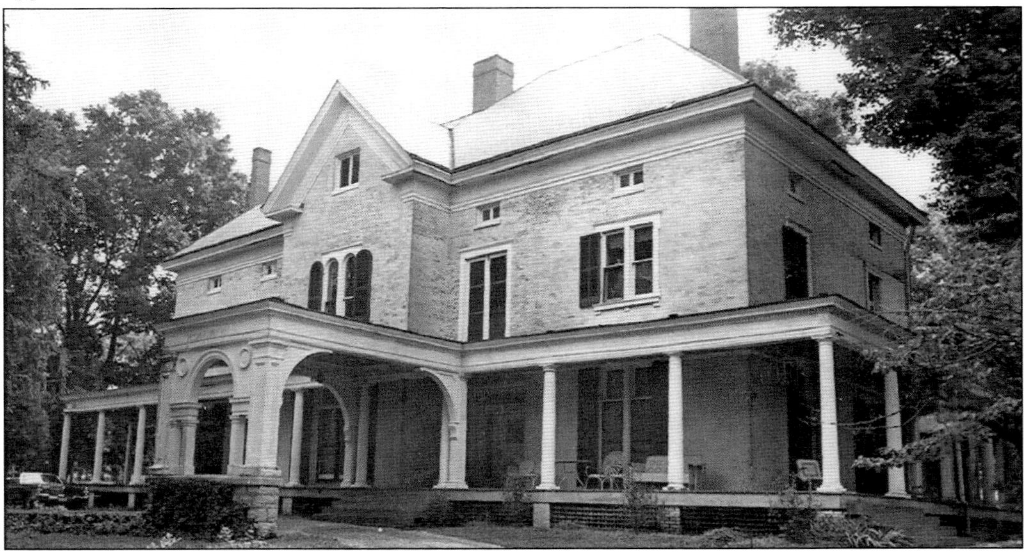

Mansfield, the estate of Henry Watterson, was located about a mile from the square in Jeffersontown on land originally owned by Joseph S. Hite. Watterson left Hite's original four-room house intact, but added countless other rooms and transformed the house into a 28-room mansion encircled by a lovely veranda. Watterson lived at Mansfield from 1886 until his death in 1921. Fire damaged the house in 1976, and it eventually had to be torn down. (Photo courtesy of the Jeffersontown Historical Museum.)

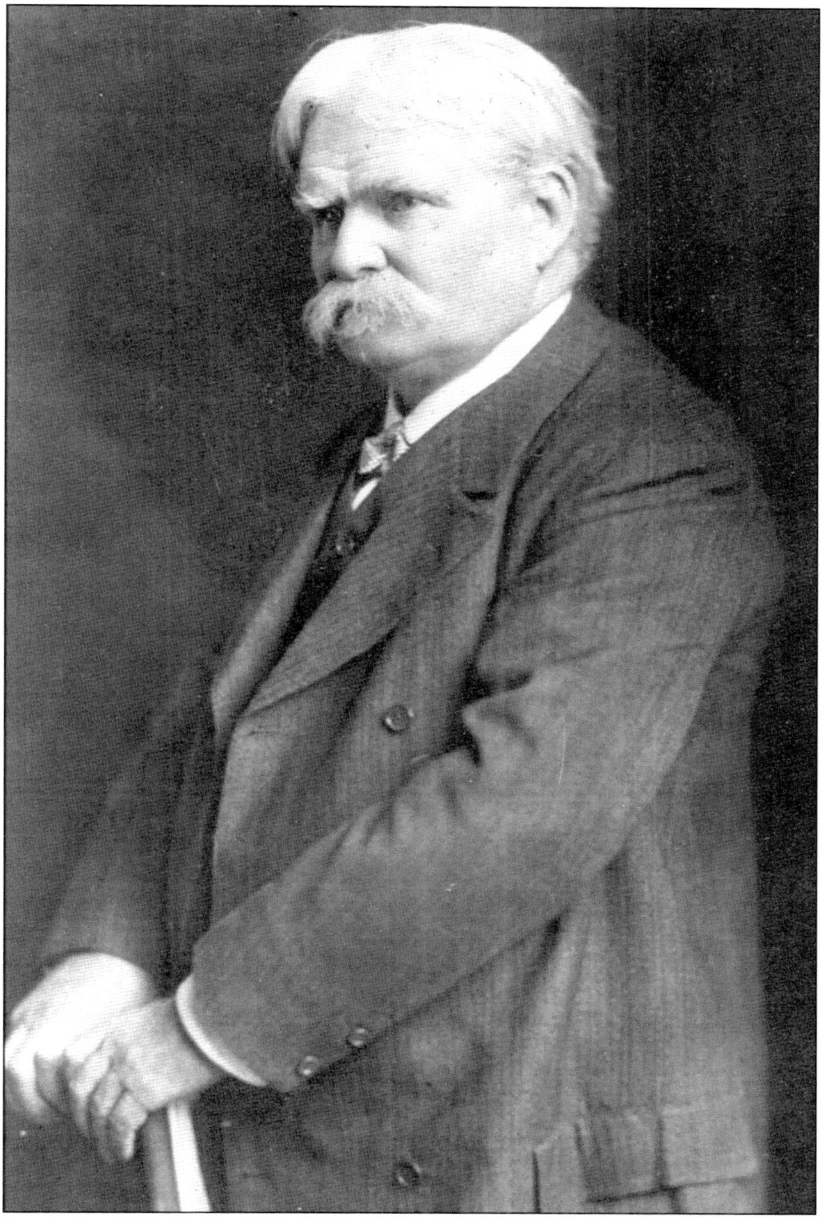

Henry Watterson is undoubtedly Jeffersontown's most famous resident. He moved to Jeffersontown in 1864 and began building his estate, Mansfield. He was known throughout the South for his outspoken editorials during the Civil War, and in the 1860s, he began working for the *Louisville Journal*. In 1868, the paper's name was changed to *The Courier-Journal*, and Watterson was its full-fledged editor for over 50 years, making it one of the most prominent and influential papers in the country. Watterson dearly loved his home, Mansfield, and spent as much time writing editorials there as he did in his downtown newspaper office. One of his favorite quips was, "I'm a Jefferson Democrat. I live in Jeffersontown in the county of Jefferson." The residents of Jeffersontown are extremely proud he chose this city for his home. (Photo courtesy of *The Courier-Journal*.)

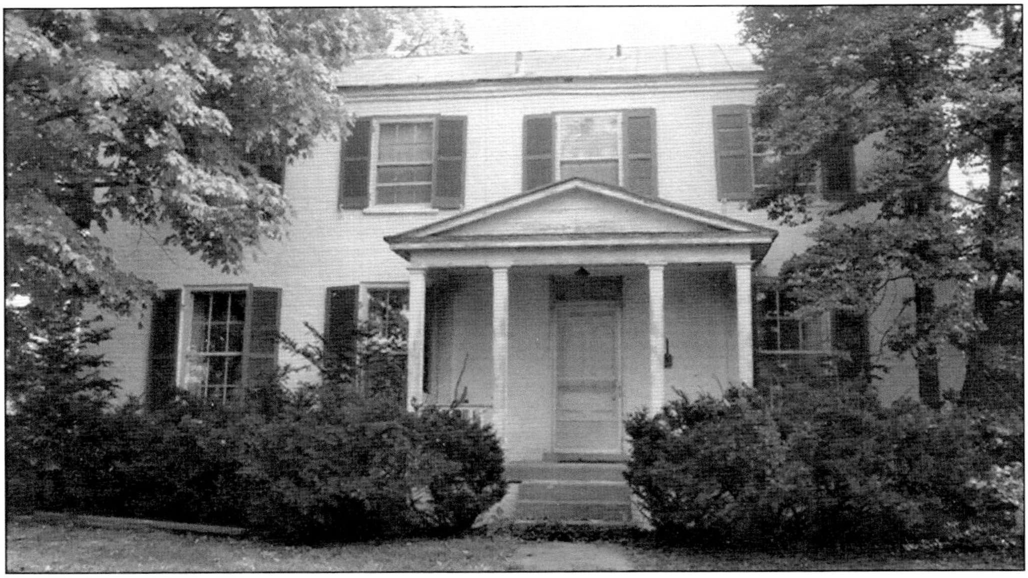

The Yenowine-Kennedy House, located on Taylorsville Road, was built by Frederick Yenowine in 1849, when his daughter, Amanda, married John Kennedy. A nearby elementary school was named for their son, Alexander R. Kennedy. (Photo courtesy of Louisville Metro Historic Landmarks Commission.)

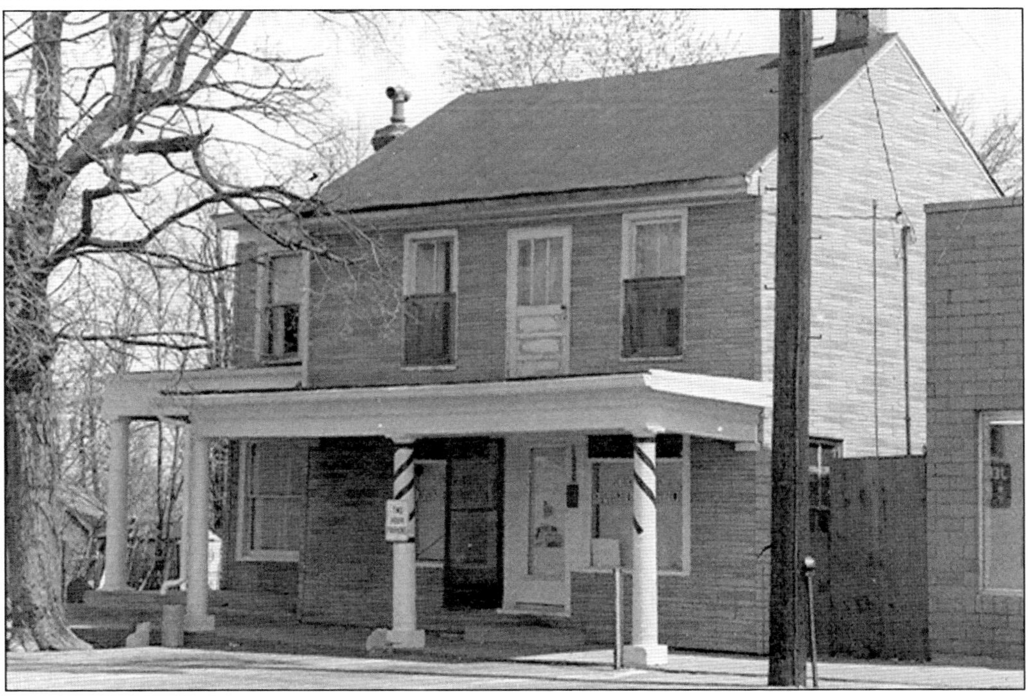

This house was built by George Zilhart (1789–1840), who purchased lot #44 on the town square in 1819. George and his brother, Philip, were wagon makers. After George died, his widow, Jane, remarried and continued to live in the house until her death in 1883. (Photo courtesy of Lt. Col. Robert C. Jobson.)

Five

Fun and Entertainment

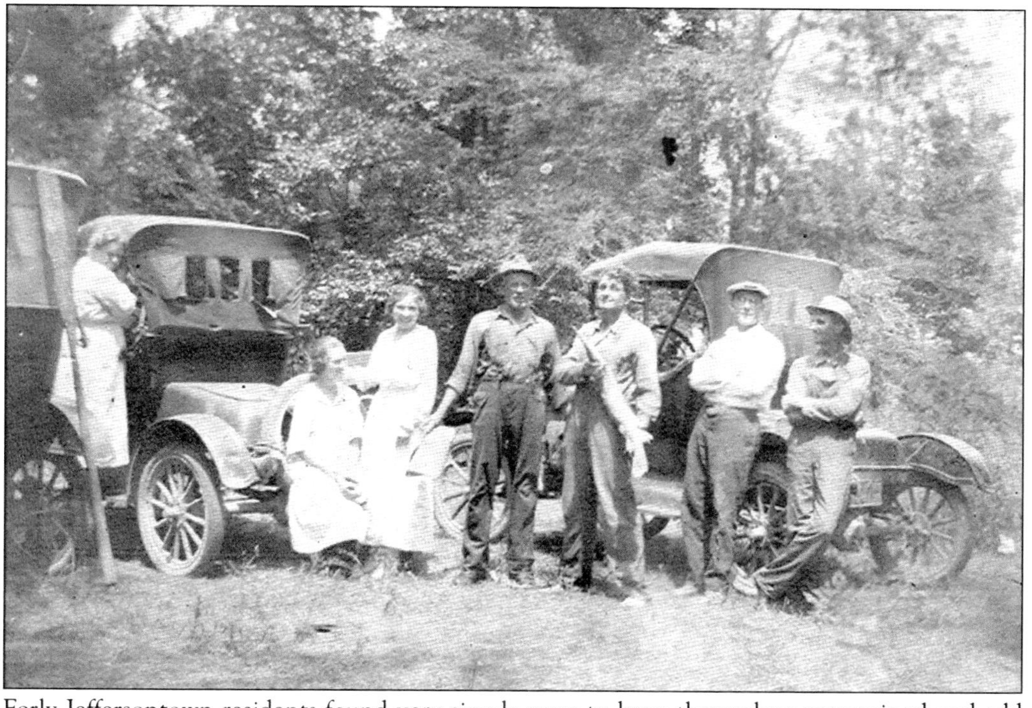

Early Jeffersontown residents found very simple ways to keep themselves entertained and add enjoyment to their lives. This July 1918 photograph shows Thomas Jones Goose, J.M. Makefield, and friends on a fishing outing. (Photo courtesy of Sallie Cheatham Smith.)

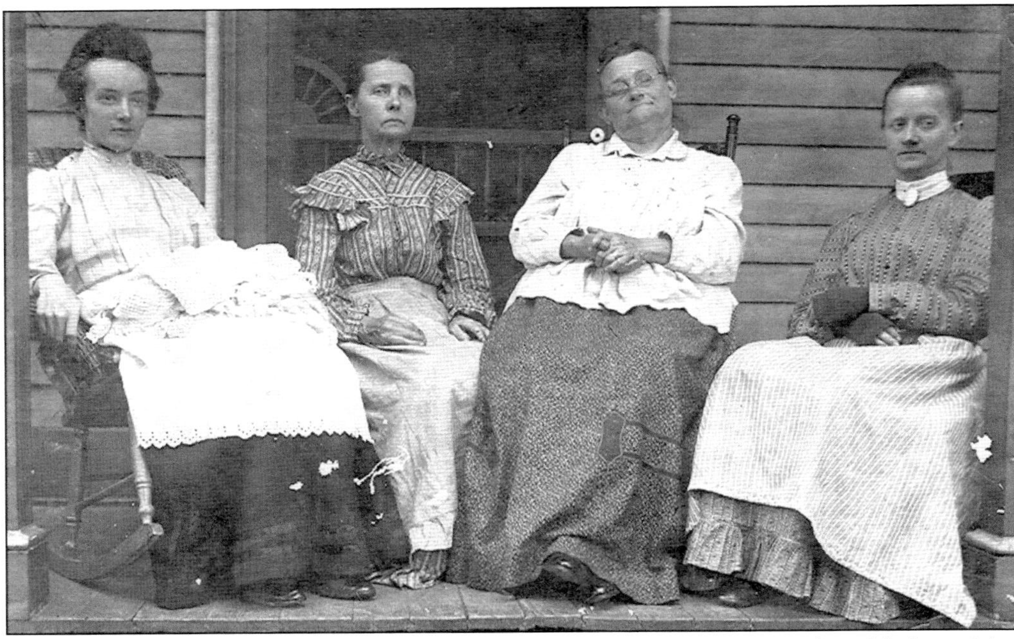

Sewing circles were one of the earliest forms of "entertainment" in the old days. Most Jeffersontown residents were farmers, and thus led very busy lives taken up almost continually by daily chores. A welcome respite for ladies was to be able to sit and chat with friends for a time—while still doing the necessary work of sewing. Pictured from left to right are Pet Wisehart, Sallie Blankenbaker, Frances Hummel, and Sallie Etta Goose. (Photo courtesy of Sallie Cheatham Smith.)

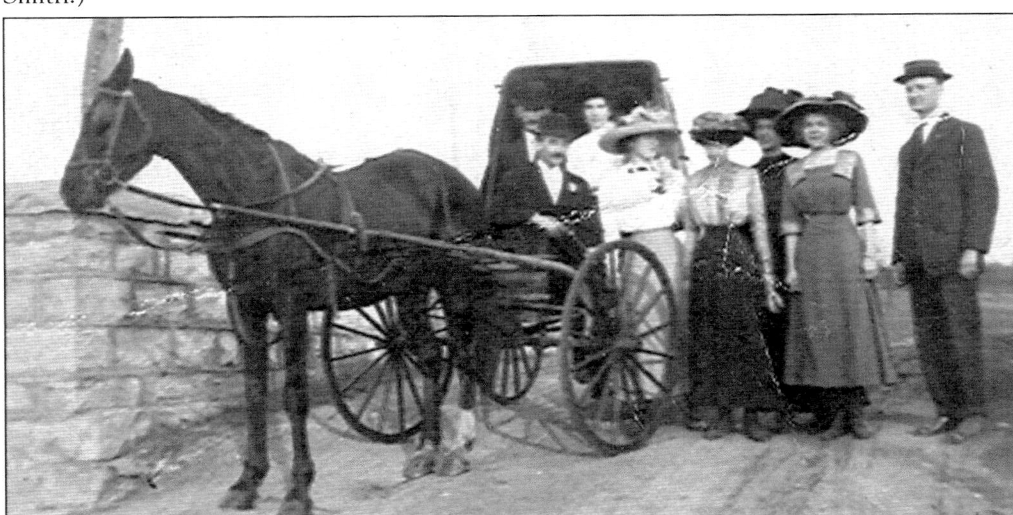

Another early form of entertainment was the Sunday drive. This turn-of-the-century photo was taken on the Chenoweth Run Creek stone bridge. The buggy may have been rented from the Jeffersontown Stable on the town square. Pictured in the front row, from left to right, are William Frederick Stucky, two unidentified women, Eva Stucky, unidentified, and Carl Hummel, editor of the *Jeffersonian* newspaper. The man and woman seated in the buggy are unknown. (Photo courtesy of Julia Smith.)

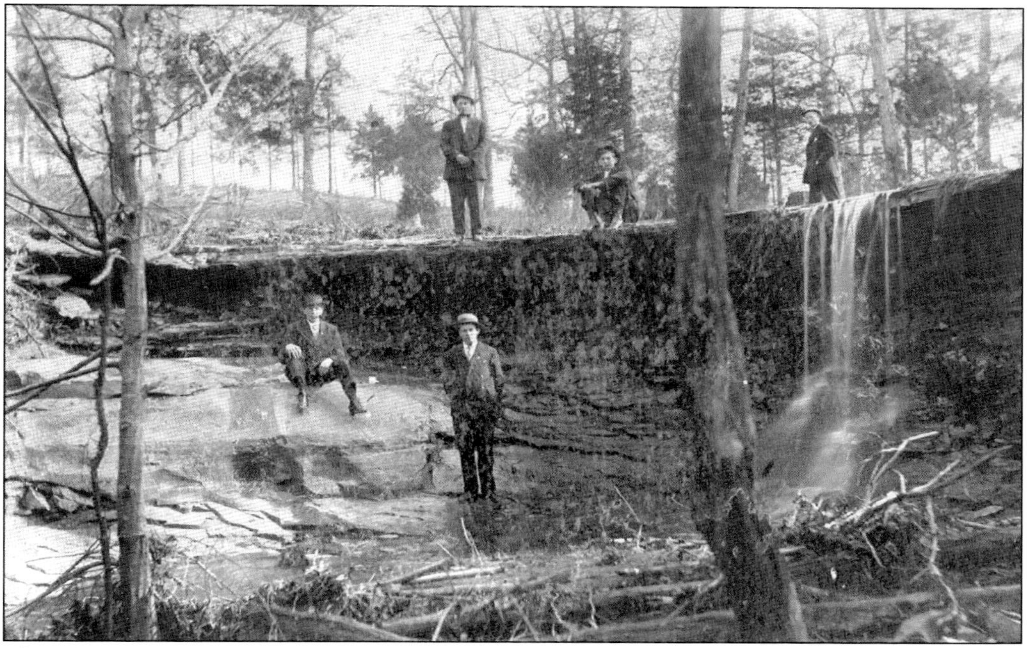

This photo, taken by William Cleary in the early 1900s, shows Carl Miller and friends from Swamp College relaxing at Chenoweth Park (now known as Charlie Vettiner Park), which has remained a beautiful place for outings throughout the years. Pictured, from left to right, are as follows: (front row) Carl William Miller and Melton Tyler; (back row) Elmer Stout, Hampton Miller, and Conner Stout. (Photo courtesy of Carole Chambers Davis.)

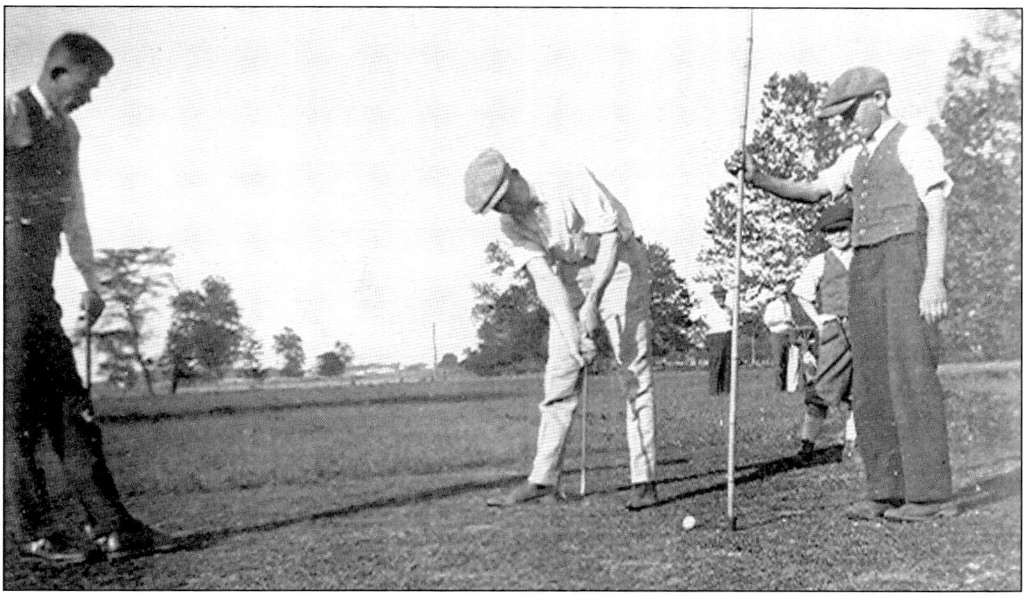

During the Depression of 1929, Claude Hunsinger built a nine-hole golf course in the cow pasture at Midlane Farm. Many picnics with golf games were held there, with good friends gathered and good food served on many holidays, especially July 4th. (Photo courtesy of Marjorie Hunsinger Weeks Babson.)

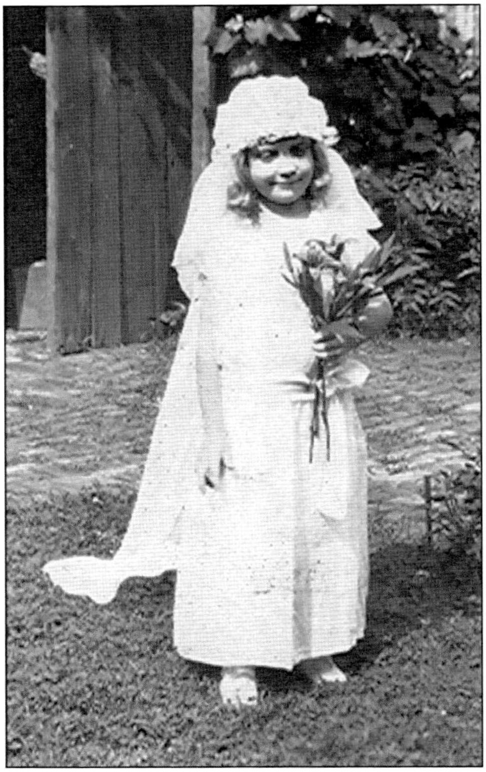

A special form of entertainment in the early 1900s was commonly known as a "Tom Thumb Wedding." During lulls in the social season, these mock weddings provided a chance for people to dress up and be amused. A young girl and boy were chosen to be the "bride" and "groom," and then dressed in miniature bridal attire. This June 7, 1928 photo is of Mary Ellen Smith preparing to "marry" G.B. Reeser. (Photo courtesy of Julia Smith.)

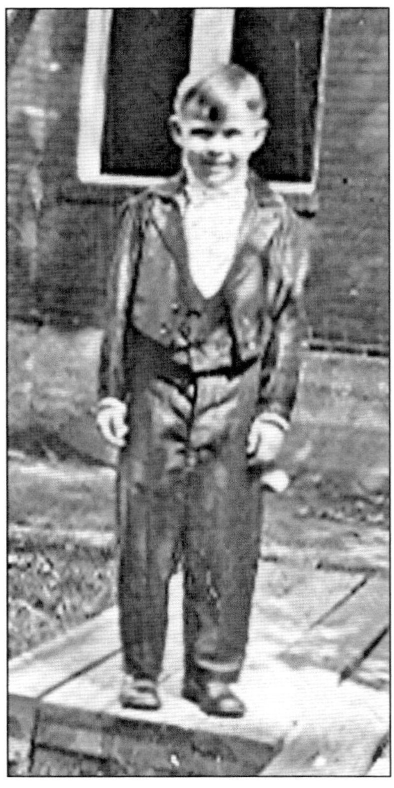

This photo, taken the same day, shows E.G. Reeser dressed as the groom for the Tom Thumb Wedding. Imagine the look on the real Mrs. E.G. Reeser's face years later, when Mary Ellen told her she had once "married" her husband! It was all in fun, of course. Quite often, entire schools would stage elaborate Tom Thumb Weddings, complete with bridesmaids, groomsmen, and "priest" (usually one of the older boys in the class). (Photo courtesy of Julia Smith.)

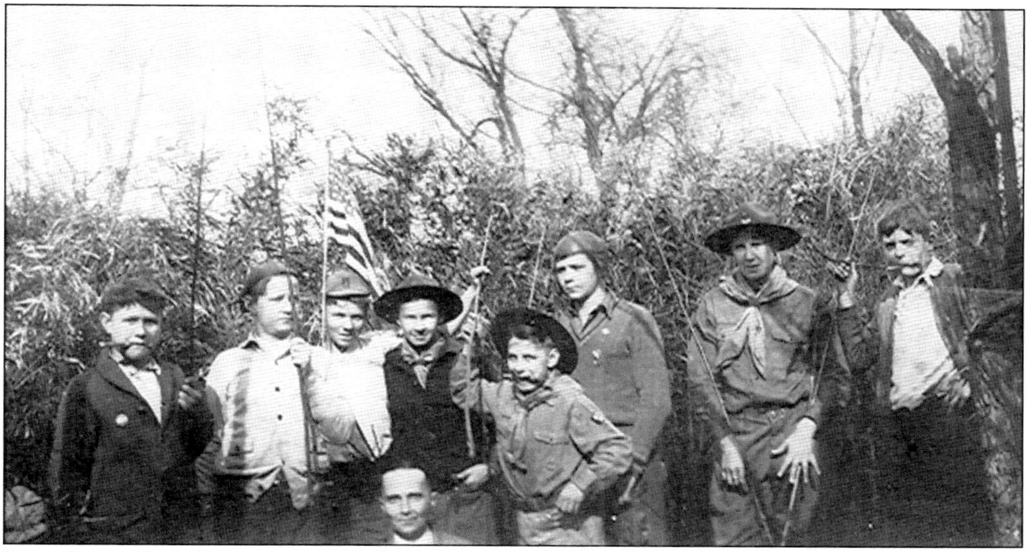

This photo of a Jeffersontown Boy Scout troop was taken about 1930, while they were exploring a cane patch around where Six Mile Lane meets Old Six Mile Lane. Kneeling in front is leader Snyder Vaughan. Standing behind him, from left to right, are Jack Brandenberg, Lee McGraw, Bill Eddleman, Stuart Adams, E.M. Allen Jr., Ted Breeding, Field Leichhardt, and Charles Bryan. (Photo courtesy of Marcia Bryan Horton.)

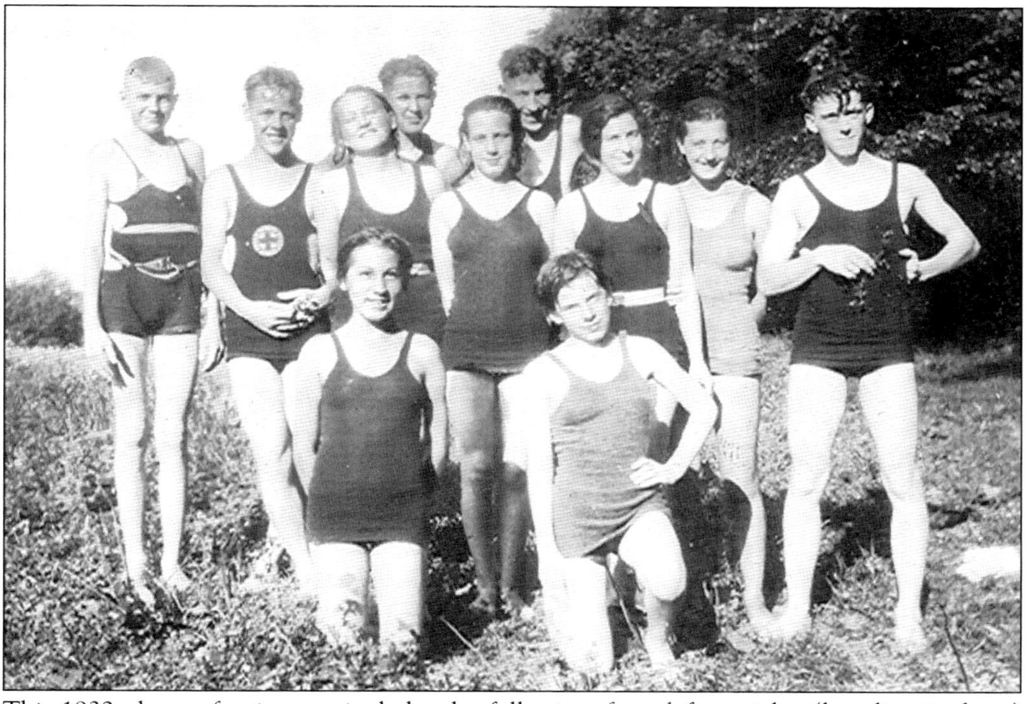

This 1932 photo of swimmers includes the following, from left to right: (kneeling in front) Julia ?, and Tiny ?; (middle row) Tods ?, Gordon ?, Marcia Bryan, Joyce ?, Mrs. Melvin, Patty ?, and Tom ?; (back row) Field Leichhardt and Beach Bryan. (Photo courtesy of the family of Irma Doran.)

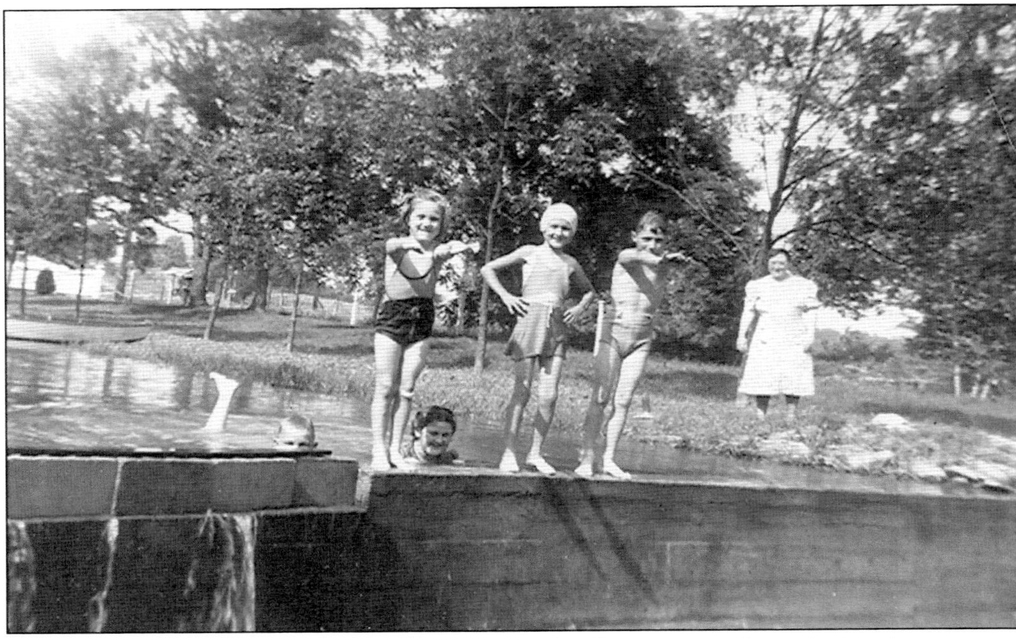

The residents of Jeffersontown loved to swim, and a favorite spot for enjoying the sport was Chenoweth Creek. The Heitzman family lived at Chenoweth Lane and Taylorsville Road, so the creek was just across from their home. This 1941 photo shows them playing on concrete blocks at the creek. From left to right are unidentified, Barbara Heitzman, Bernice Heitzman, Dorothy Heitzman, Tony Heitzman, and Rose Heitzman. (Photo courtesy of Maurice Woods.)

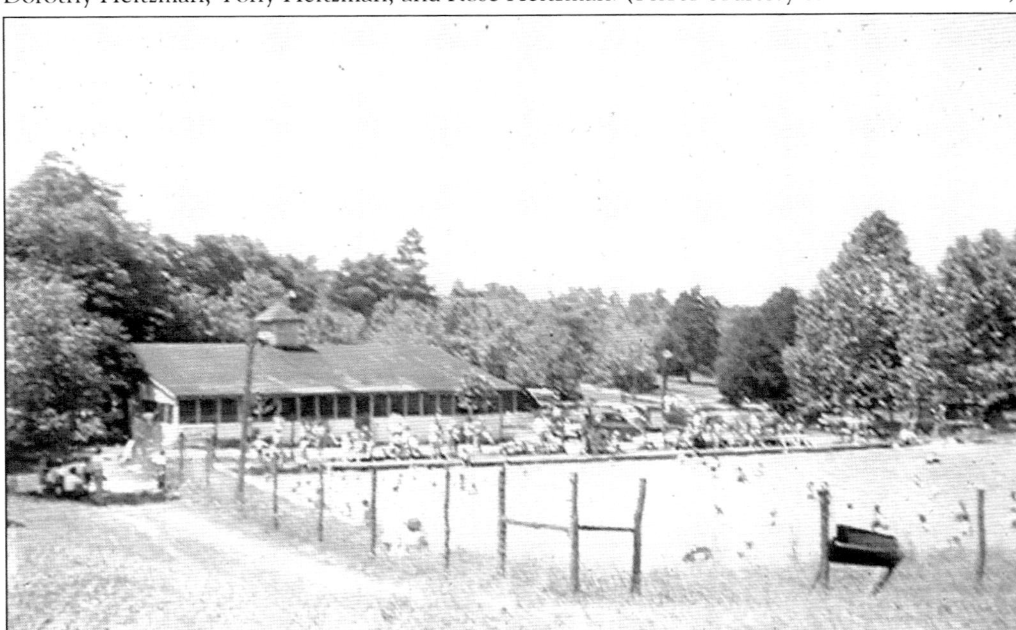

Knauer's Pool was yet another hangout for swimmers in Jeffersontown. It was originally located where Papa John's corporate office is currently housed in the industrial park. (Photo courtesy of Don Neal.)

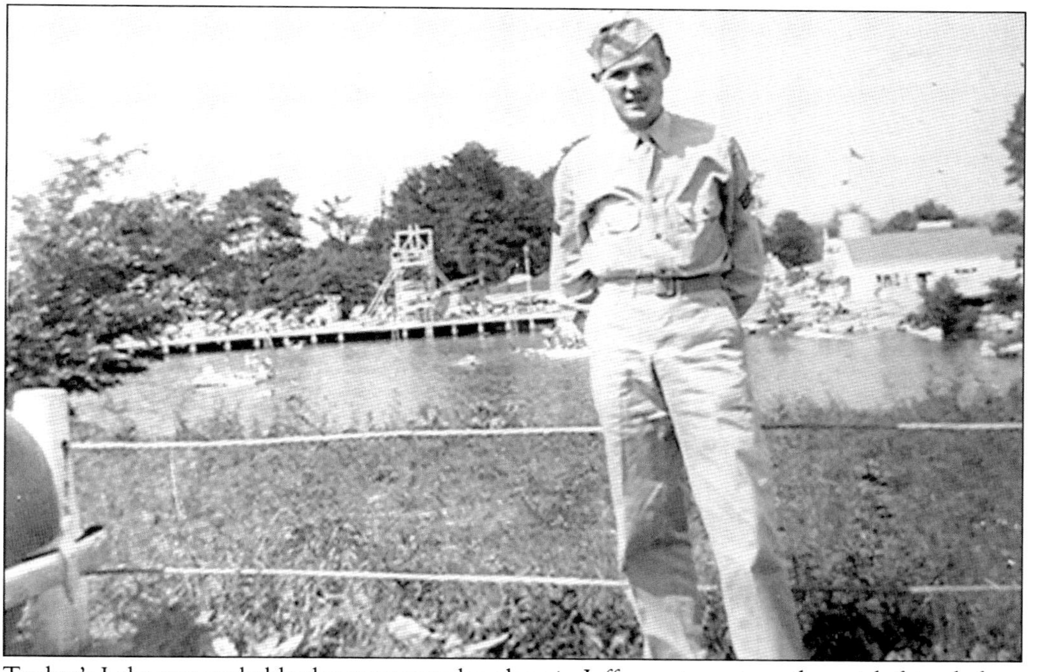

Tucker's Lake was probably the most popular place in Jeffersontown to gather with friends for a day of fun and swimming. In this *c.* 1942 photo, Franklin Chambers, all dressed up in uniform, is seen standing by the lake. (Photo courtesy of Carole Chambers Davis.)

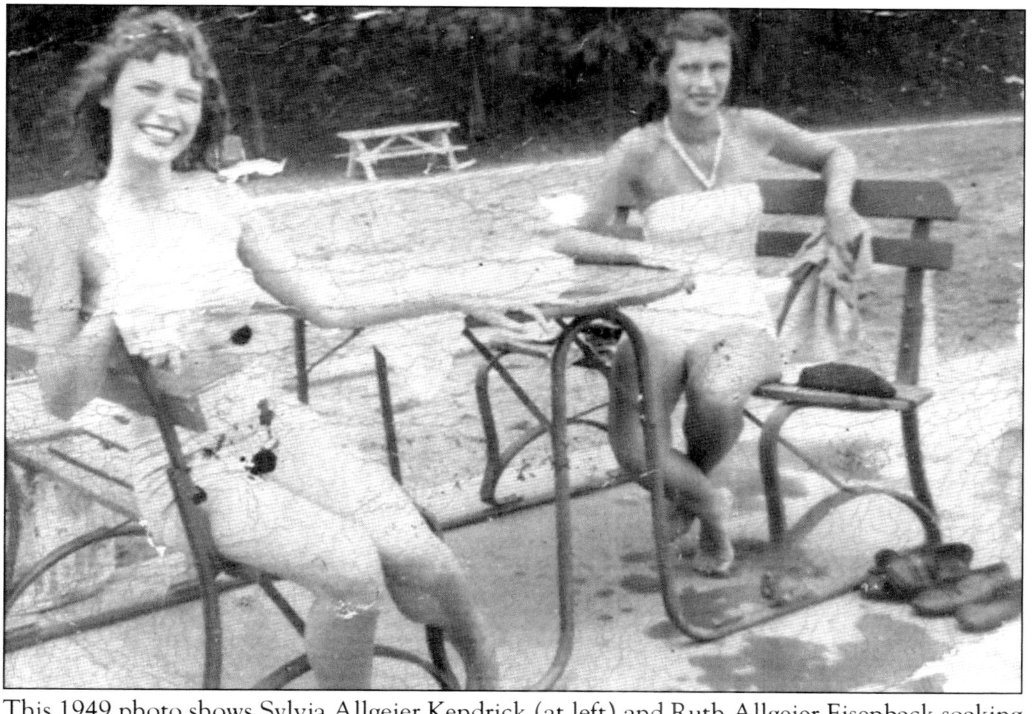

This 1949 photo shows Sylvia Allgeier Kendrick (at left) and Ruth Allgeier Eisenback soaking up the sun at Tucker's Lake. (Photo courtesy of Ruth Allgeier Eisenback.)

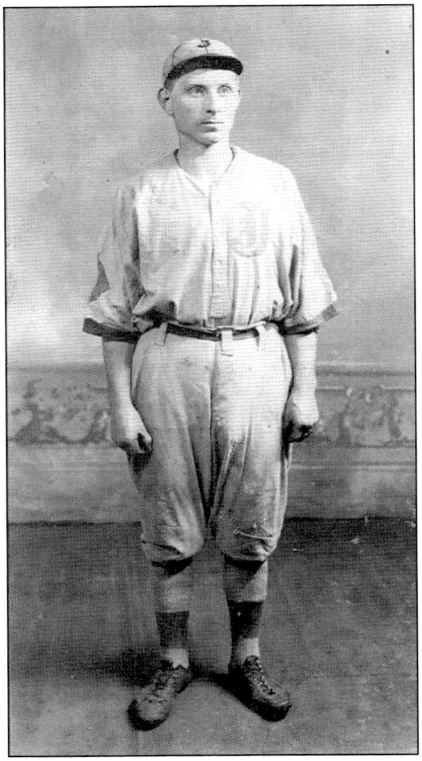

After the Civil War, baseball became a popular sport in Jeffersontown. This turn-of-the-20th-century photo is of an unknown player on Jeffersontown's team. (Photo courtesy of Jack Mittler.)

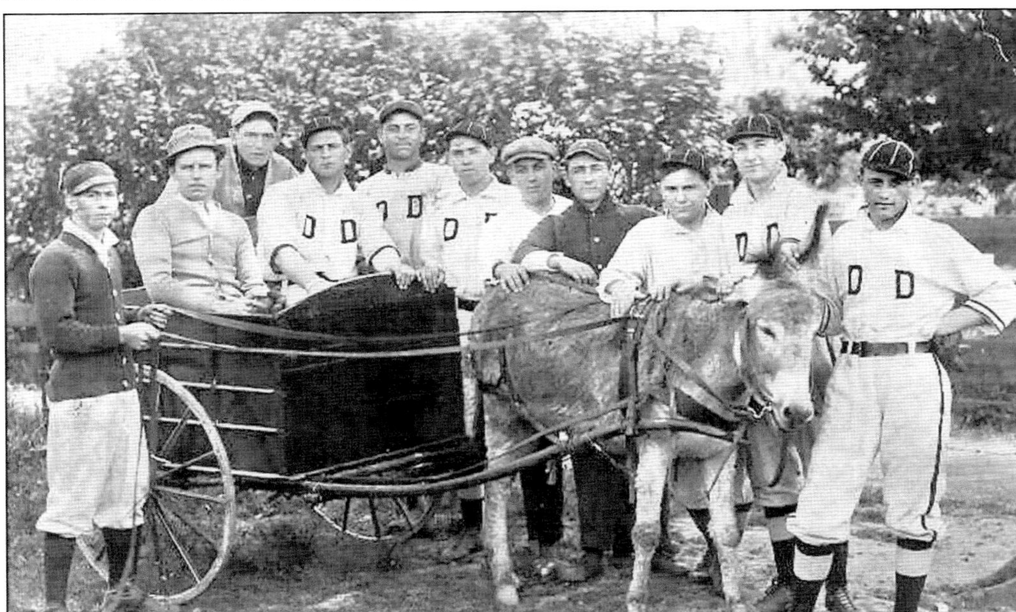

This photo shows the Jeffersontown baseball team in the 1930s era. George William Bernauer is on the far right. Local legend has it that Pee Wee Reese tried out for Jeffersontown's baseball team, but was turned down—not one of the best moves the team ever made! (Photo courtesy of George William Bernauer.)

Barto Roemele played baseball for Jeffersontown c. 1900. (Photo courtesy of Jack Mittler.)

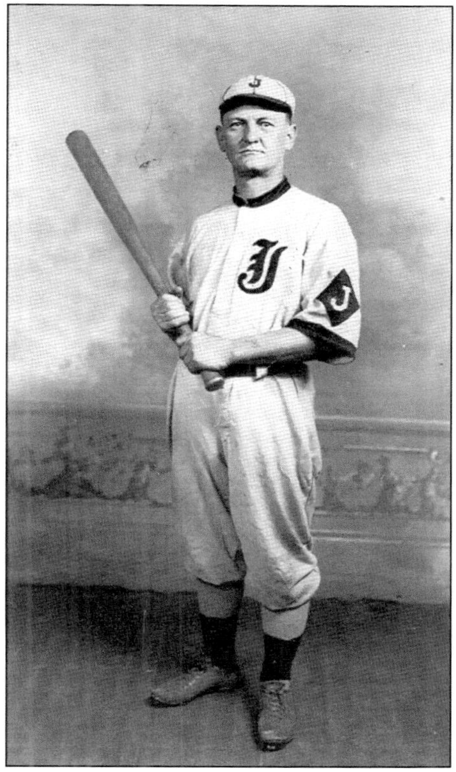

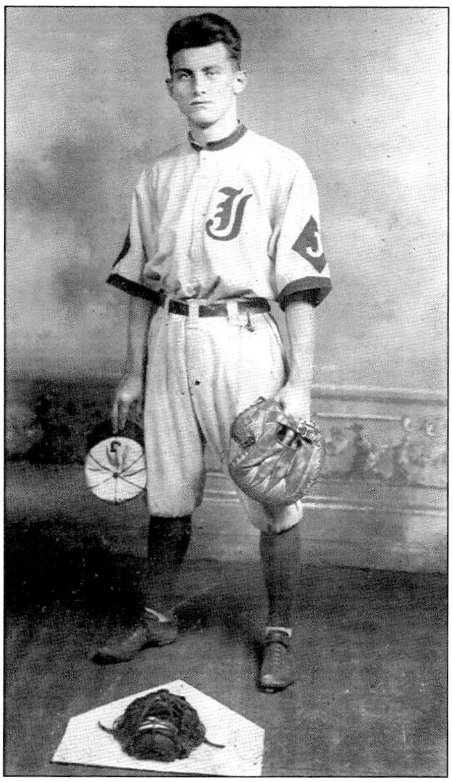

This photo shows another unknown Jeffersontown baseball teammate from the early 1900s. (Photo courtesy of Jack Mittler.)

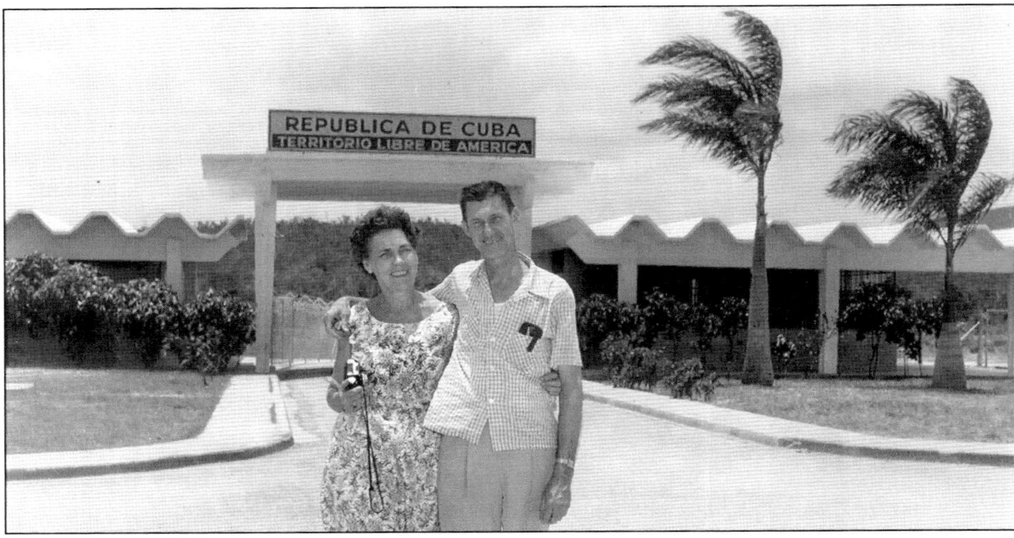

The Union Barrack-ades were an all-volunteer entertainment troupe founded in 1942. The troupe—which included a band, singers, dancers, magic acts, ventriloquists, and acrobatics—traveled all over the world, putting on shows for soldiers. Ernest and Ada Grawemeyer, who lived on Lyric Lane in Jeffersontown, were director and co-director of the Union-Barrack-ades. They are seen at Guantanamo Bay, Cuba, in this 1962 photo. (Photo courtesy of Ada Lee Grawemeyer Kane.)

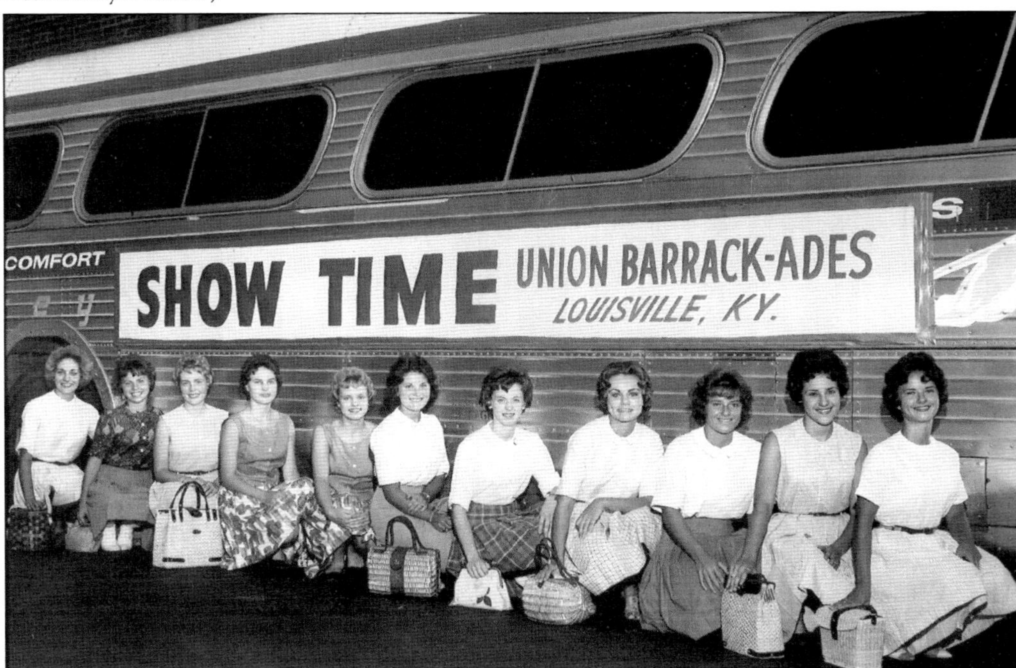

"Have Talent, Will Travel"—The Union Barrack-ades traveled by military air transport services when they performed for soldiers overseas, but when they were on tour in the United States, they traveled by bus. Here, several girls from the troupe are posed next to their touring bus. (Photo courtesy of Ada Lee Grawemeyer Kane.)

When the Union Barrack-ades first started out, they depended on labor unions to cover the cost of their equipment and costumes. This photo shows the dancers in some of their original cotton and gingham outfits, which were not showy, but were still adorable. Ada Lee Grawemeyer is seen third from left, underneath the ladder. (Photo courtesy of Ada Lee Grawemeyer Kane.)

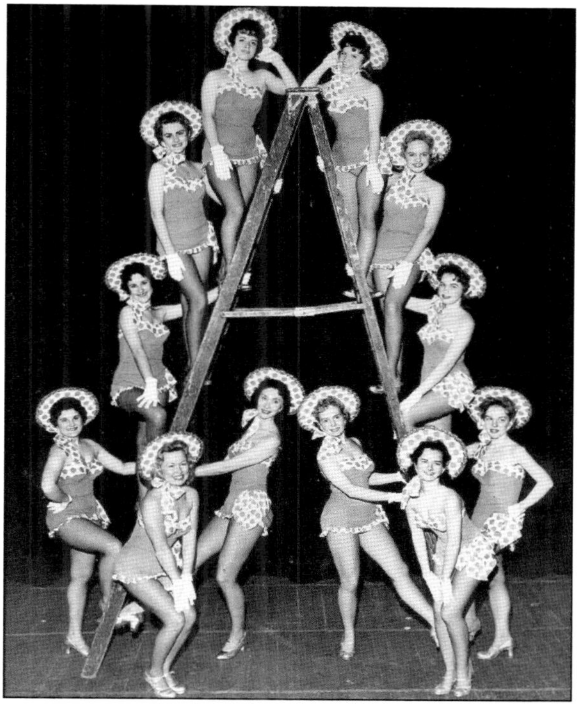

The Union Barrack-ades' mascots were known as the Brumleve Team. Marlene and Don Brumleve were a brother-and-sister act who lived in Jeffersontown. (Photo courtesy of Ada Lee Grawemeyer Kane.)

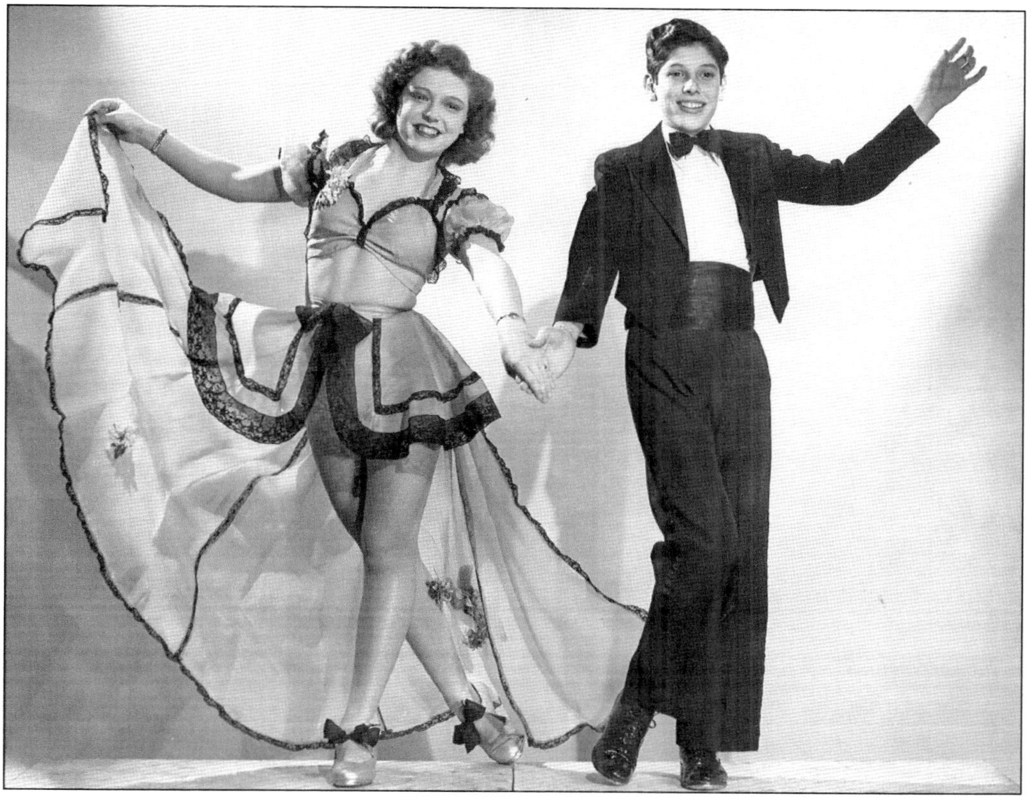

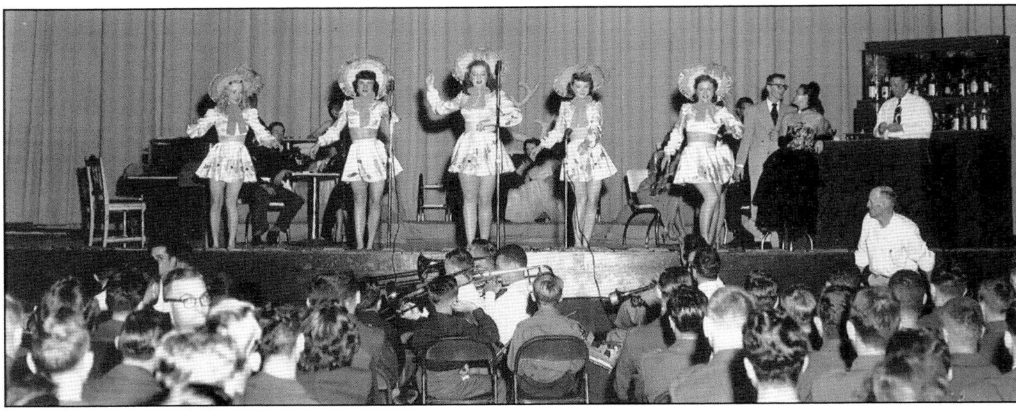

Here, the Union Barrack-ades are seen performing in a typical show at Fort Knox in 1950. The troupe performed for servicemen and veterans all over the world, and sometimes they performed for an audience of one, if a soldier in the hospital was too ill to join his comrades. In later years, American Legion posts and their auxiliaries helped the Union Barrack-ades with funds. (Photo courtesy of Ada Lee Grawemeyer Kane.)

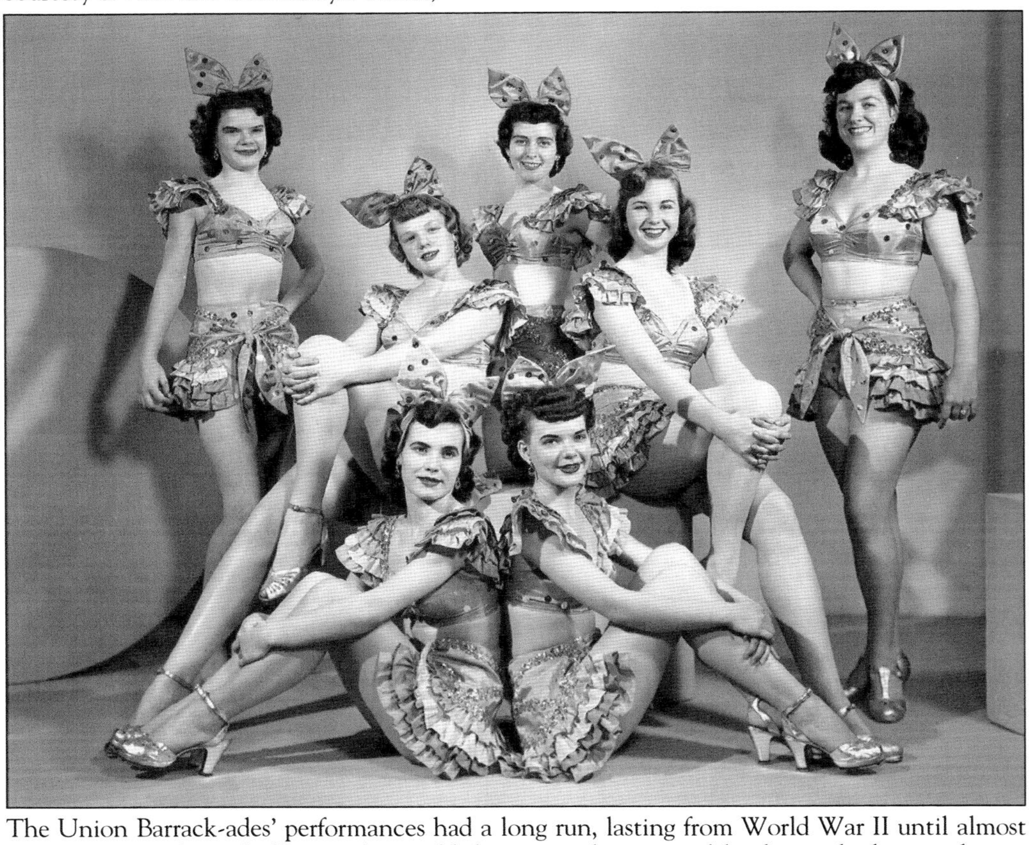

The Union Barrack-ades' performances had a long run, lasting from World War II until almost 1990. They performed all over the world, but were also enjoyed by fans right here at home, performing in local events such as the Gaslight Festival and raising money for the special needs of children in the Louisville area. The Union Barrack-ades deservedly won countless awards for their selfless devotion in bringing joy to others. (Photo courtesy of Ada Lee Grawemeyer Kane.)

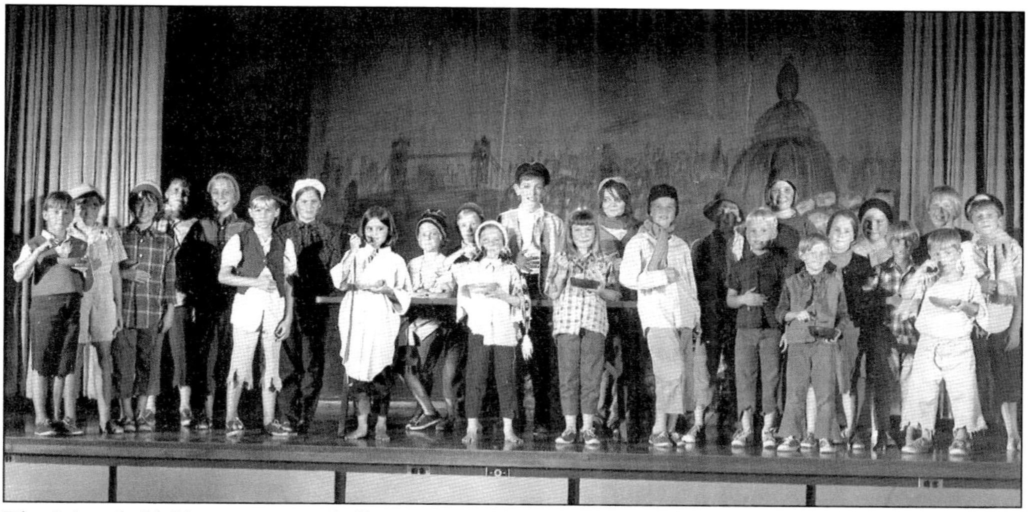

The Mansfield Players were a Jeffersontown community theatre group organized in the spring of 1970. Tryouts were open to everyone, and members of the community directed the plays and created the sets. This 1970 production of *Oliver* was one of the first to be staged by the Mansfield Players. (Photo courtesy of the Jeffersontown Historical Museum.)

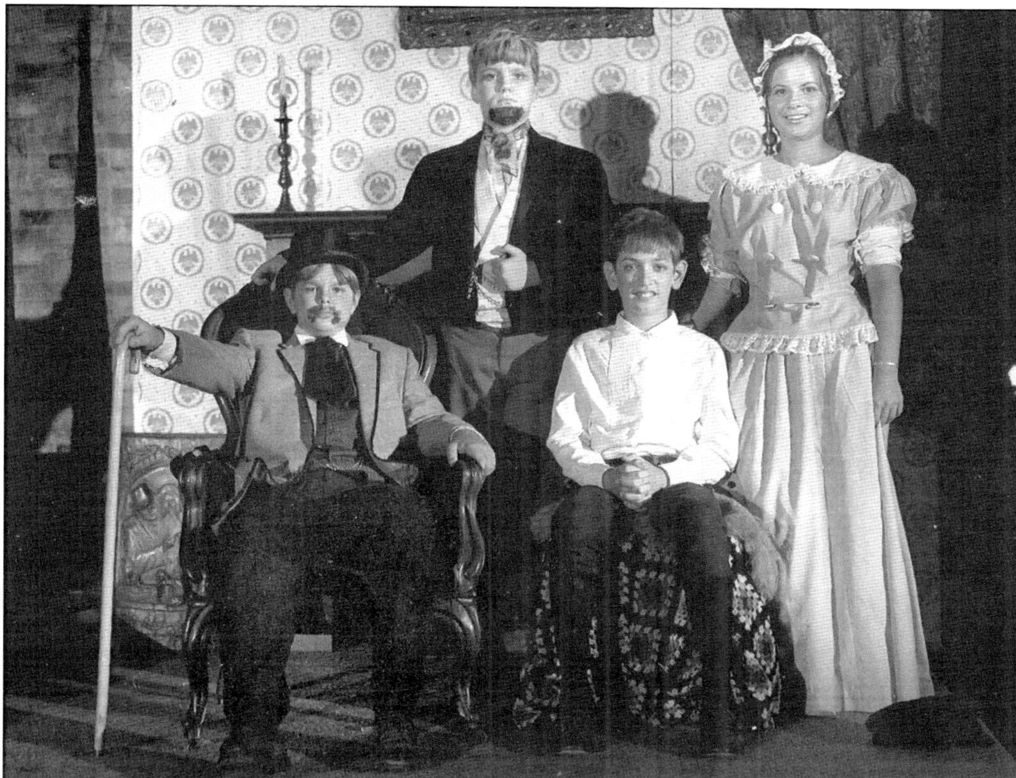

This photo of the same production includes Ricky Pierce as Dr. Grimwig, Neil Worden as Brownlow, Berry Curtis as Oliver, and Becky Straney as Mrs. Bedwin. (Photo courtesy of the Jeffersontown Historical Museum.)

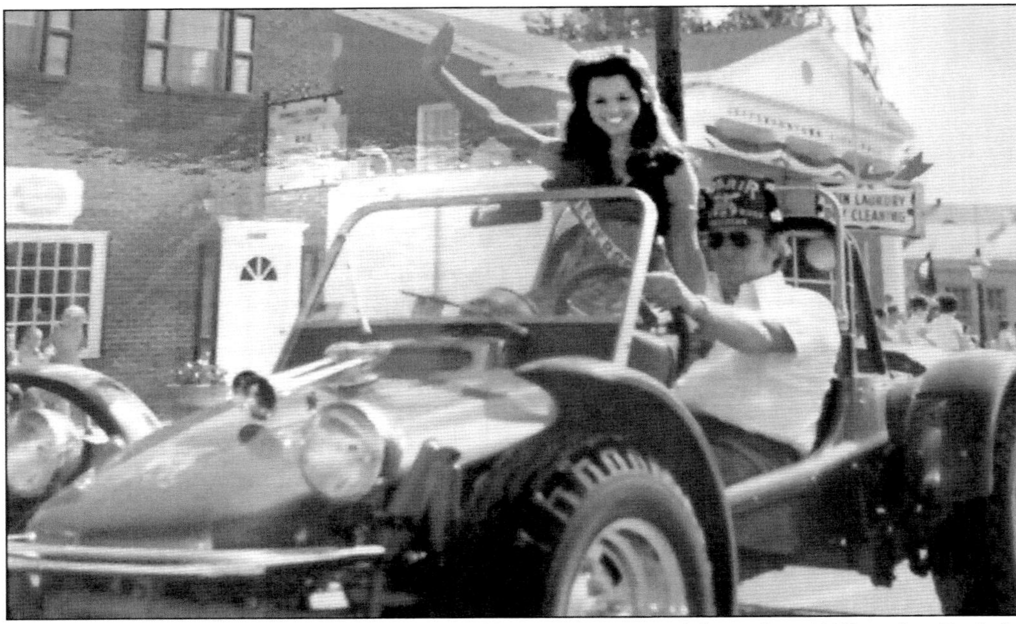

The 175th anniversary of the founding of Jeffersontown was celebrated in 1972 at the Gaslight Festival. This photo, taken at the Gaslight Parade, shows 1972 Miss Jeffersontown, Lydia Lewis, waving to the crowd from a Kosair Shriner's car. (Photo courtesy of Carole Chambers Davis.)

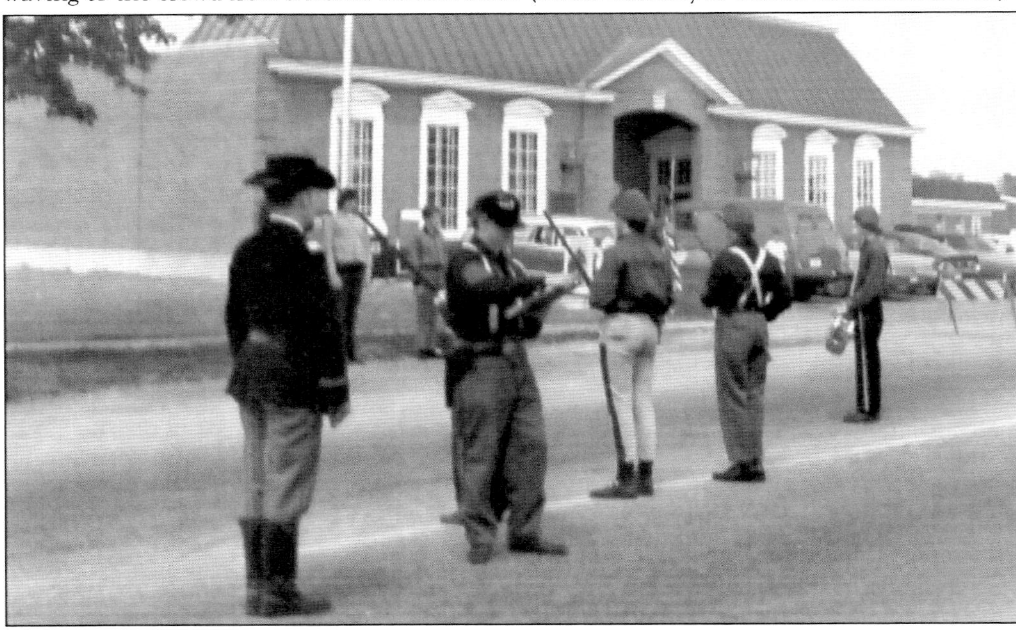

This photo, taken the same day, shows the Confederate Aerial Surveillance Corps as they reenacted the death of four Confederate soldiers here in Jeffersontown. The soldiers were shot October 25, 1864, in retaliation for the murder of a Union soldier found in Jeffersontown. The Union Army had warned that four Confederates would be executed for every Union soldier found dead. One of the four executed, however, was believed to have been a minister. (Photo courtesy of Carole Chambers Davis.)

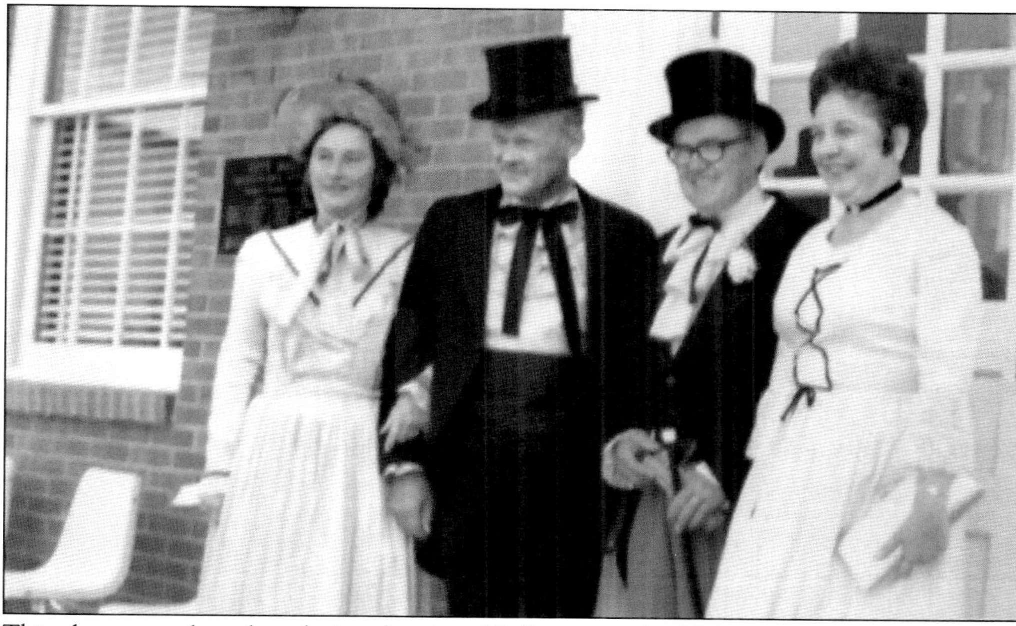

This photo was also taken during the city of Jeffersontown's 175th anniversary celebration in 1972. Here, Mayor Frank Chambers and his wife, Virginia, are seen dressed in period costume with Walter and Ruby Frederick, descendants of Abraham Bruner, who purchased the property on the square that would become the heart of Jeffersontown. (Photo courtesy of Carole Chambers Davis.)

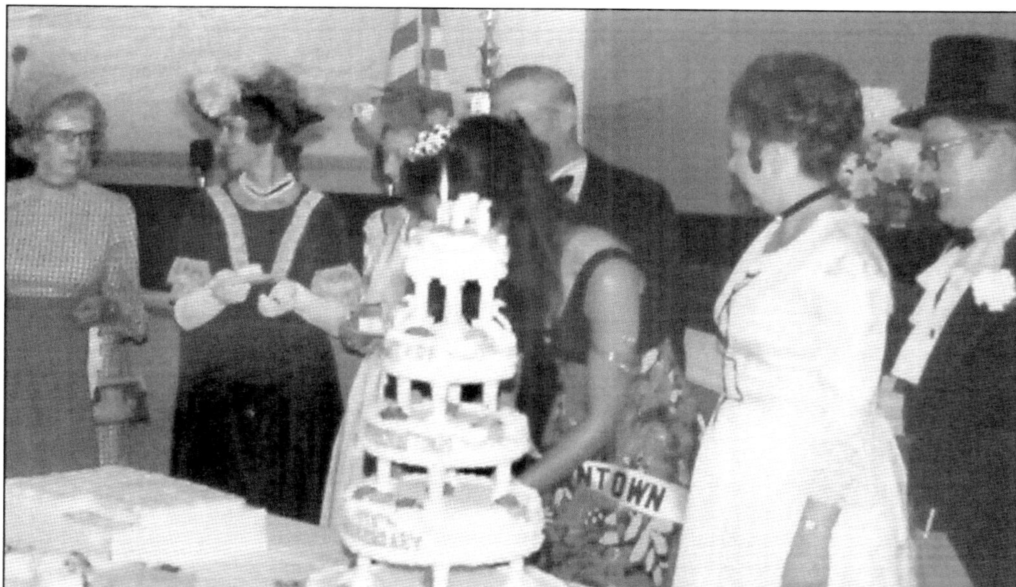

In this photo, Bruner's descendants are served a slice of Jeffersontown's birthday cake by Miss Jeffersontown. From left to right are Emma C. Wolfin, Doris Lamaster, Ruby Frederick, Walter Frederick, Miss Jeffersontown, Mrs. Franklin Chambers, and Mayor Chambers. (Photo courtesy of Carole Chambers Davis.)

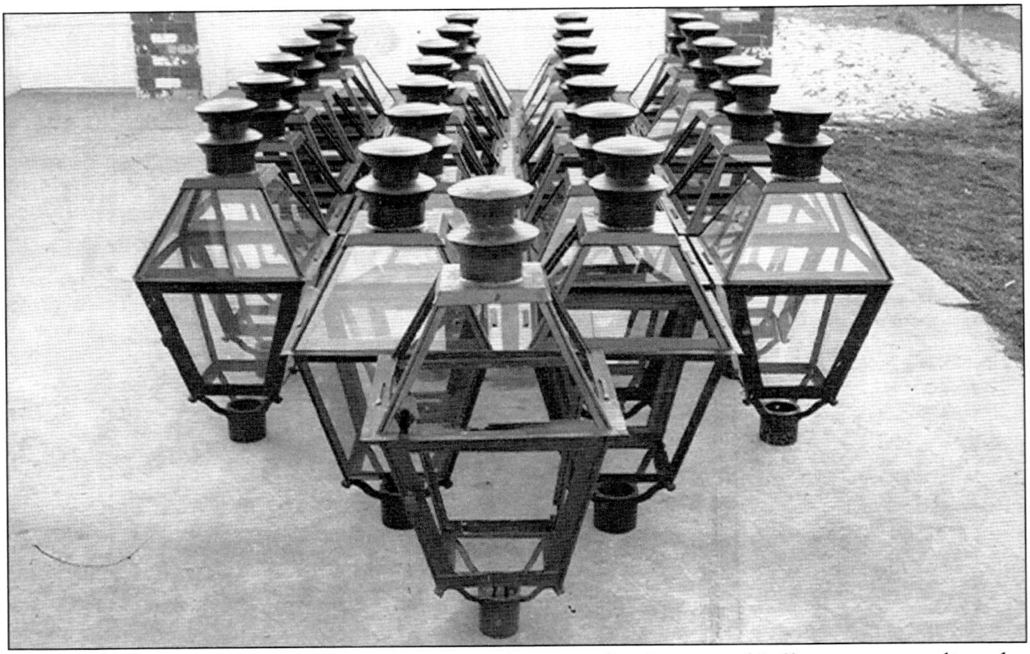

In 1967, Ozzie Oestringer fashioned about 26 lanterns for the city of Jeffersontown to line the square. The front lantern is an original 1800s coal oil/kerosene lamp that once graced the streets of Jeffersontown, and was later bought from antiques dealer Bill Claxton by Peggy Weber and Mrs. Wiehe, who then commissioned Mr. Oestringer to make replicas to decorate the square in Jeffersontown. The gaslight has now become a symbol of Jeffersontown. (Photo courtesy of M.C. "Ozzie" Oestringer.)

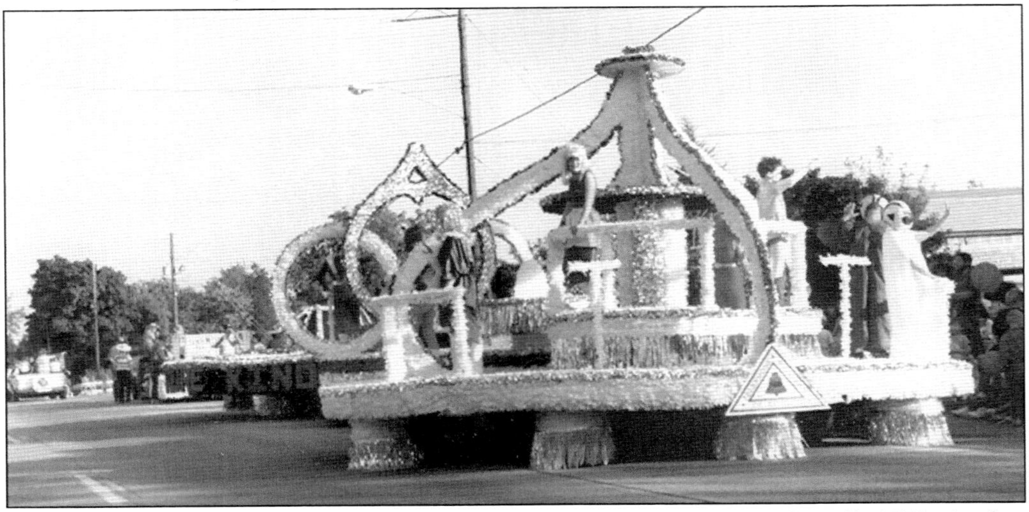

The first Gaslight Festival was held in front of the J-Town Center on June 7, 1970. At that time, Jeffersontown was renovating itself and becoming more industrialized. In 1968 and 1969, Jeffersontown won the All America City Award, and things kept getting better from there. To celebrate their pride in the city, and to build upon this recognition, Peggy Weber and Petra Williams came up with the idea of a new event—the Gaslight Festival. Seen here is one of the many rides present at the festival. (Photo courtesy of the Jeffersontown Historical Museum.)

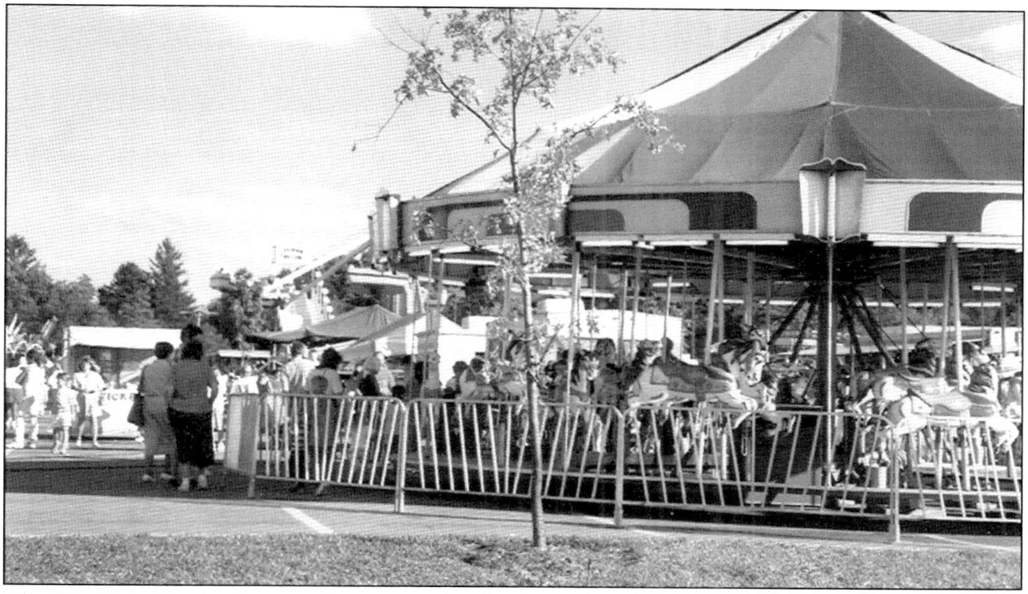

The Gaslight Festival normally occurs the third weekend in September, although the event has turned into a weeklong celebration. The days leading up to the weekend festival are filled with various races, carnival rides, golf contests, the Gaslight Parade, and even a Balloon Glow. The Gaslight Festival itself takes place over the weekend, when thousands of visitors gather to enjoy arts and crafts, good music, and great food. (Photo courtesy of the Jeffersontown Historical Museum.)

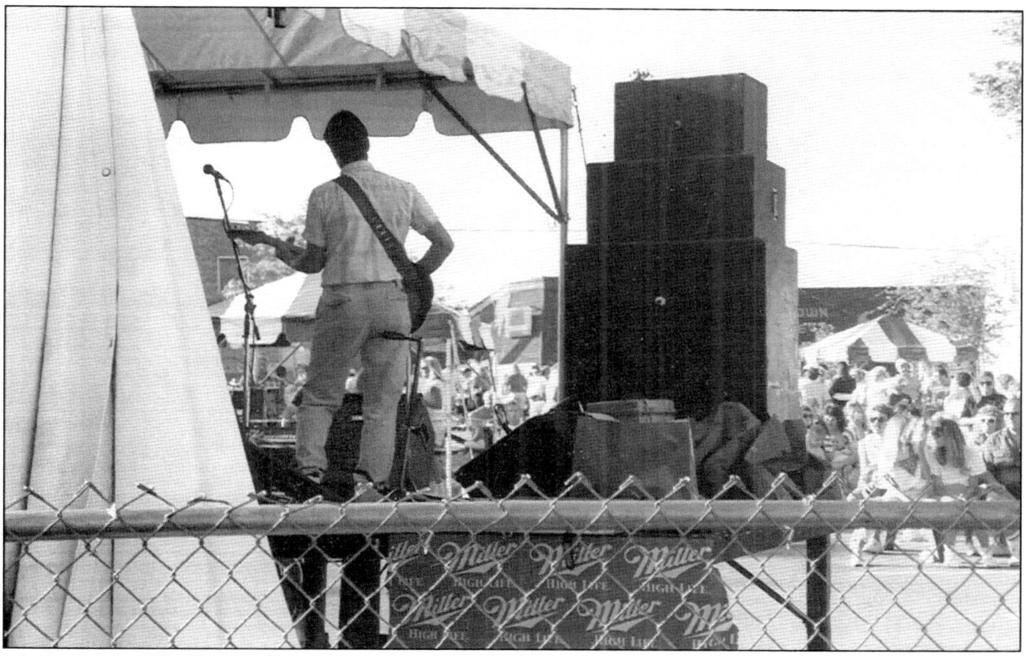

Many visitors flock to Jeffersontown's Gaslight Festival to listen to the music played live on the square. Street Heat, a group of talented Jeffersontown Police, is one of the most anxiously awaited bands to sing at the festival every year. (Photo courtesy of the Jeffersontown Historical Museum.)

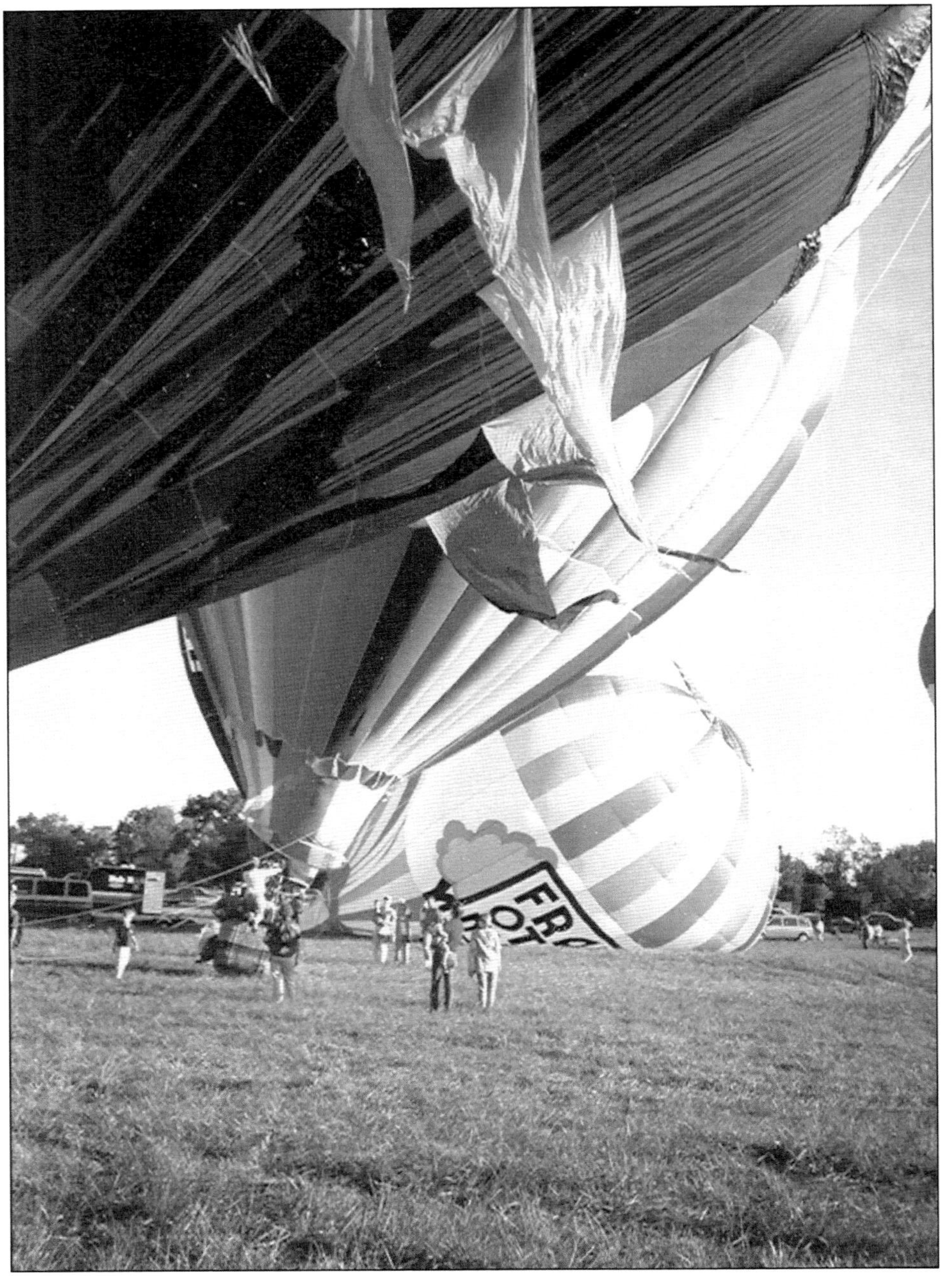

The Balloon Glow is one of the newer events that has been added to the Gaslight Festival over the years. Every year, the Jeffersontown Chamber of Commerce and the citizens of Jeffersontown try to come up with new ideas that will keep the Gaslight Festival fresh and alive, in much the same way they and our city leaders continually seek to improve the city of Jeffersontown itself. One would be hard-pressed to find a more peaceful yet productive city anywhere. The early settlers of Jeffersontown knew a good thing when they saw it, and the current residents of this wonderful city continue to reap the benefits of their foresight. (Photo courtesy of the Jeffersontown Historical Museum.)